COMBAT MISSION KANDAHAR

COMBAT MISSION KANDAHAR

THE CANADIAN EXPERIENCE IN AFGHANISTAN

T. ROBERT FOWLER

FOREWORD BY LIEUTENANT-GENERAL MARQUIS HAINSE

DUNDURN
TORONTO

Editor: Michael Carroll
Design: Jennifer Gallinger
Cover design: Sarah Beaudin
Cover image: © David Strachan, George Metcalf Archival Collection, Canadian War Museum
Maps: Mike Bechthold
Printer: Webcom

Library and Archives Canada Cataloguing in Publication

Fowler, T. Robert, author
        Combat mission Kandahar : the Canadian experience in Afghanistan / T. Robert Fowler ; foreword by Lieutenant-General Marquis Hainse.

Includes bibliographical references and index.
Issued in print and electronic formats.
ISBN 978-1-4597-3516-3 (paperback).--ISBN 978-1-4597-3517-0 (pdf).--ISBN 978-1-4597-3518-7 (epub)

        1. Afghan War, 2001- --Participation, Canadian. 2. Afghan War, 2001- --Campaigns--Afghanistan--Kandahār. 3. Afghan War , 2001- --Regimental histories--Canada. I. Title.

DS371.412.F69 2016   958.104'7   C2016-902737-6
                                                C2016-902738-4

1 2 3 4 5   20 19 18 17 16

Conseil des Arts du Canada / Canada Council for the Arts

Canada

ONTARIO ARTS COUNCIL
CONSEIL DES ARTS DE L'ONTARIO
an Ontario government agency
un organisme du gouvernement de l'Ontario

We acknowledge the support of the **Canada Council for the Arts** and the **Ontario Arts Council** for our publishing program. We also acknowledge the financial support of the **Government of Canada** through the **Canada Book Fund** and **Livres Canada Books**, and the **Government of Ontario** through the **Ontario Book Publishing Tax Credit** and the **Ontario Media Development Corporation**.

Care has been taken to trace the ownership of copyright material used in this book. The author and the publisher welcome any information enabling them to rectify any references or credits in subsequent editions.
                                                — *J. Kirk Howard, President*

The publisher is not responsible for websites or their content unless they are owned by the publisher.

Printed and bound in Canada.

VISIT US AT
Dundurn.com | @dundurnpress | Facebook.com/dundurnpress | Pinterest.com/dundurnpress

Dundurn
3 Church Street, Suite 500
Toronto, Ontario, Canada
M5E 1M2

CONTENTS

FOREWORD

Canada's military involvement in Afghanistan was a significant period for the Canadian Armed Forces as a whole, but particularly for the Canadian Army. Our participation spanned a decade and involved thousands of officers, non-commissioned officers, and soldiers, many of whom deployed multiple times. It left a lasting mark on Canadians who were either directly involved in the conflict or supported those who were overseas. Consequently, in order to truly comprehend the impact of our operations in Afghanistan on those who were there, it is necessary to understand their stories.

Combat Mission Kandahar elaborates on a number of individual experiences across the duration of our army's participation in the combat mission in southern Afghanistan from 2006 to 2011. While it does not encapsulate the totality of our national contribution, the strength of this work is that it does provide one with an idea of the diversity of Canadian involvement in the conflicted area and the effect of the fighting on those who were deployed to that region.

While a comprehensive history of Canada's activities in Afghanistan remains to be published, the separate stories of those involved stand on their own merits. Each member of the Canadian Armed Forces who was part of our mission, myself included, has a tale to tell. This grouping represents a few of those from the Canadian Army. I commend one to read them and reflect on the individual experiences contained within the covers of this book. Also, while reading these stories, I ask that the reader remember all those who were part of Canada's involvement in Afghanistan, as well as their families and friends. It is by remembering and acknowledging their vast contributions that we continue to honour their sacrifices.

Vigilamus pro Te (We stand on guard for thee).

Lieutenant-General Marquis Hainse
Chief of the Army Staff and Commander of the Canadian Army

PREFACE

What is it like to go into combat? I have wondered about that question since growing up as a young boy in the 1940s. I was surrounded by radio broadcasts about the Second World War in Europe, films glorifying the deeds of soldiers, and articles on the front pages of newspapers that contained maps of faraway places like North Africa and Italy. It was all fascinating to the mind of a young, impressionable person. After the war was over, I could not wait to solve the mystery of what it was all about by getting the first popular histories that were published.

It could be said I was easily brainwashed at that early age by all I heard or saw. This led me to join the Air Cadets, Army Cadets, and along with my buddies, the local reserve army unit. It was only a long time later after reading more realistic histories and memoirs that I came to understand that war had few redeeming features, that it is brutal, ugly, and should be avoided at all costs. I might have been fortunate that I grew up between wars and therefore did not follow the lure of excitement that in every generation causes many to enlist when wars break out.

However, wars and conflicts continued to happen, and I believe that despite our best efforts to promote peace they will persist. I still find military history fascinating, since it tells an important part of human existence. And I am not the only one attracted to military history. I have been surprised at the number of people I have met at book signings, not only male but female, as well, who are similarly attracted to this genre. They are not warmongers but probably, just like me, they want to know what happened during these critical events in history. What lessons can be learned from these histories to make ourselves secure from aggressors who still exist in the world?

My interest in the combat mission in Afghanistan is no different than my desire to understand what happened at Hill 667 in 1951, on Juno Beach in 1944, or in front of Ypres in 1915. When the Canadian Army deployed troops to Kandahar in 2006, few of us realized that our military would become involved in the most extended period of conflict in the history of our country. Most people and politicians believed the mission would be a kind of brief peace-enforcement action that would allow the new Islamic government of Afghanistan to rebuild its war-torn country. Instead, Canadian soldiers became involved in a multi-year conflict in which all their combat skills were needed to fight a determined and deadly insurgency. Soldiers were killed and wounded, and for the first time decorations for military valour were awarded.

The combat mission was well covered by Canadian journalists. However, their short reports, published in newspapers and magazines or on television and radio, could only give brief glimpses of events. A number of books came out within a few years of the end of the mission, but these only recounted a small slice of the story, as well. Perhaps the most complete picture of the intensity of the mission was provided by the book *Kandahar Tour*, but it covered only one rotation. Several books focused on Operation Medusa, but what came afterward? Any interested reader had to struggle to put the pieces together from news articles and government media releases.

An official history of the combat mission will be issued at some future date and eventually the records will be opened for historians to take a more critical look at what occurred. In the meantime, new threats of violence arise on the international stage, and the mission is rapidly fading away. I therefore felt it was important to try to give Canadians a better understanding of what their soldiers did in Afghanistan while the memory of the mission is still strong. And the story I wanted to tell is "what it was like to go into combat" in Afghanistan.

I will leave the analysis to historians whether Canada should have been in Afghanistan at all and how effective Task Force Kandahar was in fighting the insurgency. I want this book to tell Canadians what it was like for seven individual soldiers to arrive in Kandahar Airfield and to head out to a forward operating base (FOB) where they would face danger for the next six months. In accomplishing this goal, I am very indebted to those soldiers who agreed to meet with me and tell me their personal stories. It was a challenge to find soldiers who would be willing to have a civilian writer ask questions about a personal and emotional period of their career, but I believe those who did so present the kind of insight I was seeking. In finally publishing their stories, I hope this book helps Canadians gain a better understanding of the challenges their men and women faced in Afghanistan and how well they carried out their duties.

PART ONE
THE MISSION

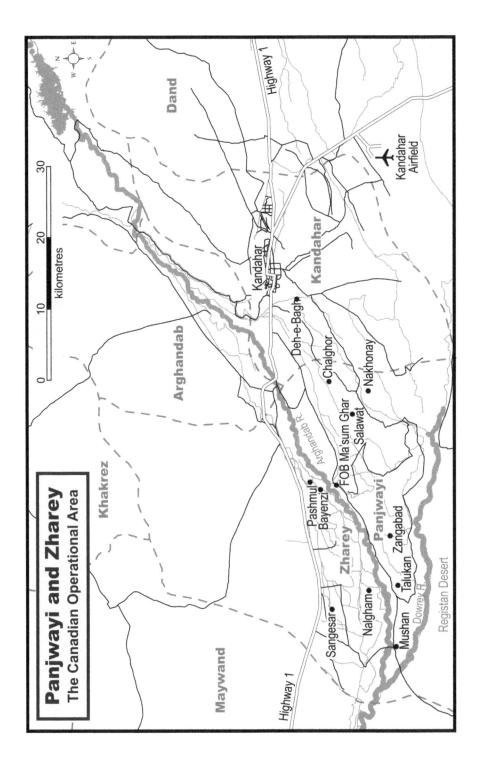

Panjwayi and Zharey
The Canadian Operational Area

At the beginning of the 21st century the Canadian Armed Forces became embroiled in a struggle to help build a new nation in the faraway land of Afghanistan. When the Canadian military first set foot on the dusty soil of that country in early 2002, it could not imagine that this commitment would become the longest foreign campaign in its history, with the last Canadian soldier not leaving until 2014.

During that period, the challenges faced by the Canadian military would change significantly as it carried out four distinct missions. The most important of these was the third mission, Operation Athena, Phase 2, which lasted from 2006 to 2011. This came to be called "the combat mission" as Canadian battle groups engaged in a deadly multi-year war of counter-insurgency in Kandahar Province. It was a war unlike any previously fought in Canada's history, with Canadians taking responsibility for the most southerly province in Afghanistan as part of a United Nations–sanctioned military force called the International Security Assistance Force (ISAF). While the Canadians were well equipped with the latest in weapons technology and could employ unprecedented fire-power, they faced a ruthless and deadly enemy that had the advantage of being hidden within the population.

This book is about the Canadian experience in Operation Athena, Phase 2, the combat mission.

1

A CHRONOLOGICAL OVERVIEW
OF THE COMBAT MISSION*

AFGHANISTAN: A HISTORY OF CONFLICT

On September 11, 2001, the world was shocked as four passenger jet airliners were hijacked by terrorists and crashed into the twin towers of the World Trade Center in New York City, the Pentagon in Arlington, Virginia, and a field in Pennsylvania, resulting in the deaths of almost 3,000 innocent victims. Five months later, as a result of this terrorist attack, 800 soldiers of the 3rd Battalion, Princess Patricia's Canadian Light Infantry (3 PPCLI), arrived at a dusty airfield in Afghanistan, a strange land more than 12,000 kilometres from Canada.

Until 2001, Afghanistan was a country that never crossed the minds of average Canadians. With an area about the size of one of Canada's Prairie provinces, it is a landlocked, largely barren territory hidden from the world's view by Pakistan on the east and Iran on the west. Unfortunately, the country remains one of the poorest in the world, with half of its people

---

* Because the events outlined in this chapter are so recent, no official primary sources are yet available to fully explain the combat mission. As a result, open sources have to be used, and regrettably these do not allow a detailed presentation of the challenges, efforts, and achievements of Task Force Kandahar.

struggling to survive below the poverty line. Afghanistan has been described as one of the least developed and most corrupt nations in the world. Afghan society is difficult to govern because it is made up of at least 21 ethnic groups speaking four different languages.[1] Of these groups the Pashtuns are the largest, making up about 40 percent of the population. The Pashtuns themselves, however, are divided into a number of clans consisting of tribes based on kinship relations or shared occupations to which members look for their primary allegiance. While each clan has a leader who is the most respected man in the community, important decisions are made by communal gatherings of elders called *shuras* if the issue is a local dispute or *jirgas* when a conflict arises between tribes.[2] Within the Pashtuns, the Durrani clan is one of the most influential, since it can claim to have created the first Afghan state. In 1747 the Durrani leader, Ahmed Shah, began a campaign of conquest from his base in Kandahar and overcame the Persians and their Pashtun rival, the Ghilzais, to found an empire that lasted 200 years.[3]

Afghanistan has a long history of conflict, and of all its racial groups the Pashtuns perhaps are the most well known for fierceness and independence. In the 21st century, little has changed in the more than 100 years since Winston Churchill, as part of a British Army expedition, described Pashtun society: "Every man is a warrior, a politician and a theologian. Every large house is a real feudal fortress made, it is true, only of sun-baked clay ... Every family cultivates its vendetta; every clan, its feud. The numerous tribes and combinations of tribes all have their accounts to settle with one another."[4] This attitude is derived from a strict code of honour adhered to by all Pashtuns called *Pashtunwali*, which requires each member to defend his personal honour, his family's honour, his tribe's honour, and his clan's honour above all other considerations. The most dramatic example of the Pashtuns' dedication to this code is their destruction of the British-Indian army that invaded Afghanistan in 1839.

Afghanistan is a Muslim country. Religion was not a contentious issue until the country collapsed into political chaos in the last decades of the 20th century. Beginning in 1978, however, the country toppled into turmoil that lasted about 20 years and ended with the disintegration of the national government. As Afghanistan became a "failed state," some regions fell under the control of local warlords or undisciplined militias while others descended into lawlessness in which criminal gangs or corrupt officials ruled. In this state of chaos, the people would welcome any group that promised to bring back order to their lives. Amid the anarchy, a religious militia called the Taliban was formed from seminary students in a town outside Kandahar City under Mullah Mohammed Omar, an obscure Muslim cleric.

Omar, a follower of an extreme ultra-conservative sect, advocated that Afghan society should revive itself by conforming to the strictest principles of Islamic law. Stories of how the Taliban formed are somewhat clouded, but they centre on an incident in 1994 when Omar led a small group of followers to obtain justice against members of a warlord's militia who had raped some local girls. This small action was a spark that started a movement, one that grew quickly as others began to see the Taliban as a group that could bring back law and order to the country. By 2000 the Taliban were in control of 90 percent of Afghanistan and had imposed religious sharia law as promised.

DEFEAT OF THE TALIBAN REGIME

During the Soviet occupation of Afghanistan (1979–89), the Islamic world rushed to support the *mujahideen* guerrillas who vigorously fought an irregular war against the invaders. One of those who had financed the Taliban during its advance to power was the wealthy Saudi, Osama bin Laden. As a result of this support, Bin Laden found a friendly haven in Islamic Afghanistan where he formed the terrorist group Al Qaeda to carry out a violent holy war against those countries considered enemies of Islam. In particular, Bin Laden issued a call for attacks by every Muslim against North Americans and their allies. From 1992 Al Qaeda organized and implemented a number of bombing missions against American targets globally, but nothing prepared the world for the horrific attacks carried out on September 11, 2001.

Within 24 hours of the terrorist acts, American authorities had identified that the attackers who had hijacked the aircraft were members of Osama bin Laden's terrorist organization. On September 12, the U.N. Security Council issued a resolution condemning the attacks and shortly thereafter authorized the use of force against the perpetrators of the atrocity. A few days later the North Atlantic Treaty Organization (NATO) announced that, in accordance with its charter, it considered the attack on the United States an attack against all its members. The United States demanded that the Emirate of Afghanistan hand over Osama bin Laden to U.S. authorities and disband Al Qaeda's training camps. When Mullah Omar refused, American and British air forces began offensive operations against the emirate on October 7, 2001.

The American-led offensive, code-named Operation Enduring Freedom, relied on fighters from the Northern Alliance of tribes still holding out against the Taliban in the northwest corner of the country. American and British air power soon shattered the Taliban defences, and the Northern Alliance fighters advanced to capture Kabul on November 13. By early December, the Taliban, along with Al Qaeda, were broken as an organized force and attempted to flee to the safety of remote areas on the border with Pakistan. With the main objectives of Operation Enduring Freedom achieved, there was now a need to rebuild the country. Following so many years of conflict, however, Afghanistan lacked the institutions required to rebuild the state and its economy. Under the authority of the United Nations, a process was thus begun to build a new government, but the surviving Taliban and other elements in Afghan society were not pleased with this prospect and were prepared to forcefully oppose the proposed new regime.

CANADA COMMITS MILITARY FORCES TO AFGHANISTAN

On October 7, 2001, Prime Minister Jean Chrétien had announced that Canada would support the United States in any action that would be taken in response to the 9/11 attack. A small team from the Canadian Special Operations Force JTF-2 arrived on the ground in December, but the first major Canadian contribution, the 3rd Battalion, Princess Patricia's Canadian Light Infantry Battle Group (3 PPCLI BG), arrived in early 2002 to assist American forces in the elimination of the last Al Qaeda holdouts in Kandahar Province. This deployment was called Operation Apollo, the first of four Canadian missions to Afghanistan. The second mission, designated Operation Athena, took place from 2003 to 2005 when Canadian troops operated as part of ISAF in the city of Kabul to provide security for the creation of a new Afghan government. The third mission, lasting from 2006 to 2011, was labelled Athena, Phase 2, to which Canada committed resources to assist in training the Afghan National Security Forces (ANSF) and improving security, economic development, and good governance in Kandahar Province. The final mission, from 2011 to 2014, was Operation Attention, in which personnel were provided for training and professional development support for the ANSF in Kabul, Mazar-e-Sharif, and Herat.

Canada had not planned to sustain a long-term military role in a distant theatre of operations, but as its role in Kabul wound down in 2004, it was under some pressure to play a larger role in Afghanistan. The tasks for establishing a stable government in Afghanistan were being gradually handed over from the U.S.-led Operation Enduring Freedom to NATO, and after some debate, the Canadian government chose to take responsibility for Kandahar Province, a decision that remains controversial. ISAF Regional Command (South) would be established at Kandahar Airfield (KAF), just outside Kandahar City itself, and would direct all civil and military activities in the six southern provinces. The Canadian contribution would come under the direction of Task Force Kandahar, which initially consisted of the task force headquarters, an infantry battle group, a Provincial Reconstruction Team (PRT), and support elements. Its area of operations (AO) would cover Kandahar Province, while the British would operate in Helmand Province and the Dutch in Uruzgan.

The May 2006 campaign plan specified that Canada's mission in Kandahar was "to conduct operations … in order to support the effort to create a secure, democratic and self-sustaining nation state."[5] The challenge Task Force Kandahar would quickly face would be to establish a sufficiently secure environment for credible Government of Afghanistan institutions to be developed along with effective Afghan security structures in a region where the Afghan government previously had little presence. With the decision to take responsibility for Kandahar Province, Canada had agreed to send its troops into what was probably the most difficult region possible. This was the home of the Taliban, where it had been created by Mullah Omar in 1994. The population of about a million people were predominantly Pashtuns who had little faith in, or even knowledge of, the government in Kabul. Some of the Pashtun tribes had historic differences and even blood feuds among themselves, which made co-operation difficult. Other tribes were so opposed to President Hamid Karzai that the insurgency in southern Afghanistan might, from their viewpoint, have been seen as a civil war.

While about a quarter of a million people lived in Kandahar City itself, the rest resided in rural areas and only about 13 percent were literate. The terrain is mostly flat and arid, bound by the Registan Desert on the south and the foothills of the Hindu Kush on the north. Between these inhospitable regions, the Arghandab River flows south, passing just north of Kandahar City and creating an 80-kilometre-long strip of irrigated farmland called the Green Belt. Here, water from the river makes the farms of the districts of Panjwayi, Zharey, Arghandab, and Maywand some of the main agriculture areas of the country. And since Mullah Omar had come from a village in this area, many still gave him their allegiance.[6] By the end of 2005, the Taliban's Quetta Shura had begun moving small groups of men back, along with weapons and other supplies that could be easily hidden in sympathetic villages. Their long-term goal was the recapture of Kandahar City as the key to re-establishing the Islamic Emirate of Afghanistan.

THE COMBAT MISSION BEGINS

Canada's mission in Kandahar for Phase 2 of Operation Athena began in February 2006 with the arrival of the first of a series of six-month deployments of Canadian units.[7] Between February 2006 and July 2011, 10 rotations were carried out, each having a mix of subunits from several battalions, all under the command of the battalion headquarters designated for that rotation. For simplicity, the Canadian experience in Kandahar for this five-and-a-half-year period could be described as occurring in three phases: the first was a wide-ranging mobile operation by 1 PPCLI BG as it initiated the Canadian presence in an area where no government control had existed beforehand; the second involved the 1st Battalion, Royal Canadian Regiment Battle Group (1 RCR BG), of Rotation (Roto) 2 confronting a strong insurgent force in a conventional battle for Kandahar City; and the remaining rotations dealt with an insurgent enemy that, having realized ISAF could bring superior firepower to bear, reverted to asymmetric warfare in a continuing effort to seize control of the province and city.

Roto	Approximate Time Period	Manoeuvre Unit
1	February 2006–July 2006	1 PPCLI BG
2	August 2006–February 2007	1 RCR BG
3	February 2007–August 2007	2 RCR BG
4	August 2007–February 2008	3 R22eR BG
5	February 2008–August 2008	2 PPCLI BG
6	August 2008–February 2009	3 RCR BG
7	February 2009–August 2009	2 R22eR BG
8	August 2009–February 2010	1 PPCLI BG
9	February 2010–October 2010	1 RCR BG
10	October 2010–July 2011	1 R22eR BG

The first rotation (Roto 1) of Task Force Kandahar consisted of a brigade headquarters for Regional Command (South) located at KAF, and an all-arms manoeuvre unit of infantry, artillery, combat engineers, and armoured reconnaissance built around 1 PPCLI BG, as well as including the Kandahar Provincial Reconstruction Team. To allow improved governance and development to proceed, however, the battle group would first have to establish security in the area by eliminating insurgent influence in the province. In these initial weeks of the deployment, the Canadians attempted to maintain the priority of identifying and initiating development work. However, as insurgent activity increased with the arrival of spring, security and counter-insurgency operations began to take precedence to the detriment of development work.[8]

By the summer of 2006, 1 PPCLI BG's commanding officer, Lieutenant-Colonel Ian Hope, realized he was facing a serious insurgent threat, and countering it absorbed all his energy. With hindsight, the Canadian task force was clearly under-resourced (as were the forces in all ISAF areas), having only one battalion without reliable Afghan National Army (ANA) and Afghan National Police (ANP) support at the time and responsibility for the entire Kandahar Province, an area of 54,000 square kilometres. In addition, as the Canadians moved into the province, they had little good knowledge of the makeup of the insurgency here. One of their first and most important tasks was to gather satisfactory military intelligence on this new region, which included forming a social profile of the area, coming to understand its internal political conflicts, identifying which tribal communities were friendly or antagonistic, and developing an effective network of reporting from local sources about the movements of insurgent fighters. To put these critical pieces together, the battle group had to overcome a lack of co-operation by local power brokers guarding their own interests, as well as different priorities at higher levels of headquarters.[9]

The first Canadian casualty came on March 4 when the battle group commander's own vehicle was struck by a suicide bomber just seven kilometres from KAF, seriously injuring Master Corporal Mike Loewen. Then, the next day, Captain Trevor Greene of the PRT was viciously attacked by an axe-wielding youth while conducting a seemingly peaceful *shura* in a village. The battle group commanding officer recognized that he was dealing with an insurgency operation of greater intensity than anticipated, not a war against terrorists, and he tailored his operations toward this type of warfare. He determined to establish ISAF's presence by making full use of the mobility provided by his vehicles, particularly light armoured vehicles (LAVs), despite the threat of improvised explosive devices (IEDs). During Roto 1's deployment, 1 PPCLI BG travelled 1,700,000 kilometres to all parts of the province and even into neighbouring Helmand Province, experiencing more than 100 contacts with the Taliban, 50 of which involved intensive firefights.[10]

During the spring, the Taliban were preparing for a renewed offensive: intelligence reports indicated that a large number of Taliban fighters from Pakistan were moving into southern Afghanistan where they could create a base with the co-operation of disaffected tribes such as the conservative Noorzai,[11] as well as with other insurgents in drug-trafficking rings. By August, senior Afghan leaders had become quite concerned with what they considered to be a fragile situation, and urged ISAF to act against the growing threat.[12]

All signs pointed to the possibility that the Taliban were planning to use the Green Belt of the Zharey and Panjwayi Districts to launch an attack to re-take Kandahar City. The Taliban appeared to be especially active near a group of villages called Pashmul on the west bank of the Arghandab River, from which they could threaten both the Panjwayi District Centre to the east of the river and also the important Highway One to the north. Confirming these reports, a large number of women and children fled the area, and local people complained that the Taliban had openly occupied a cluster of abandoned school buildings in Pashmul that the Canadians nicknamed the White Schoolhouse. Whenever elements of the battle group carried out operations in the area to clear out the insurgents, they were met with violent resistance. During one of these operations on May 17, Captain Nicola Goddard was killed, and during the fierce action on August 3 when Sergeant Patrick Tower and two others raced across a bullet-swept field to help those injured in the White Schoolhouse, 1 PPCLI suffered four more killed in action and 11 wounded.

THE TALIBAN THREAT DEFEATED — OPERATION MEDUSA

ISAF came to the conclusion that the Taliban actually wanted the Canadians to attack; they had repulsed the Canadians in their previous attempts to move into Pashmul, and as the insurgents' strength grew, they felt they could inflict heavy losses on any ISAF attack, thus demonstrating to the local population the inability of NATO to support the new Afghan government. Facing such an enemy, Brigadier-General David Fraser, in command of Regional Command (South), attempted to gather the strongest force he could. He was disappointed, however, since he received little help from most other NATO countries, which had placed restrictions preventing their military contingents being used in counter-insurgency situations. One Canadian officer complained bitterly that "we were basically told you're on your fucking own for a while."[13] For his main striking force, Fraser would have to rely on what troops were available from the newly arrived 1 RCR BG of Roto 2 and a handful of other Coalition military units, the entire force totalling only about 1,400 men.

Despite the limited number of troops, Operation Medusa was highlighted as the largest operation ever carried out by NATO. Its success was predicated on the amount of firepower that would be assembled. Expected insurgent positions would be bombarded for three days prior to the advance by combat air support from British, Dutch, and American air forces using rockets, cannons, and precision-guided munitions, and by continuous artillery fire. The sophisticated surveillance and electronic intelligence-gathering capabilities of ISAF would be used to locate enemy defences, movements, and command nodes. A final intelligence analysis estimated that the 1 RCR would be facing possibly 900 to 1,200 insurgent fighters in the area. This was normally an unacceptable ratio of attackers to defenders; however, it was felt that only about 200 of these might be first-tier "hard-core" fighters. If superior firepower could be brought to bear, the morale of the second-tier or temporary local fighters would break, leaving the hard-core caught in a trap by other enveloping ISAF units.[14]

The opening move of Medusa went badly. The plan called for a preliminary bombardment of the objective over an extended period of time. But when no reaction from the Taliban was observed on the day the bombardment began, ISAF higher headquarters began to fear that the Taliban force was escaping, and it applied pressure for the attack to begin immediately without further reconnaissance to more accurately identify the enemy positions.[15] As a result, when 1 RCR's Charles Company crossed the Arghandab River at 0600 on September 3, 2006, it ran into a trap before the White Schoolhouse at Pashmul. The Taliban opened fire on three sides of the leading Canadian elements using small arms, rocket-propelled grenades (RPGs), machine guns, and mortars. From the start the Canadians found themselves fighting for their lives. Fortunately, with support from artillery and combat aircraft, they were able to withdraw to their starting position on the far bank of the river to a height called Ma'sum Ghar. The tragedy for the men of Charles Company continued the next day when an American attack helicopter mistook them for insurgents and unleashed a deadly burst of 30 mm high-explosive rounds. Mark Graham, a former Canadian Olympic athlete, was killed and many others were wounded, including the company commander. Over the first two days of Medusa, Charles Company recorded the worst casualty record in Afghanistan, with four killed and more than 40 wounded, including a platoon commander and the majority of its platoon warrant officers and section commanders.

Task Force Kandahar thwarted a Taliban attempt to capture Kandahar City in September 2006. Here, soldiers from A Company, 1 RCR BG, conduct operations as part of Operation Medusa.

Brigadier-General Fraser quickly reoriented his plan, however, by ordering other forces to advance on Pashmul from the north while an ad hoc task force crossed the river to advance from the southwest. Air support and artillery continued to pound all concentrations of Taliban fighters as they were identified. The advance of these elements was methodical and well supported, and the objective in Pashmul was occupied on September 12. By September 15, the Taliban were fleeing the area and the battle was basically over.

The top ISAF commander was very pleased with the outcome and stated: "… what our troops did was impressive. They saved the city of Kandahar, arguably saved the country and they saved the alliance."[16] NATO also called it their "largest ever combat operation, against a well-prepared and determined enemy" and declared that the insurgents "are no longer a cohesive force."[17] Some controversy arose, however, over the estimate of Taliban casualties. Not many bodies could be found; the Taliban always removed their dead from the battlefield if possible, confounding Coalition confirmation of enemy dead. NATO's initial estimate was 512 Taliban

FOB Ma'sum Ghar became the main operational base for the Canadian battle group in Panjwayi. Here the view looks east at Bazaar-i-Panjwayi from Ma'sum Ghar. A line of trees running through the town marks the main road from the Horn of Panjwayi to Kandahar City, while Mar Ghar rises to 1,459 metres in the background.

A view of FOB Ma'sum Ghar showing sea containers used for living quarters, an observation post, and tents along mud brick walls.

killed and 136 captured, but one senior NATO general declared, perhaps overenthusiastically, that he would not be surprised if the Taliban had lost as many as 1,500 killed.[18] It was clear, however, that whatever the numbers were, the Coalition offensive had grievously hurt the Taliban and had killed at least five of their senior commanders.

Operation Medusa stands out as a high-water mark for conventional fighting in the campaign, since ISAF and the Canadians defeated the Taliban in a direct confrontation that the insurgents had expected to win. The Taliban had defeated the mighty Soviet army before and had felt they could prove superior again against the new foreign arrivals. ISAF had reason to celebrate and to believe it could now proceed with its original plan for reconstruction and stabilization.

To consolidate their victory, the Canadians constructed two major FOBs in the heart of the Panjwayi District — one on the high ground of Ma'sum Ghar, and another to the southwest on another height called Sperwan Ghar. These bases would become important strategic ones out of which the Canadian battle groups would operate from that date onward; during the last year of the Canadian mission, Ma'sum Ghar would become the permanent location of the battle group headquarters. A new four-kilometre-long paved road, dubbed Route Summit, was constructed by Canadian combat engineers to connect Ma'sum Ghar directly to Highway One, and a third major base, FOB Wilson, was built at the junction. This road was expected to be a more secure route for Canadian military operations and to bring improved economic development for local farmers.

THE TALIBAN CHANGE TACTICS

Unfortunately, it soon became evident that the victory of Operation Medusa was tactical only. Within a few weeks the Taliban began infiltrating back into the area and attacking the construction work being done on Route Summit. The determination and resilience of the Taliban was greater than anticipated. They no longer sought direct confrontation with ISAF but remained concealed in small groups among the farms, coming together only to launch quick ambushes or to plant IEDs along routes on which they expected Canadian vehicles or patrols to travel. The Taliban also increased their influence by tactics of intimidation, such as in the village of Talukan where they publicly displayed the bodies of 26 men who, in their eyes, had co-operated with ISAF.[19] Night letters were posted on the doors of mosques, warning villagers of their fate if they co-operated with the government. Institutions such as schools were burned or simply taken over to be used for their own purposes. A deliberate program of assassinations was begun, eliminating senior police officials in Kandahar City itself and moderate mullahs throughout the province. Some parts of Zharey and Panjwayi came under their control to such an extent that the Taliban were able to develop their own local parallel government as a show of their dominance. These included complaints committees and sharia courts to deal with such things as family conflicts, land disputes, and robberies.

The Taliban also increased their use of IEDs, these becoming more powerful than before and causing more severe Canadian casualties. The worst incident was the "Easter Tragedy" when a LAV escorting a convoy struck a device that blew up the vehicle, killing six men of 2 RCR and throwing the corporal in the rear sentry hatch into the air, seriously injuring him. The device appeared to be several anti-tank mines stacked on top of one another to magnify the blast.[20] Just as horrifying, on July 4, an RG-31 Nyala, specially built to withstand normal explosives, passed over another device made up of a stack of anti-tank mines that had a heavy artillery shell added. According to others in the column, the seven-metric-ton Nyala temporarily vanished in the dust and smoke, flying at least six metres into the air before falling back onto the road. Six men from 3 PPCLI inside and their Afghan interpreter were all killed.[21] Overall, IEDs killed 18 men and injured a larger number during Roto 3.

For the next four and a half years, despite such IED attacks, Canadian battle groups fought a determined battle against this enemy, inflicting heavy losses on them whenever they met, while at the same time making all possible effort to protect and sustain the Afghan population. Clearing and search operations were carried out whenever targets of opportunity were identified, and many caches of insurgent weapons, ammunition, and other supplies were uncovered. In these operations, they were assisted by units of the ANA's 1 Brigade, 205 Corps, whose effectiveness continuously

After their defeat in Operation Medusa, the Taliban began a deadly war of attacking Canadians using IEDs. Here, an RG-31 Nyala lies on an angle in a blast crater, disabled after hitting an IED near Sperwan.

The ANA began operating with Canadian troops on a limited basis beginning with Roto 1. Here, ANA soldiers from the 2nd Kandak roll out of FOB Ma'sum Ghar with 1 RCR BG, en route to Howz-e-Madad as part of Operation Baaz Tsuka in December 2006. The ANA did not have armoured vehicles for travel but used standard Ford Ranger trucks.

improved under the guidance of Canadian OMLTs. Canadian mentors had to take into account many cultural differences, such as the fact that most Afghans were illiterate, could not read maps, and would carry out their religious duty to pray even during operations.[22] One thing that was not lacking, however, was their bravery.

The 2nd Kandak of this brigade was the first to be sufficiently trained, and in mid-2007 it began joint operations with 3 RCR BG of Roto 3 during which the *kandak* gained a reputation as the most capable one in the ANA.[23] Some of the officers were already quite experienced, having fought in the army of the previous national government of Afghanistan in the early 1990s or under the Tajik leader Ahmad Shah Massoud. Having the ANA *kandaks* associated with Canadian units, partnered at times down to the platoon level, was invaluable, since the Afghan soldiers were respected by local villagers. Speaking the language and understanding local customs, ANA officers could take the lead in *shuras* aimed at gaining the confidence of villagers.

After Medusa it became clear that the Taliban remained entrenched in the area. They retained a strong influence in Zharey and the western part of the Green Belt in the area called the Horn of Panjwayi, where the Arghandab and Dowrey Rivers meet. In these areas the villagers were not sympathetic to the Karzai government, and from the Horn covert routes led easily to Pakistan, the source of supplies and fresh fighters. It seemed that after each "fighting season" — between the summer months when the opium poppies were harvested and up to the fall before the winter rains began — insurgents could find a safe haven across the border and recover their strength, ready to implement a new strategy to threaten Kandahar City the following year. The insurgents were content to be patient, smugly holding to the maxim, "the Coalition has all the watches but we have all the time."[24]

To properly bring the countryside in this part of Kandahar Province under control, a plan was developed to implement counter-insurgency (COIN) doctrine by establishing a permanent presence in each village where security was an issue. By the end of 2007, a network of police sub-stations and ANA strongpoints was built around Zharey District and into the Horn of Panjwayi to gain control of the insurgent areas. As more intelligence was gathered and the centres of insurgency became more clearly

While many development projects were carried out, operations to establish security continued to be necessary throughout the mission. Here, soldiers from 3 RCR BG advance in the Zharey District during Operation Janubi Tapu 2.

defined, targeted disruption operations were launched to gain control of these areas. Once security had been established, development projects could then be carried out to help influence the population's loyalty toward the government and support opposition to Taliban influence.

Despite their successes, however, the Canadians were unable to decisively clear out the Taliban because they had too few troops with a single battle group to fully apply counter-insurgent tactics. Successful COIN warfare doctrine is often simplified by the expression: "clear [an area of insurgents]; hold [to prevent insurgents from re-infiltrating]; and build [new political systems and economic development]." Our inability to carry out this process led one Canadian officer to complain in frustration: "You clear. You hold. And the holding can be long. It can be two or three years.... The problem is the insurgents come back, because you cannot be everywhere at once. There's only so much you can do."[25] To be fair, holding an area is not really a task the military should be carrying out by itself but

An Afghan policeman mans a checkpoint with machine gun and RPGs protected by sandbags.

was the role of the Afghan police under normal COIN doctrine. However, the ANP was incapable of doing this because it was poorly trained, had inadequate equipment, and at times was so corrupt that the local population mistrusted it. The problem of insufficient resources was not only a Canadian issue but affected all of Regional Command (South), which found itself lacking at least 3,000 troops in 2007, as all sectors struggled to gain the initiative from the Taliban.[26]

THE THREAT AGAINST KANDAHAR CITY FROM THE NORTH

By the end of 2007, the struggle for control in Panjwayi and Zharey had developed into a situation in which neither the Canadian battle group nor the Taliban had gained a clear advantage.[27] But the Taliban had not taken their eyes off their goal of gaining Kandahar City. While they continued their IED campaign in Panjwayi and Zharey, they now opened a new front by threatening the city from the north. Coalition forces were weak here, and the Taliban had held a strong influence in the adjoining province of Uruzgan for some time. They now began a campaign to gain control of Arghandab District, which lies immediately to the north of Kandahar City. The Taliban had been opposed in this district by the Alakozai tribe and its strong leader Mullah Naqib, who had allied himself with Karzai. But when Naqib died on October 11, 2007, creating a leadership vacuum, the Taliban acted quickly. Taliban fighters had already gathered in the north, and at the end of the month they surged into the district and threatened to take over the district centre. The battle group of the third battalion of the Royal 22e Régiment (R22eR, the "Van Doos") reacted quickly, assembling a force of Canadian and ANA troops supported by artillery and attack aircraft to drive the insurgent force out. They resisted only briefly, likely not wanting to face another Medusa-like defeat, and slipped away. But the October attack was only one phase of a protracted campaign that included, over the coming months, night attacks on police substations, assassinations of tribal leaders, and increased use of IEDs, all designed to undermine Alakozai morale.[28] To counter this new Taliban threat, the battle group established another major operating base in early 2008, FOB Frontenac, in the Shah Wali Kot District to watch the northern access routes to Kandahar City and guard the Dahla Dam, the source for the Arghandab River.

The Taliban made another major move against Kandahar City, however, eight months later in June 2008. This was an audacious and brilliantly executed attack in Kandahar City itself on Sarposa Prison, where several hundred Taliban prisoners, including some of their key leaders, were being held. It began with an apparently routine attack on a checkpoint about half a kilometre from the prison. With the checkpoint distracted by the small-arms fire, a tanker truck loaded with explosives raced past and destroyed the steel gate of the prison. Immediately afterward, more Taliban fighters arrived on motorcycles, some engaging the guards while others entered the prison and blasted the locks off the cell doors. Within minutes every inmate in the prison had escaped, many driven away in waiting vehicles.[29]

However, the Taliban attack was not over. Two days later, in coordination with the Sarposa Prison break, the Taliban launched a second attack into Arghandab District. Once more ISAF responded quickly by assembling a force to drive out the intruders and flying in ANA reinforcements from Kabul. As in the first occupation of the Arghandab District in 2007, the Taliban did not stay long enough to force a major conventional battle but used the move to further intimidate any local opposition. In this sense, these attacks were therefore major propaganda victories for the Taliban.

THE NEED FOR MORE TROOPS IN KANDAHAR PROVINCE RECOGNIZED

By now, even with support from the ANA and the struggling ANP, it was becoming obvious that the Canadians could not hold all of Kandahar Province alone. Under the pressure of too many demands on the limited Canadian resources, the decision was finally made in the fall of 2008 to begin reducing the Canadian presence in western Panjwayi by closing the combat outposts west of FOB Ma'sum Ghar at Talukan and Zangabad, as well as at Sangasar in Zharey, but hanging on to the strongpoint at Mushan a bit longer until finally closing it in April 2009.[30] As Brigadier-General Jonathan Vance later explained: "We didn't have enough resources.... An island [of Coalition troops] that had a 300-metre patrolling radius, and every time we did one of these river-run convoys [to resupply the bases] we risked losses. For what? Nothing."[31] In the meantime, the Canadian government had also become concerned about what was happening in Kandahar, and in late 2007 it put together a special panel to take a serious look at the problems and options for Canada's future role there. When it presented its findings in January 2008, the panel criticized the lack of a coordinated international effort in Afghanistan and presented a number of recommendations, one of which stated that continued military commitment by Canada beyond February 2009 be dependent on ISAF providing additional troops for Kandahar Province.[32]

Coincident with the report, the campaign took a strategic turn when the U.S. government similarly came to the conclusion that the lack of resources was allowing the Taliban to slowly gain strength in southern Afghanistan. In February 2009, the American government approved an increase of 20,000 troops for Afghanistan, and at the end of the year committed a surge of a further 30,000. As a result, new U.S. battalions began to arrive in Kandahar, first in Maywand District and later in Zharey, allowing the Canadians to focus their limited strength on Kandahar City itself and its surroundings, which had come under increasing threat in 2008. Canadian commanders now reoriented their campaign plan to concentrate on Kandahar City and the populated approaches to it, where they could focus more adequately on applying COIN doctrine now that the sufficient troop densities appeared to be within reach. This came to be called the "Village Approach."

In the Village Approach, instead of scattering clearance operations and aid across several districts, maximum effort would be applied to a single village — clearing this limited area of insurgents, deploying sufficient forces there to maintain security, and providing rapid progress in governance and economic aid in partnership with the local government. Once this approach could be shown to be successful to both residents of that village and others in the area, the process would be repeated village by village until the whole district was brought under control. Deh-e-Bagh, a small community of about 900 people south of Kandahar City, was chosen as the model project. It was thought to be a good candidate because it was located in Dand District where the Barakzai tribe was sympathetic to the Afghan government. The local villagers organized their own security patrols, while Afghan security forces with Canadian mentors were assembled to prevent a major infiltration by the Taliban.[33] The Taliban did try to disrupt the project by attacking convoys in Dand District and attempting to assassinate the district governor,[34] but by the end of June 2009, change had successfully been accomplished, with solar-powered lights lining the roads, irrigation canals cleared, and the local bazaar busy. The villagers of Deh-e-Bagh appeared to be proud of the progress made, and residents of nearby communities were becoming interested.[35] Despite these reports of progress, however, the picture remained imperfect, as was typical in Afghanistan; six months later, on December 29, a Canadian armoured vehicle from the PRT was blown up by a massive IED only 1,500 metres from the Dand District Centre, killing four soldiers and Michelle Lang, a Canadian journalist.[36]

The focus of Canadian operations then shifted into parts of eastern Panjwayi adjacent to Dand, to the area of the villages of Nakhonay-Salavat-Chalghowr, some 15 kilometres southwest of Deh-e-Bagh where the residents from the Barakzai, Popalzai, and Alakozai tribes were believed to be more supportive of the Karzai government.[37] In line with the emphasis stressed by the Village Approach, small patrol bases were established by 1 PPCLI BG in Roto 8 with the objective of maintaining a longer-term presence after clearing the area of the Taliban. But a strong insurgent influence remained in the area and was more stubbornly entrenched than at Deh-e-Bagh. In particular, the residents of Nakhonay were from the Noorzai tribe, known to be pro-Taliban, and this village had been under Taliban influence since 2007. Recently, it had been reported as being the seat of the Taliban's "shadow government" for the province, and most important, it was a main node on the route used by the Taliban to bring supplies and fighters from Pakistan across the Registan Desert and into the southwest suburbs of Kandahar City.[38] So the Taliban would naturally react fiercely to the establishment of any Canadian bases nearby.

In the areas held by Canadian troops, IED attacks remained as intense as ever, with mines now being laid on village paths, in farmers' fields, and in such unlikely places as trees or walls. The Taliban increased their control of eastern Panjwayi, broadening a parallel system of governance in that area. They stepped up their campaigns of intimidating villagers, ordering some elders who appeared to be co-operating with Canadians to either appear before a shadow court they had established in Zangabad or leave the district.

COALITION PRESENCE RE-ESTABLISHED IN ARGHANDAB, ZHAREY, AND PANJWAYI

With additional U.S. troops arriving in early 2010, the Coalition finally had sufficient strength to challenge the Taliban's control in southern Afghanistan. The first major operation took place on February 2010 in Helmand Province where American, British, and ANA troops broke a long-time insurgent hold on the town of Marjah.[39] Coalition focus then turned to the more strategic province of Kandahar where, in Operation Hamkari, American and ANA forces cleared out Taliban strongholds in Arghandab, Zharey, and Panjwayi Districts over the summer and fall of

2010. From October 2010, Canadian troops from the 1st Battalion, Royal 22e Régiment Battle Group (1 R22eR BG) of Roto 10 had a role in this last phase of Hamkari as they occupied blocking positions in western Panjwayi to prevent insurgents from fleeing the southward push of U.S. troops toward the Arghandab River. On December 7, 2010, troops of 1 R22eR supported by Leopard tanks occupied the Zangabad cluster of villages, clearing out an area that had been a Taliban stronghold for a long time. In previous operations there, so many IEDs had been found that Canadians had nicknamed it "Zangaboom."[40] Over the winter, 1 R22eR troops would remain in the area to establish a permanent Coalition presence and develop improved living conditions in consultation with local elders in western Panjwayi following the approach used in Dand District.

Although Operation Hamkari had eliminated this area as a Taliban safe haven, the insurgents still had not been decisively defeated; they had simply gone undercover as they had done after all other Coalition successes, making IEDs and sniping a continuing threat. In December, to strengthen the Coalition presence in the area and to improve local farmers' access to markets, 1 R22eR began construction of a road named Route Hyena that would replace the present cart track that linked the western end of the Horn of Panjwayi to FOB Sperwan Ghar. The insurgents made a concentrated effort to disrupt this project with IEDs and ambushes: one Canadian soldier was killed, two Canadian and five American soldiers were wounded, two civilian truck drivers were killed, a village elder was killed in a suicide attack, and 10 Afghan civilians were killed and 30 injured by a roadside bomb.[41] The construction work had to be carried out with well-organized security in place: each day the work site was first checked out by explosives-detection dogs and then guards were placed around the entire perimeter. But despite this opposition, the construction steadily pushed ahead throughout the winter and spring.

Meanwhile, in the rest of the Canadian area of operations, counter-insurgent actions continued as usual from a network of platoon outposts located to establish a presence near targeted communities. Building on the experiences of previous rotations, Canadian troops of this last rotation had success in the winter operations, uncovering 300 caches of insurgent supplies and 250 IEDs, and capturing a number of Taliban fighters as they returned from Pakistan to prepare their 2011 summer offensive.[42] As a result of these successes, insurgent strength was thought to be significantly weakened and the expected 2011 summer offensive did not happen. At the same time, the continued Canadian presence allowed for better progress in development projects to occur; for example, more than $1 million was spent repairing or building new schools and mosques. The most significant of these might have been in the village of Salavat where the former school building was rebuilt. Because it had previously housed a Taliban command centre, the building had to be searched room by room to clear any booby traps prior to reconstruction.[43]

THE END OF THE COMBAT MISSION

Canada's combat mission to Afghanistan ended on July 7, 2011, when, at KAF, Brigadier-General Dean Milner formally handed over Task Force Kandahar to a brigade combat team of the U.S. 4th Infantry Division. Two days earlier, 1 R22eR BG had concluded Canada's 10th rotation in a similar ceremony at FOB Ma'sum Ghar by handing its responsibilities over to an American infantry battalion. These ceremonies concluded Canada's combat missions in Afghanistan, which had lasted nine long years. To have some influence in world affairs in the 21st century, Canadian troops had accepted a most difficult role in a strange and faraway land in response to the call for help from the government of Afghanistan, the United Nations, NATO, and Canada's close neighbour, the United States. In doing so, Canada had found itself caught up not in peacekeeping and redevelopment as many had expected but in intense combat operations against a surreptitious and deadly enemy. Despite lacking sufficient numbers of soldiers, and in the beginning, inadequate equipment, the Canadian battle groups had met the enemy head-on in a struggle for the decisive terrain on the approaches to Kandahar City. And even while being involved in an all-out struggle, Canadian soldiers continued to work with the local Afghan people to try to help make a better life for them.

As the last Canadian combat troops departed from Afghanistan, some in the military and others back home in Canada questioned whether the effort had been worth the cost in lives and money. In this, the longest combat mission in Canadian military history, there was no great victory with which one could identify as there had been in wars of the 20th century. But this criticism ignored the fact that this was a unique mission like no other before — an ongoing war of insurgency that by its very nature could take years to resolve. There was no question whether this struggle could be "won" in the short period Canadians were there. The only questions were: Did Canadian soldiers carry out their mission as effectively as possible with the limited means and time at their disposal? And had they made some improvement in the lives of those Afghans who sought their help? In the turbulent arena of an insurgency where there were many protagonists, the answer must be that they had made a difference. Canadians had done their duty to help. The final verdict about the mission itself will have to be left to the future pages of history. Gratitude for the effort Canadian soldiers had made, however, was expressed in the closing remarks of Brigadier-General Ahmad Habibi, commanding officer of the ANA 1st Brigade 205 Corps: "You have all earned a great name in the heart of people in Afghanistan and please take that with pride to your homes."[44]

2

COUNTER-INSURGENCY (COIN) WARFARE

A fghanistan would be a strange battleground for Canadians — a far-away land with unfamiliar customs; an environment containing threats from strange insects and unusual infectious diseases; a people whose living conditions are clearly some of the poorest in the world; but, most of all, an enemy who would wage a type of warfare that could frustrate and disorient a professionally trained army.

A couple of things stood out in the memories of those who served in Afghanistan. One was the ever-constant dust that had the consistency of talc. Stirred up by the wind, it got into everything, matting your hair and clogging equipment. The most impressive thing about Afghanistan, however, was the unbearable heat of the summer fighting season when the temperature could soar to 50 degrees Celsius and above. Soldiers on operations had to guard themselves from becoming casualties not only from the Taliban but from heat exhaustion, as well. Already weighed down with their heavy fighting kit, weapons, and ammunition, men and women in the field had to add four or five litres of bottled water to their load in order to avoid it. Despite their thirst, they had to force themselves to drink this water after it reached air temperature, and became hot and unpalatable. Infantryman Ryan Flavelle gave an impressive description of his experience while on patrol under the Afghan sun and experiencing the onset of heat exhaustion:

> As I walk, laden down underneath my kit, the heat seems to be absorbed into my every pore. The sun becomes an iron that presses on my helmet and body armour, warming my core temperature as I fight to keep lurching one foot in front of the other. I have to make a conscious effort to maintain the basics of patrolling ... Heat exhaustion starts as a pounding headache, and then an uncomfortable feeling of warmth spreads throughout your body. Spots appear in front of your eyes and your ears ring.[1]

During operations or patrols, as they struggled forward over rough ground, platoon leaders and senior non-commissioned officers (NCOs) had to watch their men for signs of dehydration: a face turning white, disorientation, slurred speech. If they spotted someone who seemed in trouble, they would have the man sit down, take off some of his kit, and get him drinking water right away. The men knew they were supposed to drink all the time, but sometimes they just could not absorb the water fast enough as sweat constantly drenched their clothing. If heat exhaustion had seriously set in, the medic would try to rehydrate the man intravenously. If the casualty was too far dehydrated, however, he would have to be evacuated, ideally to a nearby road where a LAV or Bison could pick him up. In the worst-case scenario, a heat casualty who could not walk would have to be carried back by four others, accompanied by a couple of other soldiers for security. Knowing that such casualties could disrupt the progress of a patrol, the platoon warrant officer would be prepared to look after the casualty while the leader kept the remaining group focused on completing their mission.

In Afghanistan, Canadian soldiers would not face a conventional war against organized military opponents, but would encounter an unconventional war against an enemy who could blend in so easily among local residents that he could not be identified. Throughout history, uprisings against existing governments in many countries around the world have been common; these seem to have become more frequent after 1945 as the last of the old empires crumbled and people were no longer submissive to governments to which they felt no loyalty.

At the start of a rebellion insurgents do not usually have the armed strength to defeat conventional military forces of an unpopular government, but instead attempt to undermine the morale of the opposing force through unexpected acts of violence and the use of psychological intimidation. Insurgents believe they can achieve a change of government by being patient and practising tactics of destabilization over an extended time. After the Second World War, the tactics followed by Mao Zedong and Ho Chi Minh became examples of successful insurgent movements. As one of the leaders of the Vietminh wrote regarding their insurgency in Vietnam: "The guiding principle of the strategy for our whole resistance must be to prolong the war … [so that we] wear down the enemy forces … [and] they will become weak and will meet defeat instead of victory."[2] Thus, in such unconventional warfare, the military units attempting to suppress an insurgency cannot use the tactics of speed and force for which they normally have been trained, but must learn an entirely different approach.

The Canadian Armed Forces facing the insurgency in Afghanistan were quick to adapt, having learned many of the skills needed for irregular warfare after years of experience in peace support and enforcement operations in other parts of the world. But adapting to COIN operations in such a complex and violent society as found in Afghanistan was a challenge for all countries participating in ISAF. The U.S. Army, the main combatant in the region, had been reluctant to recognize the need for a doctrine on COIN but was forced to do so when it struggled without much success against an insurgency in Iraq following the downfall of Saddam Hussein. While many American military leaders still had difficulty in accepting such a need, those supporting it were finally able to release a manual on COIN in 2006 to guide commanders in the field. The first Canadian manual for COIN operations came out at the end of 2008.[3]

The concepts of COIN warfare appear to be logical, but applying them in real-life situations is far from easy. Simply trying to chase down insurgents and kill them will not solve the problem. Insurgencies arise from a number of causes, but they most commonly occur when large segments of a population feel they are aggrieved by their national government. The military's role in COIN warfare is therefore to first establish or restore a sufficient level of security over the target populations, and then to assist in resolving the root causes of the insurgency.[4] In accomplishing this mission, the COIN force will normally have to carry out a wide spectrum of operations, at times going on the offensive to pursue and destroy insurgent fighters, at other times protecting the target population, all the while prepared to facilitate humanitarian aid, economic development, and the re-establishment of appropriate governance. While carrying out these actions, the COIN force will have to remain deeply involved with the population not only to restore order but most important to allow the government to re-establish its legitimacy in the eyes of the people. The importance of the political nature of the struggle against an insurgency was recognized by Sir Gerald Templer, an early leader in the concepts of COIN warfare who declared during the 1948–60 communist insurgency in Malaysia that "the answer lies not in pouring more troops into the jungle, but in the hearts and minds of the people."[5] The phrase "hearts and minds of the people" would be a key motto thereafter by those attempting to practice COIN doctrine.

The problem in combating an insurgency is how to effectively isolate the insurgents while not turning the population against the COIN forces. The brute-force method, sometimes called "draining the swamp," has been used in the past, in which the population is removed to isolate the insurgents from their support in an area where they have a strong presence. But this is usually not practical and alienates all the population. A more common tactic involves disrupting insurgent activity by cordoning off a small targeted community and then searching house by house for suspicious residents and hidden weapons. But again, troops employing this approach must be well trained to use exceptional tact and respect for residents who have not proven to be involved with the insurgency — a degree of self-control not always easily practised by combat soldiers under stress.

Perhaps one of the most successful methods of influencing an area to reject the appeals of an insurgency is the Ink Spot or Oil Spot Approach. The phrase is credited to Marshal Hubert Lyautey, who wrote about how the French Army dealt with rebellions in North Africa and Indochina in the early years of the 20th century. He believed that after securing an area from insurgent threat or control, the French colonial administration should make an effort to help the local population prosper while respecting its culture and governance traditions. He was influenced in this principle by other

Patrols went out constantly from the FOBs to keep in touch with the Afghan people and assess their attitudes. Here, a soldier from 8 Platoon, 1 R22eR BG, talks with local children, who were always naturally curious, during a CIMIC patrol through the streets of Bazaar-i-Panjwayi.

Captain Guy Noury of the Canadian CIMIC unit of the PRT discusses community needs with villagers near Pashmul. The CIMIC's work played a key role in winning the hearts and minds of the Afghan people.

French officers who were involved in expanding the French colonial empire, particularly Colonel Joseph Gallieni, Lyautey's superior in Indochina. They believed that once small localities were successfully pacified in this manner, French influence would, "as an oil stain" (*comme une tache d'huile*), spread to the entire territory.[6] By the time Western military was involved in Iraq and Afghanistan, a very similar concept called "Clear-Hold-Build" had been incorporated as part of COIN doctrine. Despite these examples of successful counter-insurgency campaigns in the past, however, successful application of these principles will always be difficult and dependent on the situation. This was the case in Afghanistan where new governance systems had to be rebuilt after decades of civil war.

For any of these approaches to work, the COIN military force must also be very professional, well trained, and well disciplined, because the tasks required of them are psychologically demanding. They operate in a space where there is no clearly defined front or rear zone, so they are vulnerable to ambushes or sudden attacks at all times. Despite these dangers, the COIN forces must continue to interact with local residents even if they are suspected of being insurgents. When they suffer casualties from ambushes, COIN forces must avoid lashing out in anger at nearby civilians, as U.S. Marines were accused of doing in Haditha, Iraq in November 2005 when 24 Iraqi men women and children were killed in retribution for an IED attack.

Canada made a decision in 2005, as a member of NATO, to lead an international assistance effort in Kandahar Province which resulted in a confrontation over several years with groups opposed to the legitimate government of Afghanistan. The insurgent opposition was immediately confirmed upon the arrival of the Canadian military contribution by repeated campaigns of violence directed toward achieving the Taliban's ultimate goal — the recapture of Kandahar City, the historic capital of the Pashtuns. The main strategy of the Taliban continued to be directed by leaders who had fled to the safety of the city of Quetta in Pakistan, and whose long-term goal remained the establishment of the Islamic Emirate of Afghanistan, which would rule again under sharia law. While pursuing this goal, the Taliban allied themselves with other elements that were quite willing to participate in an insurgency for their own profit — drug gangs, corrupt officials, unemployed youth, and disaffected tribal villagers. For some insurgents it was the simple Pashtun reaction to fight any foreign soldiers who intruded on their territory.

The war in southern Afghanistan was unlike any the Canadian Army had fought in the past. It was largely concentrated in only two districts, Panjwayi and Zharey, a small farming area bordering the Arghandab River and only about 50 kilometres long and 15 kilometres wide. In 20th-century wars, such a small area would simply be cleared of enemy forces and occupied, following which the mission would have been considered accomplished. But here no such victory was possible. In the western villages of these districts, the Taliban had begun its rise supported by local tribes such as the Noorzai and Ghilzai, conservative Pashtuns opposed to the influences of Western society. From these strongholds the Taliban directed their efforts every summer to expand their control over areas from which they could launch operations against Kandahar City.

In the more remote villages where ISAF had little presence, the Taliban used a combination of terrorism, coercion, and subversion to gain the co-operation of neutral or opposing communities. They first used family or tribal connections to achieve control. If that failed to work, they issued threats, often "night letters" posted on the doors of mosques, and, if necessary, assassination of either important elders or select residents chosen to be examples. The Taliban would then install a "sub-commander" and a small group of fighters in the village to intimidate anyone who was not fully co-operative.[7] Once ensconced in an area, the Taliban could then use this as a base to further subvert control of the legitimate government. For example, one of the more sophisticated insurgent organizations in Zharey was the Baqi network, which set up subunits for specific functions — one for carrying out ambushes, another for laying land mines, a third concentrating on preparing suicide operations, and a fourth specializing in intimidation tactics (such as distributing "night letters" or assassinating key political figures).[8] Eventually, in the areas in which they felt secure, the Taliban set up a shadow government for the province, complete with a centrally appointed shadow governor, judicial system, and military commission.[9]

Battles and firefights, when they now occurred, had significantly different characteristics from those fought 50 years earlier. They now resembled the type of military action that General Charles Krulak, the 1990s commandant of the U.S. Marine Corps, had predicted would become common in the 21st century. He called it the "Three Block War" — three types of actions occurring at the same time in a single district. The COIN force could be fighting to clear insurgents out of a stronghold in one area, carrying out economic development in an adjoining village, and at the same time delivering humanitarian relief close by. In this type of warfare, Canadian troops found themselves defending against an insurgent attack while a farmer ignored the bullets and continued to plough a field not far away, or a Quick Reaction Force (QRF) racing to help a convoy recover from an IED strike would be held up by a traffic jam on the main highway. Firefights become more difficult when Canadian troops under attack were refused permission to use artillery or air strikes because of the risk of causing civilian casualties. Military intelligence to gather and disseminate information about tribal loyalties, insurgent networks, and key enemy leaders now became of critical importance at all levels of military planning.

Canadians advancing against a suspected insurgent community had to take care not to be ambushed or to allow Taliban fighters to lure them into a built-up area where collateral damage from the resulting firefight would alienate local residents.[10] This kind of situation developed, for example, on May 16, 2007, when a company group of 2 RCR BG attempted to probe into a Taliban stronghold in the area of Nalgham-Sangasar, nicknamed "the Belly of the Beast" because of the intense insurgent resistance found there. As the Canadian platoons cautiously advanced, the Taliban executed a carefully planned ambush using the grape fields and ditches to infiltrate between the forward Canadian units. When the Taliban sprang their trap, one platoon was caught farthest from the rest of the company. It came under crossfire from AK-47s and machine guns, with its lead section pinned down in an open field. It could have been a disaster, but the combat skills of the troops and cool leadership by the NCOs saved the day.

The lead section was caught in the open, but its commander, Master Corporal Gerald Killam, remained in control, and despite being personally exposed to enemy fire, issued clear fire-control orders to his men. At the same time the platoon commander deployed his remaining troops to return maximum fire against the Taliban positions. Private Michael Richard Stephen MacWhirter and Private John Williams ran across a 40-metre, fire-swept field to a position where they could set up their C-6 machine gun and bring down its heavy fire on the insurgents' flank. The coordinated action of all troops allowed for a safe withdrawal without casualties. Master Corporal Killam was later awarded the Medal of Military Valour, and Private MacWhirter and Private Williams received Mentions in Dispatches.[11] This was but one example of many actions in which Canadian troops proved themselves to be a first-rate professional army that could best the enemy in open combat.

The Taliban seldom confronted the Canadians openly with large units. When they did, as in Operation Medusa, they could exhibit a surprisingly good understanding of effective military tactics. In Pashmul in 2006, they had constructed well-prepared and concealed trench lines and bunkers with interlocking zones of fire and good supporting positions. Defensive positions were designed using canals and obstacles, along with mines placed to channel any Canadian advance into traps. Their fighters exhibited good fire control, often allowing Canadians to penetrate into a prepared killing zone and only then opening fire simultaneously on different targets. The Taliban fighting force was organized into small primary groups of up to 20 fighters called *delgai*, the members tied to the leader through kinship or other personal relationships. More than 30 *delgai* may have been based in Zharey District, making it one of the most difficult for the Canadians to operate.

Following the Taliban defeat at Pashmul in 2006, the *delgai* were reduced in number to as few as five members as they switched to more stealthy tactics of unconventional warfare. Ambushes and hit-and-run attacks were common. For this type of tactic, one or more basic fighting *delgai* of about five insurgent fighters would meet at a pre-arranged assembly point, travelling by unobtrusive means such as on motorbikes or in a nondescript Toyota car. Weapons and supplies would be recovered from concealed locations that had previously been scattered throughout the district. For raids and ambushes, surprise was relied on to inflict casualties on the Canadian or Afghan targets within the first few minutes. The Taliban force would not linger longer than necessary but try to move to another ambush position along the line of Coalition advance or break off contact before Canadian artillery or Coalition aircraft could be brought to bear.[12]

The basic Taliban fighting unit usually included at least one man armed with an RPG launcher and another with a Russian PKM 7.62 mm machine gun. The main personal weapon used by the Taliban was the widely used, inexpensive, and simple Kalashnikov AK-47 assault rifle. While it fires 600 rounds a minute, some have criticized it as being accurate for only the first burst of fire because the recoil mechanism throws it off target afterward.[13] For this reason and from lack of training, the Taliban have been unable to cause many Coalition casualties in firefights. It was also likely that the Taliban had the same attitude that the ANA had about marksmanship: training was unnecessary because on the battlefield God would direct the bullets.[14]

The RPG-7 is popular with insurgents everywhere, firing an 85 mm explosive rocket that can destroy a lightly armoured vehicle, damage a tank, or bring down a low-flying helicopter but is accurate up to 300 metres. During the advance on the White Schoolhouse by RCR's Charles Company in Operation Medusa, the first casualty came from a Taliban RPG hit on a LAV III, sending shrapnel throughout the interior and killing Sergeant Shane Stachnik instantly.[15] Three months earlier, Captain Nichola Goddard had become the first Canadian female soldier killed in the line of duty when her LAV was hit by RPGs during a Taliban ambush in the same area of Panjwayi District.

The Taliban also seemed to have a good supply of 82 mm mortars, as well as 107 mm and 120 mm rockets, which they intermittently fired at Canadian FOBs. The most deadly and most commonly used weapon, however, was the use of IED. These could be fashioned from old anti-tank mines or simply from an accelerant and a variety of damaging objects such as ball bearings, all meant to kill or maim. They could be buried in a road or trail and detonated by a pressure plate, or they could be activated by a nearby observer using the signal from a cellphone. IEDs could be hidden in parked cars alongside the road, or in walls, trees, and farm fields. As time went on, the Taliban brought in foreign specialists (Arabs or Chechens) to establish bomb-making cells, and these devices became more sophisticated and difficult to detect.

An equally deadly weapon of terror was the suicide bomber, an Islamic fanatic carrying an IED either on his body or in a car driven by him. These attacks were perhaps worse psychologically in some ways than IEDs because a suicide bombing is such a personal act. Overall, both IEDs and suicide bombings became the main weapons of the Taliban, and were the cause of

109 of the 157 Canadian deaths during military actions in Afghanistan to the end of Operation Athena.

Canadian troops had fought against insurgencies before: in 1900 Canadian soldiers were sent to South Africa to help defeat the Boers. In Afghanistan in 2006, there were some similarities with that distant era — in both cases, Canadian troops were often on the move on open terrain, sleeping under the stars when necessary, experiencing extremes of temperature, sometimes suffering from thirst, constantly alert against an enemy who was expert at concealment and could strike at any moment. However, if the men who had chased the Boers on the veldt in 1900 could have foreseen the war that was being fought in Afghanistan in 2006, it would have seemed like a science fiction tale written by Jules Verne. An infantryman now did not travel lightly but carried about 70 kilograms of equipment, including a ballistic helmet with infrared night-vision goggles, a bullet-resistant vest, a C7A assault rifle with 30 rounds in the magazine, six spare magazines with 180 rounds, four grenades, and several litres of water to avoid heat exhaustion. His rifle could fire up to 900 5.56 mm rounds per minute on full automatic, giving each soldier more firepower than an entire infantry platoon had in 1900.

In Afghanistan each rotation of Canadian troops was organized as a combined arms battle group, able to sustain itself for independent operations by having, in addition to its infantry component, its own engineer, reconnaissance, medical, and supply elements. It was also very mobile, compared to the Canadian Army's past experiences in major conflicts. In 1900 Canadian soldiers wore their boots out marching across the Orange Free State; in Afghanistan Canadian infantry were now fully mechanized, equipped with armoured fighting vehicles, mainly the General Dynamics Land Systems LAV III as standard equipment for all infantry battalions.

The LAV III weighs about 17 metric tons and can travel up to 100 kilometres per hour with a range of 500 kilometres. It has a crew of three men and carries seven infantrymen in a cargo compartment, an experience that has been described as "hell for the claustrophobic."[16] The LAV could bring the combat infantrymen into action quickly, but on nearing the objective the infantry would exit the vehicle to approach on foot. The vehicle could then position itself to provide valuable close support from its primary 25 mm Bushmaster chain gun and two 7.62 mm machine guns during the assault.

Each battle group was also equipped with a squadron of Coyote armoured reconnaissance vehicles. The Coyote was also well equipped for fighting with its Bushmaster 25 mm gun and two machine guns, and it was lighter and could reach speeds of up to 120 kilometres per hour. Its great advantage, however, was its suite of sophisticated electronic equipment especially designed for remote surveillance and intelligence gathering. This included night-vision devices as well as video and radar equipment that could detect medium-sized targets as far away as 12 kilometres and larger targets like trucks up to 24 kilometres.

To provide heavier support when required, each battle group in Kandahar Province included a battery of field artillery. The typical artillery weapon deployed in Afghanistan, the M777 howitzer, uses a standard 155 mm shell with a range of 24 kilometres. This is an amazing increase from the range of five kilometres of the "15-pounder" in 1900, or even of the range of 14 kilometres achieved by the 5.5 inch Mark III medium gun employed in the

Gunners from X Battery reload their 155 mm M777 cannons to fire on enemy positions in the north of Kandahar Province. The artillery provided valuable support to Canadian, ANA, and Coalition forces throughout the combat mission.

Second World War. The increased range proved its worth for Canadian infantry caught in firefights in every corner of southern Afghanistan.

Task Force Kandahar received a big increase in firepower in December 2006 when the first squadron of Leopard tanks was added to its strength. These massive 42-metric-ton fighting vehicles were at first thought to have no place in the back roads of Kandahar Province, but this belief was revised when the Canadians faced well-dug-in insurgents during Operation Medusa. The tanks proved their worth because their 105 mm main guns were able to blast through hard mud walls that could not be penetrated by a LAV III's 25 mm guns. They became especially valuable in leading columns against known Taliban strongholds along narrow approach lanes, since they could clear mines by using specially designed rollers attached to their fronts. The tanks had a strong psychological impact on the Taliban, and attacks on convoys were noticeably reduced when accompanied by escorting tanks.

As Canadian casualties from IED attacks on the road-bound convoys increased, the Canadian government realized that air support from Coalition air forces was not always available. Canada needed to have its own helicopters if it wanted to airlift supplies to remote outposts and to provide its infantry with the mobility to carry out rapid missions effectively. Consequently, on December 6, 2008, a milestone in Canadian military history was established as the Joint Task Force Afghanistan Air Wing was formed at Kandahar Air Field with an aviation unit of CH-147 Chinook heavy-lift and CH-146 Griffon escort helicopters. On March 7, 2009, for the first time, a Canadian helicopter took part in an airmobile operation when it joined two British helicopters to carry men of 3 RCR BG along with allied troops into an anti-insurgent operation. Having the helicopters in Afghanistan quickly proved their worth, and during their deployment they flew more than 23,000 hours on Coalition missions, transporting more than 91,000 passengers and carrying 3,200 metric tons of supplies.[17]

One of the most advanced assets employed by the Canadian military in Afghanistan was the tactical unmanned aerial vehicle (TUAV), which gathers video imagery for intelligence, surveillance, and target acquisition. As early as 2003, four CU-161 Sperwer TUAVs were obtained for use in Afghanistan, but they took a while to become operational because of problems caused by heat, dust, and wind patterns from the mountains around

Anticipation runs high as soldiers of 3 RCR BG prepare to board Chinook helicopters that will fly them deep into Zharey District for Operation Sanga Fist, a one-day airmobile deliberate operation. Helicopters were very important in getting troops into action without suffering casualties from IEDs on ground routes.

Two soldiers of 5e Régiment d'artillerie légère du Canada (5 RALC) launch a mini unmanned aerial vehicle (MUAV) outside a new strongpoint near Sangasar in Zharey District. The new compound was established as part of 3 R22eR BG's Operation Tashwish Mekawa.

Kabul. By 2006 these problems were resolved and the Sperwer operated daily in Kandahar Province. In early 2009, the Sperwers were replaced by CU-180 Heron TUAVs, the new aircraft having an improved ceiling of eight kilometres along with a flight-endurance time of four to five hours and a range of 90 to 150 kilometres. By the end of their deployment in Afghanistan, Heron TUAVs had flown more than 15,000 combat flight hours in support of Canadian ground forces.

For more immediate support of small-unit tactical operations, a number of mini-TUAVs (or MUAVs) were also obtained, like the Scan-Eagle and Maverick drones. These lightweight units had a more limited endurance and range but could be launched and controlled in the field. Acting somewhat like the spotter planes of the Second World War, they could provide immediate information to a forward artillery observer (FAO) who could then call in combat support aircraft when their visual systems detected a target. The MUAVs also proved invaluable in reconnoitring convoy routes, following suspected insurgents, and locating IEDs before damage could be caused to ground troops. By June 2010, Scan-Eagles had flown more than 1,700 day and night combat sorties totalling over 17,000 flight hours.

While the LAVs made the Canadian battle group very mobile, the full battle group was not always available for focused combat operations. Some of the infantry strength had to be used for other missions in the broad area of operations, or were needed to hold the main FOBs and smaller platoon outposts while engaging the local population. In the later rotations, battle groups were able to use their strength more effectively as the area of operations became smaller. While the larger FOBs were relatively comfortable, they were always under the threat of attack. The sounds of gunfire around FOB Ma'sum Ghar were so common that soldiers got used to them, but everyone wore all their protective gear whenever outside of their bunkers, since rockets could land at any time. Soldiers in one FOB came to treat these attacks with typical infantry humour, putting up a sign near one of the bunkers reading PROUD TO BE ROCKET-FREE FOR XX DAYS.[18]

Smaller platoon outposts were established for limited periods to guard critical infrastructure or to establish Coalition presence in the vicinity of a community. Living conditions in these posts were always uncomfortable, such as in FOB Lynx, as described by medical officer Captain Ray Wiss:

All the Canadians are packed into the remnants of an old school building. The walls are still solid enough to stop most of the shrapnel from the various things that are shot at us, but the roof is completely rotten. It is patched with duct tape in a number of places, and dust falls down on us whenever a tank drives by…. As for the environment, we are on the very edge of a desert. The heat [in November] is not the killing 50°C of July and August, but the dust is overwhelming. And in a few weeks, the rainy season will arrive and transform all this into a sea of mud. There is the usual assortment of bugs, including monstrous spiders, scorpions and a thing that looks like a wasp but (I swear) the size of a hummingbird, which I call a "Talibug."[19]

The FOBs and patrol bases were not rest areas. They were bases from which focused operations were constantly being launched and daily routine

Nakhonay remained a village with a strong Taliban presence throughout the combat mission. A soldier from Bulldog (Bravo) Company 1 R22eR BG checks a Nakhonay villager before allowing passage through an area being searched for caches of weapons and IED-making supplies during an operation by Canadian and Afghan soldiers in February 2008.

patrols issued into the countryside. The goal was to never let the Taliban rest. Sophisticated electronic intelligence units in KAF constantly monitored Taliban radio and cellphone traffic to provide specific warnings of imminent Taliban activity. In applying COIN doctrine, company commanders, too, sought to constantly take the initiative in getting to know the people in their areas of operation, gather intelligence, and take action whenever something appeared suspicious, much like the policeman whose beat is in the lawless part of a city. Even when there was no obvious Taliban threat, daily patrols continued but were tense as they passed through an environment that could turn deadly at any time. Journalist Josh Wingrove described a typical patrol from an outpost just outside the village of Nakhonay:

> Every day, the platoon mounts a patrol, with times, lengths and paths ever varied. "No matter what, you always have a goal. But you want to keep it as direct as possible, so the guys don't feel they're just putting on the kilometres," says the patrol leader, Sergeant Paul Rachynski.... As the soldiers walk back through Nakhonay, children swarm the streets, asking for money, candy, pens and paper. But the troops are wary of stopping in any one place for long.... Soldiers are always told to watch where they walk — compact earth is a good thing, but loose soil could mean something has been planted there. Here, large holes punctuate the road, left by Canadians digging up explosives.[20]

Canadians continued to try to win "hearts and minds" by interacting with the local residents by means of village *shuras* and attempting to converse with local people while on patrol. These attempts to communicate could often be discouraging; sometimes no one would show up for a scheduled *shura*, at other times elders had little response to the speeches made (through interpreters) by the Canadian officer making the presentation. But this was not always the case. At times, when they felt they were not being observed by anyone else, villagers would respond by providing information about insurgent activity or locations. Positive responses could more often be expected from residents of villages that were made up of tribes not hostile to the Karzai government; in one case a village that was close to a Taliban stronghold even expressed its desire for Canadian soldiers to remain. Most often, local residents attempted to remain neutral, not opposed to Canadian assistance but not wanting to appear to co-operate, since that would bring Taliban retribution, atrocities such as cutting offenders' throats or beheading. In one case, the Taliban executed a boy who had simply been working as a cook at an Afghan police post, beheading him and then hanging his body in the centre of the village as a warning to others.[21]

Some Canadians could not help becoming cynical after clearing a village like Nakhonay time after time, only to find the Taliban infiltrating back as soon as the troops left. Canadians on patrol would suffer casualties from IEDs, but would still have to deal with the local elder, even though they believed he knew where the IEDs were located and who had placed them along the patrol route. No wonder one soldier called this village "the Devil's Anus." COIN warfare was, in some ways, more difficult psychologically than conventional warfare. Following a severe IED attack, Captain

Shuras were one of the ways used by the battle group to keep in touch with local residents and assess their needs. Here, leaders of villages surrounding Sperwan Ghar meet with a Canadian officer in a *shura* near the FOB to discuss security in the region.

Some *shuras* attended by prestigious leaders were more formal and ceremonial. In this *shura* a group of Afghan leaders sits, with small glass tables in between two rows. The interpreter and some elders are on the left; soldiers and other elders are on the right. The scene contains a bright red carpet, yellow and red curtains, tea on the tables, and some candy in bowls.

Sean Ivanko felt like lashing out at someone, but as a professional soldier he was able to rationalize the need to remain under control:

> I'd never experienced anything like that in my life. Literally, I was consumed with rage, every single cell of my body was screaming for vengeance, was screaming out with this blind rage. Obviously, at the end of the day, that's what separates us from the bad guys; that we understand that it wasn't the villagers who did it, we understood that most of the people in Afghanistan want us to win, most of them want to help us.[22]

There were always some, however, who managed to remain optimistic and take their own initiative to deal with local villagers. In 21st-century wars, the term "strategic corporal" has been used to describe the fact that success in COIN warfare is dependent on the initiative of junior ranks and their interactions with the local population. Sergeant Dwayne MacDougall, for example, got the idea that he could make a positive impression on the villagers of Salavat by buying supplies such as eggs from the local store:

> We were trying to figure out how we could work ourselves into the community…. On the first patrol we saw the bazaar and then immediately when we got back I just thought "let's start to contribute by buying the local produce or, if we could, even a goat." Our idea was to use the bazaar to have that big feast that we had…. So I walked right into their store, into the bazaar, and there was interaction, a business thing and a friendship-building moment, too. The men were actually pushing their kids to come see me, and it's only been a week and we can see the fruits of our labour already, it's already starting to show.[23]

As many experts have stated, the struggle against an insurgency can go on for a long time. It takes patience and a completely different mindset than what is needed for a conventional war, since the objective in this type of warfare is not to control terrain but to win the trust of the population. Afghanistan was a learning process and had not yet come to a successful conclusion by the end of the combat mission, but Canadian soldiers showed they had the skills both in combat and in dealing with the Afghan people. Success in Afghanistan was to a large extent up to the other major actors to play their part with equal effectiveness.

PART TWO
THE SOLDIERS

Seven soldiers. Seven military specialties. Seven stories.

What was it like to serve in the Canadian combat mission in Afghanistan? Reports from journalists between 2006 and 2011 only give a brief glimpse of what happened to soldiers during their tours over those years. The following section of this book is meant to give Canadians a better understanding of the breadth of those experiences by describing what happened to seven soldiers during their deployment in Afghanistan.

These seven men have been selected with no other criteria than they each had very different duties while in Afghanistan. They represent a cross-section of ranks from corporal to captain and were from different combat arms, providing the reader with a diverse picture of the challenges faced throughout the combat mission. All of these men were eager to serve, and those not in the regular forces volunteered without reservation. Their duties took them "outside the wire," which meant they travelled throughout the most dangerous districts and at times were at risk of being killed or injured while trying to help the Afghan people. Of course, there will undoubtedly be others whose experiences could be considered more dramatic or those who faced greater dangers, but it is hoped that this sample will give readers an appreciation of what the combat mission meant to men and women who went outside the wire. The soldiers are:

- Captain Jonathan Mineault, a combat engineer who played an important role in counter-insurgency warfare by helping Afghans reconstruct their villages and improve their lives.

- Corporal François Dupéré, who joined a team trying to fight the insurgency not only in combat but psychologically, as well.
- Master Corporal Sean Chard, the leader of a crew of an armoured reconnaissance vehicle equipped with the most advanced electronic technology in the fight against a deadly hidden insurgency.
- Sam, a combat engineer trained in one of the most important and dangerous occupations in Afghanistan — removing and disposing of the Taliban's deadliest weapon, the IED.
- Captain Robert Peel, who became a leader in an OMLT carrying out the critical task of training the ANA to take over the battle against the Taliban when the Canadians eventually left.
- Master Warrant Officer Richard Stacey, the senior NCO of an armoured squadron who provided ongoing leadership to men who drove their tanks out daily to face IEDs and Taliban ambushes.
- Lieutenant Simon Mailloux, the leader of an infantry platoon that in a counter-insurgency struggle was the basic unit fighting to bring security to ordinary Afghan citizens.

Lieutenant Simon Mailloux and Corporal François Dupéré were the first of the seven soldiers to step off the plane at KAF when 3 R22eR arrived in August 2007 as Rotation 4 of Operation Athena, Phase 2. A year earlier the Taliban had been defeated in their bid to capture Kandahar City, but it was still proving difficult to eradicate them from their heartland in Panjwayi and Zharey Districts. Simon and François were both based at FOB Ma'sum Ghar, but they would not have crossed paths, except by chance in the mess tent, as they carried out very different tasks in trying to win the hearts and minds of local villagers and eliminate the influence of the Taliban.

Captain Rob Peel arrived with the next rotation in February 2008. A network of combat outposts and police substations manned by ANA troops and ANP officers had been established to bring security to the key districts, but the Canadian battle group was not strong enough on its own to eliminate the Taliban, which was using unconventional tactics. As this insurgent violence increased, the need for the ANA to take over more of the counter-insurgency battle was stronger than ever. Captain Peel and the other mentors in the OMLT played an important role in making this happen.

Sam and Master Corporal Sean Chard both arrived with the troops of Rotation 6 in the late summer of 2008 to find the Taliban IED offensive continuing. Sam and his explosive ordnance disposal (EOD) team would be based at FOB Ma'sum Ghar where they quickly found themselves called out daily to IED sites discovered throughout Panjwayi and Zharey. Sean and his crew, on the other hand, would be based in the north at FOB Frontenac, from where the Coyote armoured vehicles of the Royal Canadian Dragoons' reconnaissance squadron would cover the Arghandab and Shah Wali Kot Districts. Unfortunately, the Taliban had moved into this area to threaten Kandahar City from the north, and the recce squadron would find itself bearing the brunt of the IED threat in this part of the province. The danger became a deadly reality for Sean when his vehicle struck an IED within days of his arrival.

When Master Warrant Officer Richard Stacey and the men and women of C Squadron of Lord Strathcona's Horse arrived to man the Leopard tanks operating out of FOB Ma'sum Ghar in Rotation 7, the battle group was closing down the combat outposts in the western part of the province to focus on the territory closer to Kandahar City. Joint operations, however, were carried out throughout all districts in the coming months to disrupt insurgent activities and uncover IED cells. The Leopard tanks provided valuable support, leading the way into dangerous areas. The presence of tanks tended to deter insurgents from directly attacking a force carrying out an operation, but this was not always the case. A Canadian convoy escorted by tanks was ambushed by the Taliban while returning from an operation in the Horn of the Panjwayi, and MWO Stacey needed all the skills he had learned during his career to help get his men back safely.

In late 2010, Captain Jonathan Mineault and Corporal François Dupéré were the last of these seven soldiers to deploy to Afghanistan as part of Roto 10. Captain Mineault's area of operations was around Bazaar-i-Panjwayi where the insurgent threat had by now become low, although was not completely eliminated. This allowed Jonathan and his team to carry out numerous construction projects to help improve the life of the population in that area. Corporal Dupéré, on the other hand, headed out with a psychological operations (PSYOPS) team into western Panjwayi where the Taliban still posed a threat. François found himself working out of a combat outpost at Talukan, and it was here that a suicide bomber ended the corporal's second tour in Afghanistan.

These are their stories.

3

INFRASTRUCTURE DEVELOPMENT AT BAZAAR-I-PANJWAYI: CAPTAIN JONATHAN MINEAULT

In COIN warfare, success depends not only on the conventional offensive actions of military forces clearing an area of the enemy, but also on additional efforts to stabilize areas by removing sources of discontent in the population. As kinetic operations move out of the "clearing" phase into the "holding" and "building" phases, the emphasis grows on initiatives taken to counter the influence of the insurgents on local residents by demonstrating that they can benefit from supporting the national government rather than the insurgents. Counter-insurgent forces must therefore have the capability to continue to interact with the population to support improved governance, restore essential services, and promote economic development, even while they continue to provide security to prevent the return of insurgents.

Chapter 5 of the Canadian Army's manual on counter-insurgency operations defines the need to carry out infrastructure projects as part of an overall COIN strategy:

> 503. Many activities conducted by military forces [in a COIN campaign] will seek to build confidence within a local populace and to convince them to support the campaign vice the insurgents. Thus the military will conduct influence activities.... Many stability operations, such as

the construction of infrastructure ... may be considered part of influence activities.

522. Even before non-military agencies arrive in the area to begin long-term development projects, military forces may begin the process to alleviate suffering, spark development and gain campaign support. Measures will involve quick-impact projects such as repairs to wells ... and delivery of basic tools for work and agriculture.

— Counter-Insurgency Operations,
B-GL-323-004/FP-003

When Canada took on the responsibility for Kandahar Province in 2006, it prepared itself to carry out infrastructure support programs as part of its counter-insurgency strategy. In 2010 Task Force Kandahar therefore included not only a battle group but also a combat engineer unit, the Task Force Kandahar Engineer Regiment, which was responsible for developing defences against IEDs, managing construction projects carried out by Afghan contractors, and carrying out other engineering work required by the task force. Units of the regiment therefore had the capability to work with local Afghans on programs that would improve their quality of life, such as building roads, extending electrical services, digging wells, upgrading irrigation canals, and improving other structures such as mosques.

✦

Captain Jonathan Mineault was normally not nervous about walking through the town of Bazaar-i-Panjwayi, but today he was on edge; a message had been received at FOB Ma'sum Ghar the day before, warning that two suicide bombers had been reported heading for the town. Today he was taking his team on patrol through the northwest part of the town in an area known to be more supportive of the Taliban, so his senses were more alert for any negative signs. It had been about two years since the Taliban had last attempted to attack Canadians here, but the threat had not gone away. At that time, a routine patrol had been calmly passing through the bazaar area, speaking to friendly local people, when a nondescript Afghan had come up to them and suddenly shouted the Islamic call praising Allah, *"Allahu akbar!"* A moment of terror had swept through the crowd as he had raised his arms high, making the detonator in his hand clearly visible. The suicide bomber had violently pressed the trigger, which should have caused his explosive vest to detonate, but the device was faulty and nothing happened. Before he had had a second chance to detonate his charge, the Canadians had opened fire on him and ended his attempted attack.[1]

With the possibility of such an event repeating itself today, Jonathan was on constant lookout for indicators of anything out of the ordinary while his patrol wound its way through the narrow alleyways. As they passed around a street corner, the patrol suddenly came upon a small group of Afghans down an alleyway. One of them glanced up at the patrol, and a dark look passed over his face. He started walking toward the patrol, and Jonathan's instincts jumped into high gear. This Afghan was behaving very suspiciously, and Jonathan had learned during his tour to trust his instincts. Quickly assessing the situation, Jonathan immediately ordered two of his men to move to either side of the road for cover and to be ready to protect Jonathan and themselves. He then quickly moved forward to prevent the suspicious Afghan from getting closer to the main body of the patrol. Through his interpreter, Jonathan exchanged polite greetings with the man, and halted him long enough for the leader of the accompanying infantry section to come up and take over further questioning. In the end, nothing else came of this incident, and it was rather trivial in hindsight; but it was an example of what a combat engineer team assigned to development work had to watch out for on a routine day in Panjwayi District.

Jonathan was deployed as part of Rotation 10 of Operation Athena, with a tour of duty lasting from October 2010 to July 2011. The main Canadian component of Task Force Kandahar for this tour was the manoeuvre element built around 1 R22eR BG, supported by engineer and signals units. Of these, the Engineer Construction Squadron of Task Force Kandahar's Engineer Regiment had five Engineer Construction Teams (ECTs), each of which was assigned a different area of responsibility in Panjwayi, Dand, and

Daman Districts.[2] Engineer Construction Team 1 (ECT-1), for example, was carrying out the paving of "Route Hyena," a 70-kilometre road going from Bazaar-i-Panjwayi to the far western edge of the district — unquestionably the most dangerous task of all the teams. ECT-3, led by Captain Jonathan Mineault, was working in a more stable area, responsible for projects in and around Bazaar-i-Panjwayi itself. In carrying out these projects, Jonathan was clear about his role. He was not simply carrying out this work to improve the Afghan infrastructure, but more important, he was using projects to promote stability within the local communities by showing the local Afghans that life under the national government had advantages that the Taliban could not offer.

Jonathan's team was assigned a tracked M113 armoured personnel carrier for their frequent trips out of the FOB to visit work sites or hold *shuras* with local leaders. The vehicle was equipped with a heavy C6 machine gun in case they encountered an ambush. When on a dismounted patrol, on the other hand, it was normal practice for the gunner to carry the team C9 light machine gun. Mindful of the role his team was playing in trying to gain the confidence of the local population, however, after the first few patrols Jonathan decided to replace the C9 with the normal C7 assault rifle, which he felt would be less intimidating. The gun also proved to be too bulky and made it harder for the gunner to help with tasks that had to be done on the sites, such as taking photographic records and measurements. Anywhere in Panjwayi, it was never wise to remain in a fixed location longer than necessary, because it gave insurgents more time to determine the team's next step and prepare ambushes or plant IEDs. Very quickly in his tour, Jonathan decided he would make it a practice to get his job done on any project site as quickly as possible and get out.

ECT-3 was made up of four members of the regular Canadian Armed Forces, including Jonathan, and two civilians: the team's interpreter, who they needed in their constant interaction with the population, and an invaluable explosives-detection dog handler who reported directly to Jonathan when on patrol. Jonathan's second-in-command was a master corporal, a combat engineer who had already done one tour in Afghanistan and proved to be a great help in all their operations. The driver for the M113 was a corporal who had also previously deployed to Afghanistan, and although he had recently transferred to the air force, chose to come back for another tour. He therefore knew his way around and what to watch out for — ideal for a driver in a dangerous land. Jonathan had a high opinion of him, rating him as the best corporal he had ever met. The fourth team member was another corporal from the air force whose trade was that of a radar operator, which had no relation to what was needed on this job. Despite this lack of appropriate army experience, however, he was very keen on going to Afghanistan, and when the ECT opening was advertised, grabbed at the opportunity. He got all the training needed prior to deployment, and in the end, Jonathan found him to be a great help. The former radar operator turned out to have such an exceptional technical aptitude that Jonathan started using him to assist on construction projects, producing a lot of the necessary documents, and even doing design work under Jonathan's supervision. For example, if a wadi or irrigation canal had a problem, the former radar operator could soon design the stone masonry walls needed to support its sides.

Sometime during his teenage years Jonathan had decided he wanted a career in the army, and immediately after graduating from high school, joined up. He graduated from the Royal Military College in 2006 and trained as a combat engineer, serving afterward in the 5e Régiment du génie de combat and finally in the 33 Combat Engineer Regiment. While with the reserve unit, he applied to serve in Afghanistan, and in the summer of 2010 was notified that a position had opened up for a combat engineer officer to mentor troops of the ANA. That role suited him well, and he was soon going through the first phase of pre-deployment training in an OMLT at Valcartier, Quebec.

Upon arrival for final training in Wainwright, Alberta, however, he was reminded of the old adage that plans were meant to be broken. The first thing they told him in Wainwright was that he would no longer be going over as an engineer mentor because they needed him to lead an Engineer Construction Team. Of course, he was disappointed, especially since he would now be leaving the soldiers with whom he had trained for weeks. But by the time he arrived at KAF in November 2010 as part of Task Force Kandahar Rotation 10, he was ready to go with his new team. Within 72 hours of being moved to the ECT, Jonathan realized he would, in fact, be very happy with the change. In his role as an ECT leader, he would now interact much more with the local population, make use of his engineering training, and find himself more challenged and rewarded.

ECT-3 was based in FOB Ma'sum Ghar, the main Canadian base in Panjwayi District, located a short distance from Bazaar-i-Panjwayi, the largest town in the district with a population of about 5,000 people (among the difficulties in estimating the total population is the Afghan custom of concealing their women). The town is about 40 square kilometres in size and is made up of typical one-storey mud compounds. The residential part of the town is divided into numerous neighbourhoods, each with its own mosque, where the residents are usually from a common extended family or clan. The town has a bazaar area — featuring little shops made of concrete or brick, selling all kinds of goods from clothing to food — that runs for several kilometres along both sides of the main road, which leads to the town from Highway One. The businesses include two bakeries, some bicycle and motorcycle repair shops, a gas station, and many meat shops where a sheep or goat is killed in the morning and hung all day on hooks out front. With no refrigeration this attracts about a million flies to the raw meat during the day — all part of the local atmosphere. When Captain Mineault arrived here in 2010, the bazaar was bustling, having benefited

A view of the northwest part of Bazaar-i-Panjwayi shows the height of Ma'sum Ghar rising in the background. FOB Ma'sum Ghar can be seen faintly near the foot of the hill in the far distance. Captain Jonathan Mineault and ECT-3 carried out their construction work around this major town.

from the security provided by the Canadian base that overlooked it since 2006, and from the construction projects that enabled many residents to earn an income they would not otherwise have.

The town is located just south of the Arghandab River, making the land along the river one of the fertile farming areas of Kandahar Province. Crops such as grapes, pomegranates, poppies, and marijuana provide support for the economy of the town, whose residents are mostly farm workers. The town is also important because the district centre is located on its outskirts. The district governor operates from here, calling together a *shura* of local elders whenever a major decision on the administration of the district is required. When Jonathan arrived in Panjwayi, Haji Baran was the district governor. He was a controversial figure, said to have gained his position because he was favoured by Ahmed Wali Karzai, the equally controversial brother of Afghanistan's president. It could be considered typical of the uncertainty and suspicion that accompanied an insurgency that conflicting rumours swirled about him — that Haji Baran was indirectly helping the insurgents, or that some senior Canadian generals wanted Haji Baran removed, or that Haji Baran could not be removed because the Canadian military was protecting him. Who knew what was true?[3]

Bazaar-i-Panjwayi is located in a kind of bowl overlooked by several rocky heights, with Ma'sum Ghar rising about 300 metres above the town. The hill immediately became important when the Canadians first arrived in the province. Both Panjwayi and Zharey Districts were Taliban base areas, and the insurgents reacted violently whenever Canadians made sorties into their territory. When 1 RCR BG arrived in mid-August 2006, Operation Medusa was launched from the hill to clear the town of Pashmul, just across the river from Bazaar-i-Panjwayi. However, the Taliban did not wait for the Canadian attack but launched a strong pre-emptive attack, capturing the height of Ma'sum Ghar and threatening to take the town. The Royal Canadian Regiment's 1st Battalion managed to hold the district centre, and as one of the first moves in Operation Medusa, recaptured Ma'sum Ghar and turned it into a firm base for the main advance across the Arghandab River. When Operation Medusa came to an end, the strategic advantage of the hill had become apparent, since it dominated much of Panjwayi and Zharey Districts and was a naturally strong defensive position. The combat engineers of the battle group began construction of FOB Ma'sum Ghar,[4] and by the end of that year, it had become the main Canadian base for operations in the district.

For his duties in leading ECT-3, Jonathan worked out of an office in the FOB — actually a sea container he and his second-in-command used for their office, living quarters, and team equipment storage area. Afghans who wanted to submit a request for a construction project were allowed into the base and met with Jonathan just outside his sea container. When Jonathan had arrived at the base, he'd found that there was no proper area available for such meetings, so he asked his carpenter-driver corporal to build a picnic-style table with overhead cover about 15 metres from the sea container for this purpose. He did not like the previous meeting arrangement, which was an open area near the camp entrance with no privacy. With vehicles constantly entering and leaving the camp, everyone could hear and see them, and this could easily make Afghans reluctant to come forward with a request. They would rightly be concerned that at this exposed position they could be observed by hired Afghan security guards and could suffer reprisals if the Taliban were informed. It had already happened in ECT-2's area, where one of the local leaders who had requested a project had been assassinated by the insurgents as a direct consequence of meeting and talking to the Canadians. In ECT-3's area, however, Jonathan never sensed any reluctance from local people to come into the FOB. Word that ECT-3 was doing good work spread, and by the end of the tour, Afghans with petitions came from as far away as Zangabad. Jonathan took care to properly receive and listen to them, and when needed, put them in touch with the ECT responsible for their area. He tried hard "to keep the customer happy."

Jonathan also recognized that most of the civilians he met were locals of some influence, so he felt it would be a good gesture to improve relations if he treated them with as much respect and dignity as possible. This approach proved better than expected, and after a few meetings many of these Afghans opened up with useful information about potential danger areas and insurgent supporters. On one occasion, 3 R22eR's parachute company, to which the ECT was attached, investigated a compound that had been identified in one of the project meetings and did indeed confirm insurgent activity there.

ECT-3's makeshift project meeting room inside FOB Ma'sum Ghar was built by Captain Mineault about 30 metres from his camp accommodation. Mineault and his interpreter are on the left, while the representative of the local power broker and the contractor are on the right.

Jonathan could not actually approve any requests for help from local residents who came to him directly; approval could only come from the district governor. Following the proper procedure, a resident had to approach his village leader and ask that a petition be put forward for discussion at the district government assembly. Before that could happen the village leader first had to determine whether the situation affected a large enough part of the community to warrant consideration. For example, if a villager complained that his wall had collapsed because of heavy rains, the village leader would look to see if the rains were damaging the walls of other compounds. If the problem was only with the villager's own compound, the request would be rejected. If, however, the problem was more widespread, the request would be passed on to a council made up of key local leaders, and if this group felt the project affected the community as a whole, it would forward the petition to a district-level *shura* and eventually to Kandahar City for approval by the provincial governor. Despite any preliminary discussions, Jonathan therefore always made sure the petition was signed by the district governor before he began working on a project.

The ECT's primary purpose was to help promote stability within its areas of operation, while one of its secondary purposes was to support the official local government and make it as relevant as possible. If Jonathan received a petition that was not signed by the district governor, he informed the local resident that the project could not be done without that official's permission. According to the formal process, once the petition was signed by the district governor, it was, in theory, sent to the district centre. If the proper procedure was followed, the staff of the district centre then met with the non-governmental organizations (NGOs) operating in the district and with the Engineer Construction Squadron staff who then prioritized the requested projects. In practice, however, when the signed petition was given back to the civilian who requested it, and he brought it to whoever

ECT-3 required that a local villager requesting a construction project provide a petition approved by the district *shura* and signed by the provincial governor before work could begin.

he thought could make it happen; sometimes that would be a Canadian Forces civil-military co-operation (CIMIC) operator, sometimes an infantry officer, sometimes an NGO, and other times one of the ECTs. As a result, most of the time Jonathan received the signed petition directly from the civilian who had originally come to see him at the FOB.

Once the funds were obtained, the Engineer Squadron Headquarters went to the Contracts Management Cell to find an Afghan civilian contractor through a competitive bidding process. When the contractor was chosen, Jonathan met with him along with the local leader at the village, and together they walked over the ground to agree on how the work would proceed. Jonathan found himself often rejecting the contractor's estimate twice or more times before an agreement was finally reached. Once these were approved by Jonathan, the contractor was then given 72 hours' notice to commence working. It was understood that the contractor would provide the technical expertise, material, and equipment, while the village leader arranged for whatever unskilled labour was needed from the men in his village to move earth, gravel, or stone by hand tools and wheelbarrow. It was these types of construction projects that not only made needed improvements to Afghan infrastructure as an objective, but were also important in providing work for local Afghans. The fact that they had asked for these projects also made it less likely that IEDs would be planted to destroy the work they had just done.

As these projects were being carried out, there was one particular Afghan who was often involved, since he was interested in everything going on in the town. Bazaar-i-Panjwayi did not have a mayor; instead, a power broker made things happen. Haji Mahmoud was the man who was in touch with all the neighbourhoods, who had the money and his own militia, and who influenced most things that happened. He was called "the unofficial mayor" of the town. In fact, this power broker owned a construction company and benefited from contracts to pave the roads around and to the south of the town. One could ask if a man of such influence was undermining efforts to establish the national government's presence in the area. The answer is no, not really, because this was Afghanistan and that was how things were done. You had to deal with these men who were considered the leaders, officially or unofficially by the community, as long as their behaviour stayed within reasonable bounds. In Jonathan's opinion, Haji Mahmoud was as clean as an Afghan power broker could be. Most of the local people trusted him, and they went to him when they needed help from the district governor. If his signature was on their petition, it was usually approved by the district governor. In his daily work around Bazaar-i-Panjwayi, Jonathan had a lot of contact with the district governor, and from all reports, Haji Mahmoud seemed to be the fairest man to deal with among the choice available. Taking everything into consideration, Jonathan believed Haj Mahmoud actually helped make the town safer.

Besides dealing with Haji Mahmoud, Jonathan's job brought him into contact with many other Afghans, not only those coming into the FOB but also notables such as *maliks* and local elders while attending *shuras* in out-lying villages. In these interactions an interpreter was an essential addition to Jonathan's team. Over the duration of the tour, he had to deal with three different ones. The first one, Malim, was respectful and spoke English well, but his understanding of the language was not very good. If Malim was asked to translate something he really did not understand, he felt it was dis-honourable to admit his lack of understanding. As a result, instead of asking for clarification, Malim would produce a translation from his imagination.

After a couple of weeks of this, Jonathan became suspicious and told him, "Listen, you know, it's normal that you don't understand everything. For both of us, English isn't our first language, and even if it was, nobody understands everything all the time. So I don't consider it a problem. Just ask me to repeat it and I'll be happy to do so again until I'm confident that you understand. That's no problem at all."

Whenever Jonathan gave him this lecture, Malim replied, "No, no, that's not a problem with me."

But one day they went to a meeting attended by another Canadian officer who also had an interpreter. After the meeting, the other interpreter came over and quietly said to Jonathan, "Sir, your translator is horrible. He translated everything wrong the entire time!" Jonathan asked him if he had an example. The other interpreter thought about it and said, "Yes, actually, sir. When you said you aren't here to fight the Taliban, you're here to help the people and build projects for them, your interpreter said, 'We like Haji Mahmoud. We think he is a good guy.'"

Jonathan was angry. The meeting had been very important for him to get across the idea to the Afghans that the construction squadron was in the country to listen to their problems with water control and to make improvements while employing people in the village. This message had been completely lost. The next day Jonathan sent Malim back to Kandahar.

Jonathan then got a replacement interpreter. Abdul's English was at first obviously not fully satisfactory, so it was not clear whether he would be any better than Malim. When it appeared that the interpreter was under stress on this new job, however, Jonathan's gunner stepped up on his own initiative to help him out with his English, spending several hours a day coaching him. The gunner taught the interpreter words that specifically related to their work, like "irrigation," "erosion," "retaining walls," and "bridges." It made a big difference, and Abdul became a very effective interpreter for the team. Unlike Malim, he would not hesitate to say, "Sir, I do not get this," when he had a problem in a conversation.

After about three months on the job, however, another problem cropped up when Abdul became entitled to about 10 days' vacation time. When such leave came about, interpreters were not supposed to just walk out the gate but were sent back on a military convoy to their company in KAF, which would arrange transportation to their homes. Ideally, this might take about two weeks. However, around the time that Abdul should have been on the way back, he phoned Jonathan to say, "Yeah, I know I'm supposed to be back, but there's no plane available, so, well, I won't be back for another week." Then, when he finally did arrive at KAF for transfer to Ma'sum Ghar, for some reason he sat there for about another week. Jonathan kept sending messages trying to contact him, but nobody could tell Jonathan where he was. In the end, Abdul was gone for almost a month. Jonathan was able to get a temporary replacement interpreter for this period so he could carry on working with his Afghan contacts. Unfortunately, he found that this third interpreter's command of English was even worse than Malim's, but Jonathan had to put up with him until Abdul finally came back.

Despite these problems with his interpreters, Jonathan managed to make the availability of his construction team known in the area, and the Afghans responded well. It seemed to be a sign of success for the Canadian

COIN strategy that more Afghans started showing up at the FOB gate as a result of presentations at *shuras* and during other meetings. From all these requests, Jonathan discovered there was one type of construction work that seemed to be most in demand — improvements on existing drainage and irrigation canals or the building of new ones. These were needed to control the flood waters that resulted each year from heavy winter rains. While Bazaar-i-Panjwayi was located close to the Arghandab River, a small ridge just south of the river created a barrier where the land sloped away from the river toward the town. This became a significant problem, since the town was also overlooked by mountains. Heavy runoff from the rains flowed toward the town from all directions, and the hard, desert-like terrain could not absorb the water. Even as far back as 2006 when the Canadians first came to the area, 23 Field Squadron had suddenly found itself facing flash floods in November. All of the combat engineers at that time had quickly found themselves engaged in flood-mitigation work to save both the new supply road to FOB Wilson and the defensive strongpoints they had just built to protect it.[5] By the time of Jonathan's tour, a lot of drainage work had already been done, but more was needed. Jonathan's first project upon arrival was, in fact, to complete a plan that had begun with the previous rotation: a 12-kilometre drainage canal that followed the main road.

There was never a shortage of projects, only funding. During his time in Afghanistan, Jonathan received petitions for about 60 projects. Out of these he did all the paperwork for about 25, spending many hours over several weeks on it, but only got funding for about 15 of them. Of the rest, he did varying amounts of work on the proposals, but for various reasons never got them through the approval stage. The average project that he was able to complete took between six to eight weeks and employed perhaps 150 Afghans each day. So he was kept quite busy overseeing multiple projects in various stages of planning and construction.

Besides making sure that projects were done on time and within their budgets, Jonathan had to keep an eye on each site to ensure the work was done to acceptable standards. He found that Afghan work methods did not always match what would normally be done in the West, but getting the contractors and workers to change was a challenge. The issue was not one of trying to get them to use Western methods but to use techniques that met minimum-quality standards in order for the work they did to last more than a year.

Afghans did things the way their fathers had done before them and as their fathers' fathers had before that. Take mixing concrete, for example: they would shape a kind of pool out of sand and earth on the ground and eyeball the proportions of the concrete mixture, add a little water, and if it seemed to need a bit more sand or gravel, add that. The result was usually poor-quality concrete. Ongoing projects assigned to Jonathan upon his arrival had walls that were already failing as a result of this method of mixing concrete. In some places many retaining walls had already collapsed, blocking the ditch and making the project useless. But even with that evidence in front of them, it still took an effort for Jonathan to convince the Afghan contractors to bring in a concrete mixer from Kandahar City and do the job properly. To avoid this issue recurring, Jonathan soon decided that for every project that would normally be done with a concrete wall, he would specify that a stone wall be used instead. That type of wall would be more expensive, but he knew it would last much longer.

Captain Jonathan Mineault talks to the Afghan contractor and a representative of the local leader during a surprise quality-control inspection.

Left: Afghan children play in a drainage ditch under construction by ECT-3, with the concrete already poured to make the bottom.

Below: Local Afghans work on the Panjwayi District Centre drainage project.

Construction methods used by Afghans on ECT-3 projects are seen here in Bazaar-i-Panjwayi. In the background the contractor has brought in a machine excavator to dig the drainage ditch, while in the foreground workers prepare a pool into which water, sand, and cement will be mixed, using approximate proportions; a local method that Captain Mineault found resulted in poor-quality concrete.

Another problem Jonathan came across was that some of the smaller drainage ditches previously built along some village roads did not work because they were clogged with debris. These ditches, put in by previous teams, worked well at first and kept the heavy downpours from damaging the mud walls of compounds that lined the road, but these rains lasted only about a month during the winter rainy season. For the rest of the year, the drainage ditches became an obstacle for local residents as they tried to exit their front doors with bicycles or motorcycles. Many solved this problem by pulling rocks and dirt into the ditches to make rudimentary causeways to cross them. However, when the rainy season came, most villagers did not bother to remove the debris in front of their compounds. The water then backed up, and houses downhill were flooded. Residents not directly affected did not try to remove the blockage, causing neighbours down the road to complain. The previous team had tried to solve this problem by creating concrete slabs to pass over the ditches, but unfortunately the problem of poor concrete quality resulted in these slabs eventually collapsing. Jonathan solved this by rebuilding the overpasses and making the slabs twice as thick with reinforced concrete.

It was very important to monitor projects once they had started, so Jonathan tried to do a snap inspection at least once a week to ensure everything was going as agreed. To do this, Jonathan's team could not simply climb aboard their M113 and head off out the gate. For security reasons it was standard procedure in Afghanistan that no patrol leaving the base could have fewer than three vehicles if mounted, or fewer than 10 people if dismounted. Since ECT-3 was actually attached to the parachute company of 3 R22eR, Jonathan had to organize an escorted patrol with Major Frédéric Pruneau, the infantry commander.

Jonathan met with Major Pruneau to tell him what projects he wanted to visit. They then agreed on a date, at which time Jonathan and his team met their infantry escort at the gate, and the combined patrol headed out to the site. Once outside, they remained alert, constantly on the lookout for potential combat indicators, such as the sudden disappearance of children from villages. They were cautious whenever approaching any spot that seemed a likely location for an IED, such as a major intersection or culvert, where they stopped and assessed the situation. Even at the work site, if anything appeared odd, Jonathan sent in their dog handler to sniff around. If the dog seemed to sense something suspicious, they brought out their metal detector to confirm whether there was anything dangerous lurking in the ground.

Upon arrival at the work site, Jonathan did his inspection by walking around the site with the Afghan manager while another member of his team took photographs. The remaining two members of the team provided over-watch of the two on-site, rifles ready, with the infantry escort acting as an outer security cordon. Jonathan and his team always remained within view and covering fire of the escort with weapons ready. When the inspection was over, which could take from 15 minutes to an hour and a half, Jonathan's team fell back on their escort and the infantry commander took over for the remainder of the patrol. The combined patrol then headed out to complete whatever mission the infantry section had for the day, such as searching a suspicious compound. A patrol like this typically lasted about a full day.

Whenever Jonathan and his team ventured outside the FOB, safety was the biggest concern. That meant cancelling a planned patrol at times or even aborting an inspection after arriving at a site if something did not seem right. Jonathan was not going to take any unnecessary risks, because they could always come back another day. In general, however, Jonathan felt quite safe walking around Bazaar-i-Panjwayi compared to the situation that had existed a couple of years earlier when Taliban infiltration had created a sense of fear in the community. Violent acts were now down significantly; during Jonathan's tour, there were very few rocket or mortar attacks against the FOB, and no sniping that he was aware of. The Afghans they came across while on patrol appeared to be relaxed, friendly, often smiling, easy to talk to, and even casually approached the Canadians to ask questions. Jonathan normally did not experience any anxiety about the patrols; he figured there was nothing he could do about threats, and the team's training had prepared them as well as was possible.

Jonathan did experience a number of small incidents that indicated insurgents were still around. On one occasion, he was out to inspect a project to the south of the town. As they approached the site, they expected to see work going on but were surprised that no one was around. Their senses went on alert as they noticed a vehicle nearby that suddenly accelerated away from them as they approached. As the team got closer, travelling down a narrow alleyway, Jonathan's second-in-command spotted two young boys looking over a wall near the end of the lane, one of them holding his hands over his ears. This was too suspicious, since the Taliban had started using children to lay or trigger IEDs. There were too many negative indicators, so Jonathan decided to turn the team around and cancel the inspection for that day.

On another occasion, one of Jonathan's projects was behind schedule, so the construction company decided to bring in workers on a Friday, which is usually a day off in a Muslim country. When the first worker put his shovel into a pile of gravel, he uncovered an IED. More surprising, this was only 30 metres from the ANP checkpoint in the city. Were the police doing drugs, paid off by insurgents, or just sleeping? The workers pulled out the IED as an Afghan police truck passed by and yelled at the policeman in the cab, "Here, we found a mine!"

Captain Jonathan Mineault poses with an Afghan security guard hired by the contractor at one of ECT-3's sites.

The policeman got out of the truck, looked at the IED, and casually said, "Yes, that's a mine." Then he calmly picked it up, put it in the truck, and drove away to deposit it at an explosives and ammunition collection pit near the gate of the FOB, where Canadian combat engineers would eventually dispose of what had been collected. Canadian investigators came to look at the IED and concluded that insurgents had probably brought the main charge and wire to the gravel pile on Thursday night, expecting to come back on Friday night to connect the battery. It was very common for insurgents to place IEDs in multiple stages over the course of a few nights. In this case the change in work schedule foiled that plan, and the workers had to believe this had been their lucky day.

In another incident, a remote-controlled IED detonated at one of Jonathan's project sites while the workers were labouring. The IED had been quickly hidden in a pile of loose rubbish. The rubbish, which included loose earth and a lot of garbage. That time Jonathan had been lucky, because the IED was not detonated until the day after he visited the site. However, while one worker was slightly injured, no one was killed.

There were still insurgents around, but they had simply gone underground and had shifted their focus away from the Canadians to intimidating local Afghans. But the surge of American troops and Operation Hamkari had significantly damaged the Taliban and pushed their influence to the west and south. As far as Jonathan was concerned, the incidents he experienced were trivial, and he considered the area around Bazaar-i-Panjwayi to be stable. He could recall that while acting as an intelligence officer in Quebec in 2007, he had seen reports from Afghanistan indicating that the area had been very dangerous at that time. Even Major Pruneau, who had been on an early rotation, was puzzled that throughout this 2011 rotation there had been no resurgence of major attacks during the summer fighting season.[6] This unexpected stability had allowed Jonathan to easily carry out his role in fighting the insurgents by improving the lives of Afghans in many small ways in his area of operations.

As Rotation 10 ended and Captain Jonathan Mineault returned to Canada, he had the satisfaction of believing he had accomplished something positive in Afghanistan. He was realistic enough to know that the conflict remained to be fully played out, and only time would tell what longer-term effect his work would have in the larger scale of future events. But while he was there, he had interacted with many Afghans who had welcomed his presence. He had given them useful work, which they were eager to do, earning money to improve their lives despite threats made by the Taliban. The same could be said for the other engineer construction teams of the Task Force Kandahar Engineer Regiment.

By the time the change of command ceremony was held in July 2011, the regiment's headquarters had been deployed for 11 months and could report that during its tour 103 kilometres of roads had been completed and 56 kilometres of irrigation and drainage canals had been constructed or improved in Panjwayi, Dand, and Daman Districts. These projects provided, on average, much-needed work for more than 700 Afghans each month, significantly improving the economic life of the districts involved and showing a number of Afghans that they had some hope for a better life.[7]

4

THE PSYOPS WAR AGAINST THE INSURGENCY: CORPORAL FRANÇOIS DUPÉRÉ

In June 2009, a U.S. Army truck passed along the main road in a large city in eastern Afghanistan. It was a routine supply run and there was no indication of any threat as the vehicle wound through the traffic and pedestrians. One of the truck's tires had a blowout, however, and the driver was forced to stop and change it. Stopping in a crowded street of an Afghan town was never a good idea; a stationary American truck was all that was needed for a target by the Taliban, who lurked everywhere. While the driver carried out his repair, a large crowd of local people, always curious about foreign soldiers, gathered around to watch. From the edge of the crowd, an inconspicuous man stepped forward, quickly pulled out a grenade, and tossed it toward the truck. In the resulting explosion, many of the curious onlookers were killed or injured. The Taliban propaganda machine quickly went into action, spreading rumours and accusing the Americans of purposely using the truck as a lure to kill local people. They made sure the rumour spread throughout the city, and within hours angry people in the bazaar began to shout, "Kill the Americans! Protect Islam!"[1]

In the insurgencies of the 21st century, the main battle is often said to be a fight for the "hearts and minds" of the people, a psychological battle as to whether citizens give their allegiance to insurgents or to the legitimate government. In Afghanistan the Taliban know this well and are adept at using every opportunity to present ISAF forces as foreign invaders and the Karzai government as illegitimate. An incident in which Afghans are killed or injured is craftily made to appear as a planned assault by ISAF. When a foreign-aid project is successfully carried out in remote regions, the Taliban either take credit for it or claim they were instrumental in approving its work.[2]

Insurgency wars are not new; they have occurred since ancient times. What is new is the ease of access now made possible to the latest instruments of technology, and the insurgents' readiness in making use of them. Insurgents in Afghanistan have equipped their fighters with mobile phones to enhance their own communications, such as coordinating the activities of their fighting groups or rapid reporting on ISAF troop movements. They produce videos to broadcast propaganda messages to local viewers and to international audiences over popular media channels — on YouTube, Al Jazeera, or their own Internet sites. Islamists believe that an attack that is not publicized is an attack that has not succeeded. The most popular method they use to spread their messages is by posting threatening notices on the doors of targeted individuals. These "night letters" are designed to intimidate local people to conform to their edicts, and have been used to declare death threats against individuals such as teachers if they do not abandon their posts, or against the families of interpreters if they do not stop working for ISAF, using wording like "you will be killed, we will kill your family ... you cannot escape from us."[3]

The military forces of Western countries have been aware for some time that a key aspect of insurgency warfare is the battle to influence people. Throughout the wars of the 20th century all sides gradually developed the use of psychological operations (PSYOPS) to influence both their opponents' military forces and population. In the U.S. military, however, the emphasis on PSYOPS became more significant during the Vietnam War, when a dedicated psychological operations group comprised of four battalions was established to support combat operations in that conflict. By the 1991 Gulf War, the role played by American PSYOPS units was sufficiently successful that the British military decided to form its own permanent unit, which has taken part in every significant British military operation since.

The decision to create a permanent PSYOPS capability did not come easily to most militaries. Mandating and training soldiers to carry out a range of activities under the vague term of "psychological operations" was not easily understood by soldiers who were trained to fight an enemy in operations using conventional tactics and weapons. Questions arose such as: Were the use of sophisticated psychological tools, commonly employed to sell consumer products, just another form of brainwashing? Did these tools resemble the methods used too often by authoritarian regimes to deceive their citizens? And was such an effort simply a waste of time? Successful psychological operations were carried out, however, in the Gulf War against Iraq, and lessons learned there sharpened PSYOPS doctrine. Many critics had to be impressed when on television news from that conflict they saw thousands of Iraqi soldiers readily surrendering to Coalition forces.

The Canadian Army's attitude to PSYOPS probably softened in the 1990s as some commanders recognized the need for such methods during their peacekeeping experience in places like Bosnia, Rwanda, Kosovo, and East Timor, where reducing tensions among different racial groups was a big part of the challenge. Senior officers recognized that characteristics of conflicts were changing during the latter part of the 20th century, so the Canadian Armed Forces commissioned a study of what would be required by the Canadian military to meet future threats in this new environment. As a result of the recommendations, in November 2003, Lieutenant-General Rick Hillier ordered the army to develop an ongoing PSYOPS capability.

In Canada the first formal PSYOPS group was created in January 2004. It had an authorized strength of 24 reservists from the Montreal area, but so great was the response that within a few weeks more than 60 personnel were enrolled. A U.K. PSYOPS course was given in the summer of 2004 by experienced British PSYOPS personnel, supplemented with contracted courses dealing with technical subjects such as information technology, radio production, and photography. After a six-month probation period, the PSYOPS unit pared itself down to its authorized strength as those candidates who did not meet the PSYOPS standards were returned to their home units. The first PSYOPS section was deployed to Kandahar with the Canadian Multinational Brigade in Operation Athena, Phase 2, in 2006.[4]

The mandate of the unit, as formally stated, was to "carry out planned psychological activities using methods of communications and other means directed to approved audiences in order to influence perceptions, attitudes,

and behaviour affecting the achievement of political and other objectives."
More specifically, within this broad definition, psychological operations
could now be employed by a Canadian task force commander in operational theatres to support combat operations by deceiving or weakening the
will of an enemy combatant, and for gaining the support of the uncommit-
ted local populations.

Because of the broad range of skills needed to achieve such results,
taking into account resource restrictions in the army at that time, the
decision was made to staff the new PSYOPS unit mainly with reservists,
while maintaining the option to draw on contracted civilian expertise such
as psychologists, marketing specialists, and graphic designers. Regular
Canadian Army personnel could be injected in subsequent years. Personnel
from the tactical PSYOPS platoon headquarters who were deployed to the
operational area had access to the special skills required for the particular
mission and were able to develop whatever print, audio, and other media
products necessary to accomplish the PSYOPS programs. The headquarters
had the critical responsibility of using social science methods to identify
target audiences, gathering data about them, developing new products for
influencing the behaviour of this audience, and assessing the effectiveness
of these products as they were disseminated by the tactical sections.

Actual contact with target audiences was carried out by three tactical PSYOPS sections each made up of five tactical operators led by a
sergeant. They normally executed their duties independently in three- or
four-man teams, guided by the PSYOPS objectives set out by the PSYOPS
commander, but in coordination with a combat unit to which they were
attached. The operators were trained in skills that allowed them to constantly assess the attitude of the population they were dealing with and
report on what issues they could identify. They even looked for non-verbal
indicators such as what goods were selling in the bazaar, were the people
dressed properly, and whether they were looking at the ground or at the
Canadians in the eye. Normally, one of the operators engaged Afghans
who were considered the "target audience," while a second was responsible for close protection, and a third watched for body language or other
non-verbal indicators. Formal interactions with the audience were largely
done by taking part in *shuras*.

At the end of each mission the section documented what they had learned by preparing a mission report for the task force headquarters, detailing what happened on the patrol, the topics discussed, and the reactions of the local population, concluding with an analysis of what was going on in the area just assessed. Reports from the tactical sections describing both formal meetings and informal contacts that had been made with the population were then assembled at the PSYOPS headquarters to produce an informed picture of the population and its needs and interests, as well as to assess the effectiveness of the PSYOPS programs being used.

✦

François Dupéré stared ahead of him at the knife-edge ridge rising at an 80-degree slope leading to the narrow summit that marked the top of Island Peak at 6,188 metres in the Himalayas. He paused, gasping for oxygen at this altitude, and thought, *No way. You've got to be kidding me!* But that thought quickly passed through his mind and was put aside. It was simply another challenge to him and that was what he lived for. The past training he had had in the Canadian infantry had simply reinforced that natural attitude; when you get into a difficult situation, simply get on with it and do it without complaint. All the members of the expedition reflected the same attitude because they had a lot in common, all having been injured at some time during their service in the Canadian Armed Forces. But that did not stop any of them from volunteering to join this expedition, organized by the True Patriot Love Foundation as a means to raise money to support mental health programs and rehabilitation for Canadian veterans and their families. The 12 volunteers would show the world that they could still overcome physical and mental challenges despite their injuries. Now, on October 23, 2012, 16 days after arriving in Kathmandu, Nepal, they were about to conquer the peak.

François is small in stature and does not stand out in a crowd. But he has always kept himself in good condition, ready for any physical challenge. His most notable feature is his optimistic and energetic attitude toward life. With an outgoing personality, readiness to come out with a joke under any circumstance, and an easy smile on his face, he is someone you could readily recognize as having that characteristic called "joie de vivre." He had served in two tours in Afghanistan with PSYOPS, but during his second he was so seriously injured by a suicide bomber that he should have died. François only survived that incident thanks to exceptionally good medical care.

By 2013 he had finished all his physiotherapy when two friends informed him about the True Patriot Love project. They knew a challenge like that would attract him. He responded by sending in his application, but then promptly forgot about it. A couple of months later, while relaxing on his boat on a lake in the Laurentian Mountains, he was surprised to get a call on his cellphone informing him that he had been chosen to join the pre-selection process for the Himalayan expedition. Within weeks he found himself in Canmore, Alberta, training for the climb, and then a few weeks afterward he was off to Nepal.

Now, high in the Himalayas and bracing himself against a strong, cold wind, with the icy ground dropping off on each side, he faced his final challenge — a last push to reach the summit — while out of breath for lack of oxygen and struggling to use his one good hand to both hold an ice axe and manage his jumar, the ascending device he needed to remain securely fastened to the safety rope. But he made it to the top, and was proud to cheer with the others as they celebrated their success by hugging one another while revelling in the sight of the massive peaks soaring around them. François felt a great personal satisfaction from the successful ascent, grateful that he had overcome his injuries enough to accomplish this physical challenge, but he did not dwell on it long. To him, it was just another milestone along the way. His motto was, "check off the box. Let's do something else!" He was already looking for another challenge, an ambition that had grown stronger since surviving the Afghan mission.

François developed this attitude at an early age while growing up in Laval, north of Montreal. He was a normal boy living in a typical middle-class neighbourhood. But in high school he was shy, with a small physique, and larger boys sometimes bullied him. One day he decided this had to stop. He began to take karate lessons, becoming stronger and more

Corporal François Dupéré remembers his regiment as he celebrates reaching the top of Island Peak in the Himalayas at 6,188 metres.

confident, until one day, when one of his tormentors tried to push him around again, he stood up to the bigger boy and thrashed him. After that the gang stopped bothering him and his attitude to never back down from any challenge took hold.

François's interest in the military started at an early age because he saw it as a source of adventure. He had always had an interest in the military, so he joined the reserve battalion of R22eR as soon as he was old enough. In 2001 he had his first overseas deployment when he volunteered to go on a peacekeeping mission to Bosnia, where he served as a LAV III gunner. Soon after his return to Canada, he saw the notice that the army was looking for volunteers to join a new unit being formed in Montreal called PSYOPS, which sounded like a good source for new experiences.

This strong instinct François displayed to seek out new challenges despite the risks they might entail resembles one of the personalities described by J. Glenn Gray, an American intelligence officer in the Second

World War, who wrote about his observations on how war affected men. Gray believed there was one type of soldier who was not reluctant to face death in battle, because

> action is their element, and their hearts are in the future as it enfolds itself every day. They look out upon the world as adventure and upon themselves as capable of storming its ramparts. They are not naive enough to regard themselves as indestructible, and do not even desire to be. What they desire is experience, and the fuller and more intense that experience is the more content they are…. If death be the issue, they are normally fatalists by instinct and can accept it more calmly than the prospect of a boring, empty period in their lives.[5]

When François heard that people in PSYOPS were sure to be deployed to Afghanistan, it was not surprising that he decided to volunteer. But there were other things related to PSYOPS that attracted him as well. It was a small self-contained unit, more informal than a regular infantry section, whose members received training beyond basic combat skills, and were expected to make a special impact on the mission. When he joined the unit in 2004, he was sent on the first tactical PSYOPS operator course given in Canada at Longue-Pointe, just outside of Montreal. Here they were given lectures by specialists from outside the military who trained them in such atypical subjects as the ability to study people in foreign theatres of operations and sensitivity to factors like cultural beliefs and demographics.

To enhance the lectures, the trainees were presented with scenarios in which they practised interacting with villagers from foreign cultures. At that time the Canadians only had previous experience in the areas around Kabul, so the training was designed to deal with rebels in Sudan. Choosing this country was as good as any, since the scenario's purpose was to teach students to examine all possible political, military, economic, and social issues that might be involved in a foreign deployment. To make the course more realistic, members of the Montreal Syrian community were brought in to play the roles of local villagers. They weren't Afghan, but they spoke several foreign languages that none of the trainees understood and were very knowledgeable about the challenges a Westerner might face when immersed in Middle Eastern cultures, presenting situations in which foreign habits had to be considered.

François was keen to go to Afghanistan as soon as he could, and almost went on the first rotation to Kandahar in 2006, but complications in paperwork prevented that from happening. Jason Warren, an acquaintance of his from the Black Watch of Canada, went instead. Unfortunately, that July, the shocking news came back from Afghanistan that Jason and another soldier from PPCLI were killed when their convoy was hit by a suicide bomber just west of Kandahar City. Warren's death, as well as the many others who had already died on the mission, was on François's mind when he was finally selected for deployment on Roto 4 in August 2007.

By now it was clear based on all the reports coming back, that Afghanistan was a dangerous place, so François expected a difficult tour when he left Canada. His concern was heightened shortly after arriving at KAF while he was getting his kit sorted out. A friend who had already been there for a few weeks asked him if he wanted to see something unusual. Naturally, François would accept such an invitation, so they drove out to the "vehicle graveyard," a site within KAF where the vehicles that had been damaged beyond repair during previous rotations were dumped. It was a strange sight, but the one that impressed François the most was a LAV that from a distance seemed to have only lost one wheel, and so appeared not badly damaged. But when François climbed up on top of it he found that the driver's hatch had been completely ripped off, and there was only a big hole remaining where the driver's seat had been. That brought him face to face with reality in Afghanistan!

It was only a short time later that François left KAF on his first road convoy, going to Ma'sum Ghar using the same road on which so many IED strikes or ambushes had taken place. The memory of that LAV was still with him, making that trip tense and fearful. But a sense of fear had never deterred him before; in fact, it had usually been a motivator that challenged him to seek out such experiences. In the end that convoy turned out to be routine, and after his second and third uneventful convoys, the fear subsided and was gone. Eventually, François became attuned to Afghan culture and began to think like the locals, accepting fate by repeating *Insha'Allah.*

The first months in Afghanistan were a whirlwind of activities for the PSYOPS team. On paper they had rooms in KAF but were hardly ever there. They were always out on operations for up to a week at a time, returning to KAF only occasionally for a brief rest. On those return visits, they had just enough time to wash their dust- and sweat-stained clothes before the PSYOPS commander alerted them about another operation. They then joined a convoy heading out from KAF and travelled to a FOB, usually Ma'sum Ghar, where they stayed with the infantry unit carrying out the next operation.

Their travels took them all over the districts adjacent to Kandahar City, but were mostly focused in Panjwayi. Here they visited villages such as Zangabad and Talukan, and as far out as Mushan at the end of the Horn, where as part of Operation Garranday Zmaray the battle group established ANA and ANP bases to secure the area from the continuing Taliban presence. Normally, their task was simply to patrol an assigned sector, stop at selected villages, talk to the leaders, and collect as much human intelligence as possible along the way. If, at the end of the day, they were too far out to return to the FOB, they stopped overnight in the middle of the desert with vehicles parked in a box formation, guns pointed outward to cover all approaches. Someone from each crew was selected to remain on watch in each vehicle while the others arranged their sleeping bags in the middle of the box.

François loved these nights when he slept in the open. The temperature in the desert could plummet from extreme heat in daytime to close to freezing at night, but the sky would be pitch-black. To François it was spectacular, with stars sparkling in all directions. The only thing he didn't like about those desert nights was the scorpions that sometimes showed up.

The five-man PSYOPS unit travelled in a multi-purpose RG-31 Nyala armoured personnel vehicle, for which François was usually the driver. The Nyala was especially designed to withstand normal IED strikes, although it was still vulnerable to the increasingly powerful IEDs the Taliban had

---

* The Islamic invocation that all will go well if it is within Allah's plan.

Corporal Dupéré kneels while on a patrol in Arghandab and Shah Wali Kot Districts.

begun to employ. Fortunately, the team was not attacked by insurgents on any of their trips. The vehicle did suffer damage, however, but it was self-inflicted. After one operation, the PSYOPS section was driving after dark as part of a convoy of about 20 vehicles. To avoid detection by insurgents, all vehicles advanced with their lights off. But at a muddy section of the road the Nyala got stuck, holding up the whole convoy. When François tried to get the vehicle going again, however, its lights got turned on and he could not switch them off — the Nyala was an unconventional vehicle designed in South Africa for riot-control work, and so had some awkward design features. The convoy commander angrily called in clearly over the radio, "Hey, you Nyala, get those damn lights off!"

Still struggling to get the vehicle out of the mud, François heard the start of incoming Taliban fire and decided to resolve the issue once and for all in his own unique way. Leaping out of the vehicle, he extinguished the offending lights by smashing them with his Gerber knife. It was not an approved solution, but he had a clear conscience when he later told the mechanic that he had hit something on the road. It was a question of saving lives — survival mode, as far as he was concerned.

The PSYOPS tactical section's main technique for assessing local sympathies and gathering human intelligence was to interact with local Afghans in their *shuras*. The section never went out alone but was always part of a joint patrol, linking up with an infantry unit from the Van Doos that provided security. The PSYOPS and the infantry units had their own objectives for the day but acted as a team to carry out whatever tasks were necessary. Each member of the PSYOPS section was briefed on what specific information was to be gathered or disseminated for that mission, and what role each operator was expected to play in carrying this out. Who they met with and how many of the Canadians would be involved depended on the circumstances.

The section attended *shuras* in a wide variety of buildings, from simple mud compounds to mosques, and might meet with mullahs, village elders, or local power brokers. Although most of these meeting places were very simple, one brought François's section to an apartment block in Kandahar City, where before getting into a conversation the power broker asked for help adjusting the television aerial on his roof. For a simple improvised *shura*, two Canadians might sit cross-legged inside while some remained outside on watch for security, with others getting into conversations with curious villagers looking on. On more formal occasions, a district *shura* was organized in which mullahs from a number of villages were invited, with 20 to 30 persons in attendance.

Shuras were not meant to be rushed or to follow any kind of script. Everyone sat, with tea and perhaps simple foods such as nuts or dates offered, and then a conversation would begin on general topics, such as the weather or the welfare of the families of those in attendance. Gaining the confidence of local Afghans required patience, and some soldiers used to the fast pace of Western life often found this lack of speed difficult. The PSYOPS sergeant might start the conversation, but then let the corporal take the initiative if a rapport seemed to be developing between that soldier and the mullah or elder. At the end of the day the mission report was prepared by the PSYOPS member who had had the main interaction. Everyone had been trained in skills needed for asking questions and listening and was

A *shura* takes place between a village elder and Corporal Dupéré's PSYOPS team leader during a patrol in Arghandab and Khakrez Districts. This is a less formal meeting with many villagers attending to hear what the Canadians had to say. This elder was a former *mujahedeen* who had fought the Soviets and for Muslims in Bosnia.

In this more formal *shura*, the PSYOPS team leader and his interpreter talk to elders during a patrol in Arghandab District.

therefore capable of taking the lead in acquiring maximum information. Questions were framed carefully. For example, to find out if the mullah was getting along with the elder, the operator might ask, "Have you seen the elder lately? How's it going with him? Have you heard anything about the location of a known Taliban leader? We know there's gun smuggling going on in the area. Who's involved in it?" Body language was observed for more clues and any emotions in the mullah's responses were noted.

In all these interactions, an interpreter was, of course, essential. PSYOPS operators had some elementary training in Pashto, such as *Salaam Alaikum*,* but they could not hope to carry on meaningful conversations with Afghans on their own. The PSYOPS section had a good interpreter named Hafiz, who remained with it for the whole tour. Hafiz travelled everywhere with the section's members, eating their meals and sleeping with them wherever they bivouacked. Because they were together for such an extended time, François got to know Hafiz reasonably well and enjoyed talking to him. François became aware of the extent of Hafiz's strict religious beliefs one day when he mentioned that in Christianity Jesus was considered the Son of God. Hafiz snapped back angrily, "No, no, no, he's not a son of God. He's just a prophet. He isn't the son of God!"

Obviously, this was not a subject that could be easily discussed. François quickly understood that Hafiz was quite conservative in his beliefs, and was sure that if he ever had the opportunity to emigrate to Canada his wife would wear a burka. Other than their differences in religion, however, there were no problems in the relationship between the team and Hafiz, and he did his job well. At the same time, he was nervous on occasion about being an interpreter because his family lived nearby in Kandahar City. He feared that if someone recognized him, word could get back to the Taliban and his family would be threatened. So whenever they operated close to the city, Hafiz wore a scarf to conceal his identity.

The team continued to be lucky and none of their convoys experienced IED strikes, though they did have contact with insurgents who fired on them from a distance. At the same time, however, there was always the chance of becoming a casualty, even when resting at FOBs, which

---

* "Hello," or more formally, "Peace to you."

were targeted intermittently by mortar or RPG fire. At Ma'sum Ghar the PSYOPS team was always given a simple transit tent for accommodation without any concrete wall to protect it. One day when the section was resting in their tent between missions, an enormous explosion knocked everyone to the floor. A mortar bomb had hit only metres away, riddling the tent's roof with shrapnel. Shards of shrapnel had torn though the tent but, by some miracle, no one suffered even a scratch. François knew they could have been badly hurt, but remained relieved that his luck was still holding out.

In all the *shuras* they participated in, François sensed no antagonism from the Afghan participants. That could have simply been a reflection of the conflicting situation Afghans found themselves in: provide hospitality to a guest, listen attentively, but make no commitment until it became clear which side would dominate. But it remained obvious that insurgents were everywhere, watching, listening, and waiting for an opportunity to do damage. The most chilling example that François experienced was on a morning when the team was out on a patrol and passed through a village where all of the people were out in the street and appeared to be in shock. Through Hafiz, the Canadians asked what was wrong. The villagers led them into the police station, where they were shown the bodies of the entire garrison. It was a sight that François would not forget. The police were all dead, gunned down, with blood everywhere.

On further questioning of the villagers, the PSYOPS team came to understand that one of the policemen had disappeared, likely a double agent from the Taliban. He had been on guard duty that night and had left just before the executioners had arrived. It was not just the sight of the dead bodies that disturbed François. There was a strong, strange smell of death in the building that struck him immediately. The odour seemed to linger in his nose and was so distasteful that he had to chain-smoke cigarettes afterward to try to get rid of it. While this scene was shocking and might have been traumatic for some, François's reaction was the same as it had always been: he was merely a witness to an experience in the real world, so he got on with his duty as usual.

Near the end of the year the PSYOPS section received a change of orders. It would no longer be based at Ma'sum Ghar but would move to the far western extremity of Panjwayi District, where the Arghandab and Dowrey Rivers converge in the so-called Horn of Panjwayi. Here they would be headquartered at Combat Outpost (COP) Mushan, the most westerly of a chain of three bases meant to secure that part of the district. It was an area with a strong insurgent influence. The Taliban needed to control the area around Mushan, since it was on their main route for moving supplies and men from Pakistan toward Kandahar City. As a result, during the summer of 2007, they built up their strength in the area and began attacking the police posts, inflicting significant losses and demoralizing the officers.[6] The Canadian battle group had managed to stabilize the situation by the fall of that year, but the conditions at COP were not something to look forward to. Ryan Flavelle, a signaller with PPCLI who went on a patrol to Mushan in 2008, described the base:

> SP [Strongpoint] Mushan is one of the most depressing places I have ever seen. It is located about one kilometre outside the village of Mushan, which consists of about 100 buildings and no more than 200 people.... The strongpoint is a tiny pimple on the otherwise flat face of the desert it inhabits. It is surrounded by about one kilometre of dried-out opium fields separated from the village proper by the deep wadi.... The architecture amounts to a square wall of HESCO bastions. Around the HESCOs is a razor wire, and the square is dotted by observation and firing positions.[7]

Now winter had arrived, with temperatures dropping to close to freezing every night and rain falling constantly. With such miserable weather, François might have expected to find Mushan quiet because the fighting season was over and the top-tier Taliban fighters normally withdrew into more remote shelters, like Pakistan, for the winter. But local insurgent cells remained in the villages of western Panjwayi where tribes were sympathetic to the Taliban, and the outpost experienced sporadic small-arms or mortar fire almost every day.

After being away on leave, François soon became aware of this insurgent presence almost immediately upon his arrival back at Mushan at dusk on a convoy from Ma'sum Ghar. He was eager to find his section and greeted them all with "Hi, bro, what's up?" Then he had a cigarette, got caught up with the latest news, and finally withdrew to his small two-man tent to get some sleep. Just as he bent to untie his boot laces, the whoosh of an RPG suddenly cut through the stillness. The rocket had just missed his tent, shaking the framework, and slammed into a Badger armoured vehicle, wounding one soldier in the face with shrapnel. François could only think sarcastically, *Happy New Year. I'm back in Afghanistan!*

To make matters worse, because of the weather, Mushan was more miserable than ever. Throughout January and February the ground turned to soft, sticky clay. Eight-wheeled and tracked vehicles got stuck, and mud gripped on soldiers' boots, making them feel a couple of kilos heavier. Everything got stuck at some point. In François's opinion, it was disgusting. This was the only time in Afghanistan when his natural optimism departed and he could only think, *Oh, man, I hate my life here!* But despite that feeling, he got on with the job that had to be done. The PSYOPS section continued to carry out its daily patrols, now mostly on foot, and put up with the weather. Winter soon passed into the spring of 2008, however, and with that the tour was over and they headed back to Montreal.

For the next two years, life returned to normal for François, and Afghanistan became just a memory. But he did not forget the country and PSYOPS. François had loved the job he had done on his first tour despite his complaints. As a PSYOPS operator, he had travelled throughout the Canadian area of operations, had seen all the FOBs and police substations, and had enjoyed meeting Afghans in their villages. His tour had given him the opportunity to get a global picture of the mission that most other soldiers were not able to have. He also felt that by delivering PSYOPS programs he had been doing something useful that would hopefully benefit the Afghan people. So, in early 2010, when he heard that some of his buddies were going to apply for another rotation, he knew he had to go again and volunteered for a second tour.

In the intervening period after François's first tour ended, the struggle against the Taliban in Afghanistan had not gotten any easier. The single Canadian battle group supported by inadequate ANA and ANP forces was not strong enough to cover the whole area of operations in Kandahar

Province effectively, and the Taliban had increased their activities in their attempt to close in on Kandahar City. As a result, in the spring of 2009, the decision was made to close Mushan and the other combat outposts in the Horn of Panjwayi so that ISAF forces could concentrate on Kandahar City and eastern Panjwayi. The Taliban moved back into the villages of western Panjwayi, where they now had complete freedom of movement. Eventually, the situation began to turn around in 2010, when a new commander of ISAF and U.S. forces in Afghanistan, General Stanley McChrystal, arrived with a revised strategy that deployed additional American troops to southern Afghanistan to regain the initiative.

In September 2010, the first phase of Operation Hamkari began, in which U.S. forces first battled to regain control of Arghandab District, followed shortly afterward by a second phase that cleared much of Zharey District. Finally, in October, U.S. infantry and Special Forces along with Afghan army units advanced into the Horn of Panjwayi, first against Mushan and Zangabad, and finally against Talukan. By this time, the Taliban had already suffered grievous losses in their attempts to oppose the Coalition advance, and the insurgents simply faded away. The emphasis for the Coalition now shifted from offensive clearing actions to regaining the confidence of the Afghan villagers in the Horn. Combat outposts were re-established on a long-term basis to maintain a security presence while the local communities were rebuilt.

The village of Talukan lies in the heart of the Horn, halfway between Mushan and Zangabad, so it had been under Taliban influence for a long time. After clearing the booby traps left by the departing Taliban, a new, larger Coalition operating base was built adjacent to the village bazaar around an old compound fort that had last been used as a *madrassa*. It was large enough to hold a company of the U.S. 2nd Stryker* Regiment,[8] which operated out of Talukan for the rest of its tour as part of the renewed counter-insurgency strategy. Journalist Brian Hutchinson visited the village later that winter, admitting that it still gave him "the creeps" after his previous experiences there. In 2006 he had uncovered the report of a Taliban

---

*   The Stryker is an eight-wheeled armoured vehicle used by the U.S. Army that is similar to the Canadian LAV III.

atrocity in which 26 villagers had been executed after being accused of co-operating with ISAF troops. Now, with the permanent presence of a large combat base, it was hoped the area could be made secure and the threats of such atrocities removed.

The last rotation of Task Force Kandahar took place in October 2010. It was built around 1 R22eR BG and included, as one of its supporting elements, a PSYOPS platoon under Major Benoit Mainville. With the main effort of the Task Force now concentrated on the Horn, the PSYOPS resources were also deployed in this area to gain maximum benefit from its methods, with a section each assigned to Talukan, Zangabad, Ma'sum Ghar, and along a new road being constructed to link Sperwan Ghar and Mushan.

During the summer of 2010, François went through his pre-deployment training again, but a family emergency delayed his deployment for several months. Consequently, he did not arrive at KAF until near the end of February 2011, having missed the first months of that rotation as well as the worst part of the winter. Upon landing he went straight out to Talukan, where he joined the PSYOPS section under Sergeant Reginald Obas. On his arrival, he found the Canadians were now operating smoothly out of the FOB alongside the American infantry unit based there, establishing a security bubble with their constant presence. Foot patrols went out every day, covering the same sectors on a frequent schedule. Because more than one infantry patrol usually went out daily and at different times, the PSYOPS section now split itself up with only two or three men on each patrol.

The mission's purpose now was to disrupt the insurgents' sense that they still retained freedom of movement here. For example, patrols were designed to regularly visit the compounds of individuals who were thought to be insurgent supporters to show them they were being watched and that Coalition troops could make a surprise appearance at any time of the day or night. These tactics were meant to unnerve a suspect over time, with the hope that he would make a mistake such as moving a weapons cache while unknowingly under observation. With such operations pressuring local insurgents, the efforts of the Canadians and Americans appeared to achieve some success in demonstrating to local villagers that the Coalition was determined to remain this time.

In April 2011, Dog Company, 2nd Squadron, U.S. 2nd (Stryker) Cavalry Regiment carried out counter-insurgency operations out of Patrol Base Talukan under the command of Task Force Kandahar. Here, Private First Class Austin Lanzrath from Dog Company provides local security during a patrol through Talukan Bazaar.

One of the main PSYOPS products that François's section was now making use of was a Radio Literacy Program designed to promote education in rural areas, as a means to enhance the image of the Government of Afghanistan. Canadians had been building schools in Panjwayi villages during the past few years, but found that these often became targets for the Taliban, who burned them down after the Canadians departed rather than allow them to continue operating. Literacy was an important element in the fight against insurgency; if Afghans could read the Koran themselves, they could challenge Islamist interpretations and make up their own minds about their beliefs. While construction projects to develop infrastructure continued, a program to deliver literacy education by radio was developed to bring schools directly to homes in villages that remained under Taliban threat. The section had gone out to surrounding villages to speak to the mullahs or elders, talking to them about the importance of education. The religious leaders had reacted positively, and readily given permission for the Canadians to proceed with their program.

Now, on their travels, one of the main activities of the PSYOPS operators was to distribute a radio powered by a hand crank along with three handbooks of instruction that covered a 45-week program of reading lessons. Whoever accepted the package just had to tune the radio in to a certain frequency at specified times of the day, and a teacher, broadcasting in Pashto, provided instructions. Near the end of the rotation the program was assessed and found to be quite successful, with 80 percent of the population giving it a positive rating. The program had been developed by the ISAF Regional Command (South) PSYOPS unit, but the Canadians actively volunteered to test it and were the first to execute it.[9]

Disseminating the language packages became one of François's main tasks over the next few weeks. His main problem was that he had to add a full load of these books and radios to his kit, which was already quite heavy. It was like carrying three Montreal telephone books stuffed into his backpack on top of his water, ammunition, and the rest of his heavy kit. But he had some satisfaction that the program was well received, because he usually returned to the base at the end of the patrol with all the materials gone. The fact that it was labelled as a program being delivered by Canadians seemed to add to its attraction for many Afghans.

Such a successful Coalition program, however, was bound to receive the attention of the Taliban, and there was no doubt they were still present in the area. Occasionally, while on patrol, a bullet whizzed by their heads, with the sniper disappearing into a cluster of compounds. A more serious incident occurred when an IED hidden in a parked motorcycle was detonated remotely as François's patrol walked past. Luckily the bomb had been placed on the far side of the motorcycle, which protected the patrol from the blast. The only casualty was an American infantryman who sustained a concussion and was evacuated for a brief period.

This incident might have been a warning sign and should have alerted the PSYOPS section that the Taliban were becoming more dangerous. Near the beginning of April, Canadian intelligence received a report at Zangabad, where the Van Doos had a platoon base, that insurgents wanted to carry out a suicide bombing attack on what was vaguely described as a

Coalition group that dressed differently and spoke to local people. Since a Special Forces unit was operating out of Talukan, it was assumed that it was the key target, not realizing that the Canadian PSYOPS supporting the Americans in Talukan might have been the actual one.

For François, April 12, 2011, started off normally. The foot patrol had been successful and he had gotten rid of all his books and radios. As they filed back into Talukan and approached the FOB's gate, they stopped in the bazaar for a few minutes to talk to the local power broker, as was their custom every time they passed through. Everyone in the patrol was relaxed because this part of the village was considered a secure area, protected by ANP checkpoints. With that courtesy done, they started off again toward the gate, only metres away.

Suddenly, François found himself flying through the air! The sound of an explosion stunned him. Then he was on the ground, with a huge cloud of dust everywhere. His mind took a few seconds to process the situation: *What the hell! Okay, something exploded. I must have hit a mine. Oh, shit!* Lying on the ground, he felt a weight on his leg. He managed to reach down and touch it. He felt sure it was his leg … broken. Touching it again, he discovered the foot was wearing a sandal. No, it was not his leg; it was someone else's! Confusion. His mind tried to grasp what was going on.

Okay, my leg is all right, he thought. *I've got my two legs, but I can't feel one of my arms. Try to raise the other arm,* he told himself. *I can raise it … okay, it's still attached.* Some relief entered his mind. *I can't see from one eye. Am I disfigured? Maybe it's full of blood?*

Shrapnel had cut his carotid artery, and he felt blood squirting out of his throat with every pulse of his heart. He lay there and looked at the sky. *Okay, I'm dead! It's over.*

That thought didn't fill him with fear. He had already mentally prepared himself for such an event, and could accept it because of the philosophy he had followed all his life: that he had had a good life, and would not be overcome with dread if he were to die, so he relaxed and lay still.

Many months later, back in Montreal, François watched the movie *Act of Valor* about combat missions carried out by U.S. Navy SEALs, and something in it struck a very personal chord with him. At the end of the film a narrator speaks the poetic words of the warrior chief Tecumseh, in which he talks of facing death without regret. To François, the passage brought back the feelings that had kept him calm as he had lain badly wounded on that dusty road in Talukan.

> When it comes your time to die, be not like those whose
> hearts are filled
> with the fear of death, so that when their time comes they
> weep
> and pray for a little more time to live their lives over again
> in a different way.
> Sing your death song and die like a hero going home.[10]

The suicide bomber had been waiting in an open-front motorcycle repair shop on the main road passing through the bazaar and leading to the FOB's entrance, knowing the patrol would have to come that way. He had only to step forward a few steps and press the trigger as the column of American and Canadian troops filed past. With each man about five metres apart in the line, François had taken the full force of the explosion, while

Seen here is the crater caused by the suicide bomber who critically injured Corporal Dupéré in front of the motorcycle repair shop on the main road in Talukan.

behind him his buddy Andrew Peddle was hit in the legs, and in front the American medic, Chad Bortle, had shrapnel rip into his buttocks.

Despite his injuries, Chad swung into action immediately, rushing to François's aid. Chad quickly got a tourniquet on his leg, which was bleeding severely, then put pressure on his throat to stop the bleeding from the

The crater caused by the suicide bomber in front of the motorcycle repair shop in Talukan.

An American medic urgently tries to save the life of Corporal Dupéré, who lies on the ground after being critically injured by a suicide bomber in Talukan. American Special Forces personnel, in the background, have raced out of the FOB on Quad bikes to get the casualties back as quickly as possible.

carotid artery, while someone else did a tracheotomy to keep him breathing. François now credits Chad with saving his life. It seemed as if his entire body on the side closest to the bomber had been damaged, and he was bleeding profusely everywhere. Small metal fragments had peppered his face, shattered the bone around his right eye, broken his jaw, and passed through his chest from one side to the other, in the process severely damaging the brachial plexus, which controlled the nerves to his left arm. Shrapnel had even ripped open his boot and mangled his ankle.

While the uninjured men in the patrol frantically tried to help the injured, some American Special Forces troops in the FOB had heard the explosion and knew it was close by. They dropped everything, jumped on Quad all-terrain vehicles, and dashed out to the bomb site. With their help François and Andrew got back to the FOB, where they were fortunate to have a Black Hawk helicopter already waiting to evacuate them. Sergeant Obas, who had been in the base when the explosion had detonated, was also waiting to make sure his corporal and friend, François, got off all right. As he was lying on the stretcher, François managed to see Obas, and although he could barely speak through the tracheotomy, he managed to gurgle, "Hey, Reg, I'm dead."

"Nobody dies here without my permission," Obas replied.

François laughed at that and said, "Okay, everything's normal then!"

"François, you're an idiot!" Obas then moved aside, and the helicopter lifted off.

When they landed at KAF, an ambulance was waiting to rush François and Andrew to the Role Three Hospital, only metres away from the landing pad. The next thing François remembered was waking up on a bed in the hospital hallway with a friend beside him. In a daze from the morphine and unable to talk, François requested a paper and pencil to ask what had happened.

"Don't you know?" his friend asked. "Man, a suicide bomber!"

"Where's the bastard. I'm going to kill him," François wrote, still not realizing the bomber was already dead.

"What? You're just thinking of getting even? You're crazy."

François passed in and out of consciousness for the next three days, and when he finally woke up, he was in the Canadian wing of the U.S. Army's

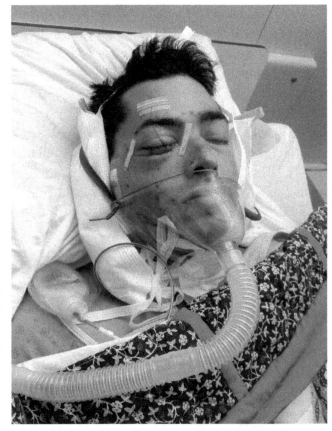

Corporal Dupéré received immediate life-saving treatment in the Role Three Medical Unit at Kandahar Airfield.

Landstuhl Regional Medical Center in Germany. There he found out that, among other things, his left arm was paralyzed, he was blind in his right eye, and his vocal cords were paralyzed. One of the doctors also told him that by remaining calm and not struggling after he had been hit, he had probably saved his own life. His wounds had been so serious that if he had been agitated he probably would have bled out and died before Chad had been able to apply first aid.

He remained in Landstuhl for the next two weeks while the doctors waited for him to stabilize. Then they got him on an aircraft to take him back to Quebec City. Once there he began a long series of reconstructive surgeries along with physiotherapy, occupational therapy, and even speech therapy, which he needed in order to recover from paralyzed vocal cords. He received great care from a number of medical specialists who continued

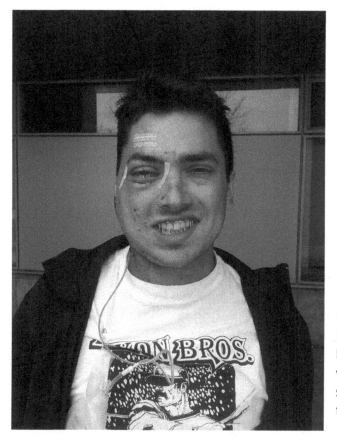

In Quebec, Corporal Dupéré has just had his first major surgery, which wired his jaw shut and installed a titanium eye floor.

to remove pieces of shrapnel from his body, reconstructed his nose, grafted on a new eardrum, corrected his broken jaw, and rebuilt his eye socket with a titanium web. In June he was finally released, but weekly physiotherapy and occupational therapy sessions continued for about a full year, as well as numerous appointments with a multitude of medical specialists.

Toward the end of 2012, François was home again in Montreal and functioning reasonably well. Despite the continuing weakness in his left arm and less than perfect sight out of one eye, his old spirit returned and he was ready for new challenges. He began by taking up skydiving, and in October 2012 climbed to the top of Island Peak in the Himalayas. That was an achievement for anyone, even without a handicap. Next, in the summer of 2013, he followed up these experiences by participating in the annual Nijmegen March in the Netherlands, in which a team of Canadian Forces personnel walked for four days, travelling 40 kilometres each day while carrying a 10-kilogram rucksack.

François left the military because he was no longer able to pass the physical tests required for remaining in one of the combat arms. However, his spirit for adventure and for seeking out new challenges never left him. In the spring of 2016, he was accepted into a program initiated by retired Lieutenant-General Roméo Dallaire and conducted through Dalhousie University — the Veteran Trainers to Eradicate the Use of Child Soldiers (VTECS). In this program, former Canadian soldiers recovering from injuries will be trained to work with military and police forces around the world to eliminate the use of child soldiers, an effort that has become a major personal cause for General Dallaire. Wounded Warriors Canada has given its support to this initiative, since it can make good use of the experience of former Canadian soldiers, like François, who are uniquely qualified to deliver such a program. François is very much looking forward to becoming part of VTECS and meeting this new challenge with his usual enthusiasm.

The True Patriot Love expedition team celebrates at its base camp at an altitude of 1,219 metres by unfurling the flag of the Mingo McEwen Foundation, one of its sponsors. Corporal Dupéré is third from the left.

5

HOLDING THE NORTH — SHAH WALI KOT AND ARGHANDAB: MASTER CORPORAL SEAN CHARD

In September 2008, D Squadron of the Royal Canadian Dragoons (RCD) began its tour in Afghanistan with a twofold mission: protecting the Dahla Dam, and patrolling the southern sector of Shah Wali Kot and all of Arghandab Districts to disrupt any insurgent activity threatening Kandahar City. Normally, a reconnaissance unit like D Squadron acted as the eyes and ears of the battle group commander and was given independent tasks that allowed it to roam throughout the battle space. However, with Task Force Kandahar hard-pressed to cover the entirety of its area of operations, D Squadron for this rotation was given a specific but more limited mission that tied it to an unusually large area of about 1,500 square kilometres all on its own.

Highway 167 running north from Kandahar City is one of the few transportation routes going from Kandahar City to Uruzgan Province. The highway follows the Arghandab River for a while, first passing along the fertile zone of Arghandab District and then through the rugged Shah Wali Kot District before reaching the provincial border more than 100 kilometres north of Kandahar City. About 34 kilometres north of Kandahar City the road passes near the expanse of Arghandab Lake, formed when the waters of the Arghandab River were held back by the massive Dahla Dam. This important dam, the second largest in Afghanistan, was built to provide water to the downstream districts of Arghandab, Panjwayi, and Zharey, enabling them to become flourishing agricultural areas. But the dam and the irrigation systems were not maintained, and by the time the Canadians took responsibility for Kandahar Province, they were no longer functioning properly.

When the Canadian battle group and the PRT deployed to Kandahar Province in 2006, it soon became apparent that the area was far more insecure than had been expected. Instead of concentrating on development and reconstruction as had been hoped, Canadian forces became involved in a counter-insurgency struggle that was costly in terms of lives and money. Consequently, the Canadian government needed to examine whether the mission should be extended past its original end date of February 2009. An independent panel of notables was assembled to review Canada's future role, and it presented its findings in January 2008, recommending that Canada continue only if a more comprehensive strategy was formulated for the country's role. One element of this strategy recommended that development and reconstruction be re-emphasized by identifying a "signature" project that would clearly provide a major benefit to the Afghan people. As a result, an announcement was made in June 2008 that a $50 million project would be established by the Canadian International Development Agency (CIDA) to repair the Dahla Dam and its irrigation systems.

The Dahla Dam is located in the southern part of Shah Wali Kot District. The terrain of the district is made up of rolling hills in the south, transitioning toward higher mountains with steep valleys in the north. It is arid and harsh, and was said by one Canadian officer to look "much like the surface of the moon with rock and sand everywhere."[1] It is an economically poor district with a population of fewer than 40,000 people, most of whom are farm labourers living in small, scattered villages. Arghandab District, just south of the dam, is more prosperous because it produces much of the fresh vegetables and fruit for the markets of Kandahar City thanks to the waters running downstream. But Shah Wali Kot is important for the Taliban, since it serves as a transit route for supplies and fighters threatening Kandahar City from the north.

The Gumbad Platoon House was established in early 2006 to disrupt insurgent activity in the area, but the supply routes were too vulnerable to

IED attacks and it was closed down by mid-year. Short-term operations were carried out in the north to counter specific Taliban attacks on district centres and police posts, but otherwise no permanent Canadian presence was situated there. Consequently, the Taliban remained in the area and posed a potential threat.[2] That threat became real in October 2007 when insurgent fighters from Shah Wali Kot and Khakrez Districts made a bold move to take over the Arghandab District, but they were foiled by a quick response from 3 R22eR BG and the ANA. Although the Taliban had been driven out of the district, it was now obvious that security had to be more permanently established if the Dahla Dam signature project was to succeed. Accordingly, work on a new base located near the dam was begun, and in June 2008, FOB Frontenac was ready for use by Canadian troops.

Given that the most important need for the infantry strength of the battle group was in Panjwayi and Zharey, the decision was made to assign responsibility for Shah Wali Kot to the reconnaissance (recce) squadron by deploying it to FOB Frontenac. While the squadron was a very small force for such a large area, recce squadrons were equipped with a unique piece of equipment that allowed them to patrol over large distances — the Coyote armoured reconnaissance vehicle. This vehicle could reach speeds exceeding 100 kilometres per hour, had a range of 660 kilometres, and was well equipped for fighting, with a Bushmaster 25 mm gun and two machine guns. Its special advantage, however, was its suite of sophisticated electronic surveillance equipment, including night-vision devices, video, and radar that could detect medium-sized targets as far away as 12 kilometres and larger targets such as trucks up to 24 kilometres away. The Coyote had a crew of four soldiers: a commander, driver, gunner, and surveillance operator (serv op). The mobility and special equipment of the recce squadron helped make up for its lack of numbers as it carried out its mission on the northern borders of Kandahar on Rotation 5 of Task Force Kandahar.

✦

As the giant C-17 Globemaster began a steep descent toward KAF on an early September evening, the sun was just setting, throwing a red glow over the harsh Afghan landscape. Some soldiers in the chalk* were probably either excited or nervous about their arrival in this remote country, especially the younger ones. But Master Corporal Sean Chard took it calmly — he had already served one tour in Kabul, and had twice deployed to Bosnia years earlier, so it was not a novelty to arrive in a foreign country. This time it had been a 36-hour trip from Petawawa, Ontario, but he had managed to rest enough on the flight and was quite alert as the aircraft began its swift descent. From his seat he could see out a window, and as he passed the mountains, he couldn't help thinking, *Yeah, okay, I'm back!*

Dusk was approaching as the aircraft door swung open. Sean's senses were overwhelmed with the once-familiar sounds and smells of Afghanistan. He heard prayers issuing from the mosques in the valley and spotted low, lingering smoke lying over KAF coming from the cooking fires of the surrounding compounds. It had a smell redolent of burning garbage, just as it had had in Kabul, and the odour was as unpleasant as it had been in his previous tour.

Sean liked being in recce, and the freedom of their role allowed them to operate with relative independence. He sometimes had minor problems fitting into the vehicles because he was a big fellow — over six feet tall and built like a lumberjack. But he knew how to get around that, removing the ring from his hatch opening to give him more flexibility when climbing in or out of the Coyote. He was not specifically excited about going to Afghanistan. What excited him was his own sense of mission for this deployment. This time, as a master corporal, he was the crew commander of a Coyote and was responsible for making decisions, right or wrong, and for the safety of the men in his crew: his driver, Trooper Brian Good; the gunner, Trooper Mike Sores; and the serv op, Trooper Richard Bride.

When soldiers worked together in the confines of a vehicle, a bond easily developed among them, and Sean had resolved that as commander he was not going to let any of his crew down on this rotation. He knew that

---

* A chalk is a military term used to identify a temporary grouping of soldiers for the purpose of transportation such as on aircraft or in a convoy of vehicles.

once operations began the team could be faced at any time with situations that were unexpected and unclear. In such circumstances he would have to do the best he could, relying on his training and experience, and if things did not turn out well, he would have to count on what he had learned in previous deployments — to brush himself off, and carry on to accomplish his patrol's mission as well as possible.

This new responsibility felt like a bit of a weight on his shoulders, but he was ready for it. He had served in all vehicle positions up to now: as driver in his first Bosnian deployment, serv op in the next Bosnian tour, then gunner in Kabul. Sean knew Kabul had been different than Bosnia had been, and Kandahar was going to be even more challenging. His goal now was to be the best crew commander possible, and he was keen to get out of KAF and get on with the job.

Sean was therefore relieved when they finally left KAF and arrived at FOB Frontenac a couple of days later, and that he could begin to familiarize himself with the mission and the strange new territory. Ironically, as one of his first assignments, he was ordered back to KAF seven days later. His mission was to command a Coyote as part of a three-vehicle patrol that was to meet and escort other RCD soldiers from the next chalk just arriving from Canada. His own crew had not yet arrived, so he grabbed another available driver and gunner and headed back down the 70-kilometre stretch of highway to KAF. Once there he found he was picking up a newly arrived crew commander, who they decided would take over the gunner's position for the return journey. The time on the road would be a good opportunity for Sean to chat with the new man and brief him on their area of operations (AO).

The return trip up Highway 167 went smoothly until the patrol approached a spot where the road crossed a series of four closely spaced culverts. Such choke points were always risky because of possible IEDs, so they left the highway and started travelling cross-country. As the column of vehicles moved along the edge of a ridgeline, Sean suddenly realized that the track they were following was channelling them into a defile that would force them into another possible choke point. He quickly told the driver to make a hard turn left, but it was too late. That was when it happened. The whole vehicle suddenly jolted violently and came to an abrupt stop. The Taliban had expected them to follow this route, and Sean's Coyote had hit an IED!

Sean had heard no sound, so they must have been directly over the centre of the IED when it exploded. But he had felt the concussion — a powerful rush of air coming up through the hatch with dust blowing under his glasses and pulling his helmet off. Sean quickly got over the shock of the impact, and his training kicked in. He went through his checklist to make sure everyone in the crew was good and was relieved to hear them report that no one was injured, although they had some bruises and sore necks. The driver was shaken up the most, but Sean got her calmed down and she was able to drive the vehicle off the blast site with two flat tires. The hull was fine, but some of the steering components were banged up.

They were now immobilized, and decided to try to drag the Coyote back to the FOB. After a brief attempt, however, they found that approach would not work. Instead, they cordoned off the area, made sure there were no insurgents hanging around, and waited for the armoured recovery vehicle to arrive. Sean then recalled that he had heard an ironic bit of news on the radio: this was International Day of Peace. It was also the day the command authority for the mission in Shah Wali Kot was transferred to the RCD squadron. What a time to hit an IED! As the adrenaline high wore off, he thought, *Holy crap, this is real. It's not training anymore. That was too close for comfort!*

FOB Frontenac was a large triangular-shaped base with a circumference of about two and a half kilometres, ringed by HESCO bastions. The Canadians were housed in standard ballistic sea containers located in the centre, with cement slabs called Texas barriers against them for protection. They had showers, an ablution tent, a gym, and a kitchen with excellent cooks, making everything very comfortable. Because the base was located in a beautiful setting with mountains as a backdrop, the Canadians in their barracks-room banter started calling it "FOB Fabulous," as if it were a holiday destination. In the fall of 2008, the Canadian strength consisted mainly of the RCD D Squadron made up of two troops of eight Coyotes each, along with the squadron headquarters and a support echelon. They also had attached to them the 3 RCR reconnaissance platoon with its vehicles, giving the squadron an effective manoeuvre force of about three mechanized troops. Adding

An aerial photo shows the Dahla Dam, which provides water to irrigate the Arghandab River Basin. One of three Canadian signature projects in Afghanistan, it was controversial, particularly as costs escalated from the original $50 million budget.

D Squadron forms up in FOB Frontenac, along with ANA reconnaissance troops in the centre and Afghans from the Tundra Security Group on the right, on the occasion of Remembrance Day 2008.

an engineer recce section and some artillery forward observation officers, the Canadian strength was about 170 soldiers. For this number of troops, the base was certainly larger than needed. Some time later the Americans would take over the AO and house a full battalion there.

The FOB had been placed on its site primarily to provide protection for the Dahla Dam. The location was picturesque, but the FOB was in a basin that was not well sited tactically for defence, with high ground over-looking it. While insurgents were not as active here as farther south, the base was not a place of rest and safety, since it eventually became the target of intermittent rocket and mortar attacks. With small rolling foothills to the south that overlooked the base, insurgents soon found some covered areas from which they began to send a few rockets into the FOB. None of these incidents caused any casualties, but they were potentially dangerous and always an irritant, since everyone had to jump up from wherever they were relaxing and stand-to. Once, when a rocket exploded only 40 metres from Sean's sleeping quarters, he awoke with such a start that he hit his head hard on the bunk above, stunning himself. During another rocket attack, he got out of his quarters so fast that he only had his pants, flak jacket, and one boot on as he ran to his vehicle. He had to joke that the rockets made for one hell of a wake-up call!

While the Canadian force was stretched thin in carrying out its primary duties, at least it did not have to take on the added task of local security. Afghan guards were contracted from Tundra Security Group SCA, which supplied 50 men who lived on the base and took care of overnight security.[3] This was an arrangement that relieved the Canadians from taking on the added burden of such a routine duty, but it took some time for most of them to get used to. The guards were recruited from outside the district so that insurgents would not recognize them and intimidate their families. They mostly kept to themselves, but to help both sides work together the squadron organized development exercises, such as going out to a firing range to fire each other's weapons. It was on occasions such as these that they could interact and find opportunities to become familiar with one another.

D Squadron had two districts for which it was responsible: Arghandab and part of Shah Wali Kot. In the latter, one of their priorities was, of course, watching over the Dahla Dam, which they did by sending occasional foot patrols across terrain that was inaccessible by vehicle to meet up with the ANP posts at the dam. But most of the squadron's time was spent on route clearances and patrols — gathering intelligence, providing security, and looking for signs of insurgent activity. On occasion they were called on to send a troop down to Panjwayi or Zharey to help with a major operation, and once they were sent to Khakrez District in the west. Then there were jobs like escorting VIPs or convoys, such as a 200-vehicle Australian packet trying to get to Kandahar City. One troop's Coyotes were provided, and the vehicles distributed with one at the front, one at the rear, and the other six spread throughout the packet, hoping that none would hit an IED or get ambushed along the way.

Ideally, a troop was split into two patrols of four vehicles, but never less than three if at all possible. They were quite aware that wherever they went insurgents were always watching them, and if anything went wrong in a remote location, they needed to have enough strength to get back safely. But they were recce, so they went everywhere — on routes that were not routinely traversed and so had uncertain risk, following routes that were merely rough dirt tracks, and along goat trails, up rocky wadis, or over passes into the mountains. All these were routine patrols for the squadron.

A typical patrol often had a combination of tasks. The vehicles might head out along a predetermined route, stopping at all the culverts to check them for IEDs before ending the day by visiting a particular village. On these types of patrols, the serv ops carried out any dismounted duties. When checking out a culvert, for example, the serv ops from each vehicle dismounted and went forward to do the actual inspection while the patrol commander remained in the lead vehicle, keeping a lookout for possible threats while watching the dismounts' movements. Occasionally, the patrol might bring along a handler with an explosive-detection dog. They rode along in the back of one Coyote and did a more thorough culvert check. If an IED was found, the patrol had to remain on site until engineers arrived to disarm the device and either blow it in place or take it away.

Despite their limited strength, the squadron's commanding officer, Major Dean Tremblay, was determined to conduct as much COIN work as possible, using his patrols to interact with the local population and gather information about insurgent activity. During these patrols, an interpreter

A Coyote armoured reconnaissance vehicle from the Reconnaissance Squadron patrols in Panjwayi District, Kandahar Province.

A wide-angle view of the terrain in Arghandab and Shah Wali Kot Districts where the Royal Canadian Dragoons conducted their patrols; dry fields and mountains rise in the background.

A typical scene of a village in Afghanistan visited during a patrol through Arghandab and Shah Wali Kot Districts.

Curious local children watch a Royal Canadian Dragoons patrol pass by.

was brought along and the vehicle might stop to allow the Canadians to talk to local Afghans either along the main route or off of it when they travelled into specific remote villages. At these times the patrol commander got out of his Coyote to make contact with a village elder, but a couple of other soldiers also dismounted to maintain a close watch while the other crew members remained alert in the Coyotes, covering all approaches.

These were important interactions between the Canadians and local Afghans, with the first questions designed to see if help could be supplied to the village. How was their water situation? How was the health of the villagers? Did anyone need medical attention? Once some measure of personal interaction was achieved, the patrol commander would move on to ask for information about insurgent activity in the neighbourhood or travel by strangers. Some patrols got through their daily route pretty quickly if nothing unusual was happening, but at other times a patrol could take six or seven hours before they were finished. They often got back to the FOB very late, grabbed some food and sleep, and were ready to do it all over again the next day. The day's mission might even turn into an overnight

A rough day for the crews in the Coyotes as they cross soft ground in the desert.

A presence patrol on a tight road passes through the agricultural area of Arghandab District. In such close terrain, crews were constantly alert for the threat of an ambush.

stay in the desert during which they operated the electronic surveillance gear after dark, watching for ingress and egress routes used by insurgents.

There were no ANP or ANA personnel based in FOB Frontenac, but the squadron still had a role in supporting governance and security. Some Coyotes might be sent up to the ANP post located in the district centre about 30 minutes north of the FOB for a joint patrol, which might involve vehicle checkpoints. For these the ANP ran the checkpoint and vehicle searches while the Canadian element provided a security cordon. Such checkpoints were maintained for no more than 20 or 30 minutes, because by that time everyone knew about them and they were no longer effective. In Arghandab the squadron had the additional task of providing resupply for a base held by a five-man Canadian OMLT with their ANA *kandak*, located closer to Kandahar City. The squadron had a good working relationship with these Afghan soldiers and occasionally did joint foot patrols with them when they did the resupply run.

The insurgents were not happy with D Squadron's presence in Shah Wali Kot and Arghandab, and made their disfavour known by firing rockets at the FOB and planting IEDs. They did not like the fact that D Squadron was in the middle of their northern transit path to Kandahar City, and became vigorous in trying to intimidate the Canadians with constant IEDs, hoping to force the Canadians to pull back into the FOB. The IED that Sean's Coyote hit in early September was the first strike the squadron suffered as the Taliban geared up their offensive action. Luckily, no one was killed or seriously injured in that strike. However, within the next few weeks, another strike occurred, injuring a driver seriously enough that he had to be evacuated to Canada. More strikes followed in the ensuing weeks — smaller ones with only minor injuries, but they were enough to impress on the crews how determined their opponents were. It was only natural that the crews began to feel a high degree of anxiety every time they exited the FOB gate — it was like throwing dice to see whether they would land on an IED.

Being threatened by IEDs day after day was hard on morale, particularly when the Canadians could not hit back against an unseen enemy who emplaced his explosives at night. Every time the Coyotes went out the gate, everyone knew there was a good chance someone was going to get hurt. That was when squadron leadership pulled them through. This was counter-insurgency warfare in which the lieutenant, the sergeants, and master corporals had to make critical decisions daily on the ground. The squadron sergeant-major, Shawn Mercer, credited the strength of the vehicle commanders who provided examples their crews could follow; these junior leaders were tactically aware, professional, motivated, and mature. Some, like Sean, had done other tours and could handle stress better for that. In his first tour in Bosnia, Sean's best friend had died in his arms after a vehicle accident. That loss had hurt him emotionally, but he had found a way to deal with it and had gotten over it. He might have felt fear after his first IED strike, but he was philosophical about it. As he put it, "I had to really suck it back, push it aside. It wasn't about me. It was about my soldiers, my patrol, my troop, my squadron. Be strong for them and be able to focus. You think about it but don't dwell on it."

None of the patrols Sean participated in had any serious contact with insurgents. That was not to say the Canadians did not have areas they were particularly suspicious of, ones they were very cautious about when approaching. They were always aware they were at risk, and because of the small numbers in any patrol, they realized they were vulnerable. Sean's most anxious time on this rotation came when he was on a long-range patrol on the other side of the mountains to the north. They ended up having to inspect a couple of points of interest along the route that took them into rough terrain and up a remote wadi. Sean felt it was a bit eerie because the route was not often travelled, and it would have been easy for insurgents to hide anything in there.

After the patrol had checked out what they had come to see, they decided to stop and shut their vehicles down for a short break. They could then have some water and report into their base by radio. After a brief rest, they were ready to go again and climbed back into their vehicles. But then Sean discovered that his Coyote would not start! Worse, the command post in Frontenac told them it had intercepted insurgent radio chatter talking about Sean's patrol. The insurgents had spotted them sitting still and knew that Sean's vehicle was broken down. Hurriedly, Sean tried to talk his driver through troubleshooting the problem and moving personal kit to get at cables to see if one had come loose. He pulled the electrical kit out of the vehicle and began frantically searching for the problem. To him it was a nightmare because he could not figure it out. Meanwhile, Frontenac was telling them, "Get out of there, now!"

The situation was highly unstable. Insurgents might close in at any time, and there was only one way in or out of the wadi. Back at the FOB the squadron's other Coyotes were deployed on another operation, and only support vehicles were available to come to their assistance if it came to that. Sean and the others in the patrol were ready for a fight if necessary, but not for a long, drawn-out engagement with an immobilized vehicle. In fact, if they ever had the opportunity, they wanted to hit back against those ghostly insurgents who planted IEDs after dark. But now Sean did not like the possibility of coming under fire in a remote mountain wadi — armoured recce soldiers were trained to operate best when manoeuvring and shooting. To Sean, being stuck here was worse than facing the threat from IEDs. Frustration mounting, he crawled into the driver's hole himself to troubleshoot the electrical components. Hurriedly going over all of the electrical connections again, to his relief he finally located a loose wire. It was the lead to a neutral start switch in the gear selector. He had played with this wire in his first check and it had seemed all right, but now he noticed that the connection was broken. This time he only had to touch the wire to the connector and the Coyote started up. With a surge of relief, they all mounted up and the patrol quickly headed down the wadi and out of there. The insurgent radio chatter stopped and the incident was over.

Sean's critical moment of the rotation came on January 7. The squadron mission started off in a routine way. His Coyote was the third vehicle heading out of Frontenac early that sunny morning as part of an eight-vehicle patrol into Shah Wali Kot. All was routine until their route took them up a side wadi, and ahead they saw a suspicious white truck. As soon as the occupants of the truck spotted the patrol, it started up and sped away — a bad sign. The patrol kept an eye on the truck but lost sight of it as it turned off into another wadi on the left. All along this route Sean's driver, Brian Good, was careful to keep their vehicle in the tracks of the Coyote in front,

Driver Brian Good gets a break from the hot driver's compartment of his Coyote.

Master Corporal Sean Chard, crew commander 62G, whose vehicle was acting as security on a vehicle checkpoint cordon.

as he always did. All the vehicles followed this practice to ensure that if there were any IEDs in the ground the Coyote in front would hit it first but their own vehicle would be safe.

Initially, Sean remembered nothing of what happened. Despite their precaution, they struck an IED, and for a few brief moments Sean was knocked unconscious. As he came back to his senses, he was startled by the clang of his swinging hatch cover and became aware of debris flying around. He opened his eyes but only saw red because blood was pooling in his eyes from a gash on his forehead. Still stunned, he felt really sick to his stomach. His heart rate was racing and he knew he had to pull himself together, so he instinctively began to practise the deep breathing exercise they had been taught in pre-deployment training. With some relief, he sensed his heart rate and adrenaline coming down, and thoughts tumbled through his confused mind. Later he easily recalled every second of what happened next.

Okay, what happened? Yeah, we hit an IED!

I'm not moving and there's smoke coming out of my vehicle. I look over at my gunner, Mike. He isn't in his usual standing position. He's sitting down in his hole. Oh, no! He's unconscious but is turned sideways. He's a big fellow, pushing 260. Back home we'd practised evacuating each other in a situation like this, because he and I are so big that it would be hard to get us out of the vehicle. Then he wakes up and I feel relieved.

The vehicle is still on its wheels. There's smoke. The engine compartment cover is blown open. My serv op, Bride, is standing because he almost got launched out of the back of the vehicle. He's talking to me, but I'm trying to get my driver to answer me. I'm telling Bride, "Check on Brian."

We have to traverse the turret because the gun is over the driver's hatch. But the controller is broken off, so we have to get him to traverse manually. While Bride is trying to get the hatch open, Mike has come up and starts telling me that I have a big gash under my chin.

My jaw is broken. Mike tries to throw a bandage on, but I don't feel anything. As they're starting to pull Brian out, my adrenaline is coming down and I feel a lot of pain in my foot and lower leg. I don't know if I still have a foot or not. I can't tell, but the pain is excruciating. So I just say to myself, *You've got to kick something.* I take my right foot, kick part of the turret, and feel my foot. *I've still got a foot. Thank God!*

Members of the other crews are starting to come up, and I give them thumbs-down, the sign that there are people down. I see another serv op running toward us, and I automatically yell out a warning that everyone should still be cautious about secondary explosive devices that might be around. "Stop! Stop! Do your secondaries!" So they first had to search around the vehicle to make sure it was clear.

Then they get Brian out. It's an image I can't get rid of. You're used to seeing someone one way and then you see him damaged, missing legs. I know that I've got to get over it and help the other guys.

I'm still in my turret. I have to get out, so I lift myself up, get on top of the turret, and then climb down through the serv op hole — there's a hatch in the back. But I'm not paying attention to what I'm doing when I step out of the vehicle, so I fall right into the crater. I go down another couple of feet.

And then I step on my foot! Obviously, I fell over because I couldn't put any weight on it.

They put me on a stretcher. Everything feels like a dream — it doesn't feel quite right for some reason. They get me halfway back to the Casualty Collection Point and the stretcher breaks! I fall over and hit the ground, smacking my head. And right then, in a second, *Shit!* Everything that happened somehow becomes clear: *This just happened!* Before, it was all hazy.

We get back to the Casualty Collection Point and go through the drills. Everybody is bang on. They're doing first aid on me, on Mike, giving us medication, painkillers. I have to ask one of the patrol commanders, Steve Slade, "How's my driver?" Even though I kind of hope that maybe he isn't dead, the possibility's there, so I have to ask. We were taught in training not to answer that question from a person who's injured. But when you work with somebody for so long … He says, "No." Okay, but at least it was quick.

The medevac helicopter got there very quickly because it was already in the area. Everything happened like clockwork — the blast area was secured by the crews on-site, the Quick Reaction Force was on its way out from the FOB, and Sean, Trooper Mike Sores, and Trooper Richard Bride were loaded onto the helicopter. In a short span of time, the casualties were off-loaded at the Role 3 Multinational Medical Unit at KAF where they were given immediate attention.

The next day, despite being loaded with painkillers and weighed down with their legs in casts, Sean, Mike, and Richard managed to attend the ramp ceremony for Brian. A couple of days later Sean and Mike were placed on a flight from KAF to Bagram Air Base near Kabul, and from there were quickly transferred to the American hospital at Landstuhl, Germany. Less than a day later they were on a commercial flight bound for Canada — first class, so that the seats could be depressed to serve as beds. Sean's sense of separation from his crew and squadron was hard, as he later recalled: "Bride stayed back, which was hard for me, because he was part of my crew — can't take care of him if he's not with me, right? So he stayed back, and it was so hard when we left Afghanistan because we didn't see anybody else. They were still on operations."

On the day of the IED strike, while the squadron sergeant-major was securing the site, the rest of the squadron was actually pulling out of the FOB in support of a three-day airmobile operation. Sergeant-Major Mercer caught up with the other vehicles after the recovery was complete and talked to the soldiers at the first opportunity to bolster their morale as well as he could after the shock of the first death in their tour. They had lost a comrade. That was bad news, but he had to emphasize that they had to carry on: "Guys, rough go today. We know we just lost Brian. But we're not going to talk about it now. We have a mission to do. There will be a time to mourn, but not now." The crews nodded as they accepted the news. Brian was on their mind, but they refocused and were ready to go to complete the operation successfully. Sergeant-Major Mercer had to admire them. As he put it, "They had just seen their best friend killed and three wounded. And they got back up on their horses and went. You can't put a price on that. Because they knew that all they had left was each other, and they didn't quit on each other. That's courage."

The squadron's trial was not over, however. On the way back from supporting that airmobile operation, the Coyotes hit two more IEDs. Fortunately, no one was killed by these, but as they finally pulled back into the FOB, four of the vehicles were in tow from either IED damage or mechanical breakdown. They had more strikes over the next weeks of the mission, totalling 18 overall. By the end of their tour, the majority of the squadron crews had suffered bruises or minor injuries from at least one IED strike. They also lost Troopers Marc Diab, Corey Joseph Hayes, and Jack Boutillier, along with a number of others sent home because of injuries.

And before they left for Canada, there was one more fatality that touched the squadron emotionally just as much as the others. The recce squadron from 12e Régiment blindé du Canada (12e RBC) began arriving to take over the next rotation at FOB Frontenac. Before the transfer was complete, one of 12e RBC's Coyotes hit an IED, killing Corporal Karine Blais. With 12e RBC's tour just starting, this was a shocking tragedy for the incoming squadron. But as RCD rushed their Quick Reaction Force out to the scene, they, too, could not help but feel an emotional connection to this loss. Professionally, they were all part of the same community, so D Squadron had come to consider her as one of their own, painting her name on their memorial wall. Along with their other missing comrades, they would not forget Karine Blais.

Five years later Sean Chard continues to serve in the Canadian Armed Forces. He recovered from his injuries pretty well, although some days his leg hurts and he is unable to run properly because of his bad ankle. But he considers himself lucky that he is able to walk and carry out his daily tasks, and play and ride his bike with his son. He still thinks about the strike, but as he has learned to do, can recognize his emotions and feels he can cope with them. Sounds sometimes bother him, like the noise of a helicopter, or grinding metal, which was the first sound he heard when he regained consciousness in his wrecked Coyote.

Unfortunately, because of the weakness in his leg, Sean could not stay in the armoured corps but instead accepted retraining for a new trade in the army. In 2016 he still misses being a recce soldier, but is focused on what lies ahead for him as he follows his new career path. Some physical pain returns at times, but he considers it a grim reminder of what happened in Shah Wali Kot, as it should. He firmly believes that soldiers carrying out their mission have to accept the possibility of death or injury, and if it happens, live with it. With this acceptance, Sean has shown himself to be a truly professional soldier. That is what makes him who he is.

6

WAR AGAINST THE IEDS:
EXPLOSIVE ORDNANCE DISPOSAL

On September 2, 2006, the ISAF Multinational Brigade, led by elements of the Canadian battle group, launched Operation Medusa to eliminate the Taliban threat to Kandahar City. Two weeks later, with all objectives occupied and the surviving Taliban fighters fleeing the area, all higher commands enthusiastically declared that a major victory had been achieved and the enemy were no longer a cohesive force. The authorities could now turn their attention to encouraging the return of the civilian population to the area and begin reconstruction. But not all commanders were ready to relax; they knew from their intelligence assessments that the Taliban were determined opponents who, as soon as they could recover, would strike back in a new and deadly way. The nature of the new threat soon became evident as the Taliban almost immediately started infiltrating the Pashmul area again, stealthily emplacing improvised explosive devices along the Canadians' supply route. By the end of the month, the Canadians had hit seven IEDs, three of which were newly laid.[1] The first death came on September 29 when Private Josh Klukie of 1 RCR BG stepped on a massive IED. A week later Trooper Mark Wilson of RCD was killed when his armoured vehicle struck another IED on the supply route south of FOB Wilson. These were the signals that for the remainder of their mission in Afghanistan the Canadians would continue to be engaged in a "War Against IEDs."

In the early years of the 21st century, great geopolitical and techno-logical changes had led to decreasing stability in many parts of the world. One of the major concerns for military leaders of major Western countries became the rise of militant dissident groups, that now had such easy access to modern weapons and technology that they were a significant threat in such places as Bosnia, Iraq, Israel, Lebanon, and Syria. The term "asymmet-ric warfare" was coined to describe how such groups, too weak to openly oppose conventional military forces, could by using unconventional tactics gain an advantage over their stronger opponents. One of the main weapons now used by insurgent groups in this type of warfare became the IED, which was employed in large numbers against Western military forces in Iraq and Afghanistan.

The IED, a homemade explosive device constructed and employed surreptitiously by a non-state militant group to create psychological and physical damage, is not a new weapon. It has been around in one form or another for centuries. One of the earliest examples can be found back in 1605 when Guy Fawkes assembled 36 barrels of gunpowder under the British Houses of Parliament in a plan to assassinate King James I. This type of weapon was again chosen by terrorists in 1880 in another attempt to kill a ruling monarch in Saint Petersburg, Russia, when dynamite charges were smuggled into the Winter Palace to kill Tsar Alexander II. Early devices were crude, but they became much more sophisticated in the 1970s when innovations by the Provisional Irish Republican Army made these weapons more effective, leading the British Army to be the first to use the term "improvised explosive device."[2] IEDs began to be employed more fre-quently in the 1980s in Afghanistan when they were used by *mujahedeen* resistance fighters against Soviet forces, but they really proliferated in Iraq after the U.S. invasion in 2003. By 2007 this weapon was responsible for 63 percent of Coalition deaths in that country.

In Afghanistan the level of violence temporarily diminished after the defeat of the Taliban in 2001 and the installation of the new Islamic repub-lic. However, other insurgent groups that opposed the Afghan government remained a threat, and IEDs reappeared in small numbers in 2002 causing four U.S. casualties that year but increasing each year after that.[3] Canadians found that this threat was something they now had to deal with when they suffered their first casualties near Kabul during Operation Athena, Phase 1. On October 2, 2003, a routine patrol returning to Camp Julien ran over a land mine that had been placed on the track only hours after it had been cleared by engineers. Sergeant Robert Short and Corporal Robbie Beerenfenger of 3 RCR were killed and three others were wounded. But the Canadians soon discovered that explosives hidden in the ground were not the only danger; another form of IED designed to create terror was the suicide bomber, a religious fanatic who was willing to die while attempting to kill foreign troops by triggering explosives they were wearing. A few months after the attack that killed Short and Beerenfenger, a suicide bomber killed Corporal Jamie Murphy and wounded three others when he jumped on their vehicle as it slowed down for a speed bump in Kabul.

When Canadians arrived in Kandahar Province in 2006 to take over responsibility for that region as part of ISAF, the Taliban had recovered and were gathering to threaten Kandahar City. During the summer of that year, the Taliban began to mass their strength in Panjwayi District to fight the Canadian battle group. At the same time they employed IEDs throughout the province to restrict the Canadians' freedom of movement and inflict casualties whenever possible. The significance of the IED threat quickly became clear to the men of the first rotation when within days of their arrival in March 2006 the LAV of their commanding officer, Lieutenant-Colonel Ian Hope, was hit by a suicide bomber a short distance outside Kandahar City.[4] On top of such attacks on Canadian lines of communication, a Canadian outpost in the north of the province, the Gumbad Platoon House, soon became the most threatened place in the Canadian Area of Responsibility. Located 90 kilometres north of Kandahar City, Gumbad became such a magnet for IEDs that the supply route to the outpost was nicknamed "IED Alley." Within weeks five LAVs were destroyed, resulting in 10 men being severely injured. The first critical losses then occurred on April 22 when a light vehicle coming out of Gumbad triggered an IED made up of a stack of anti-tank mines, killing the four men inside.

In September 2006, the Taliban suffered a significant defeat when the Canadian battle group launched Operation Medusa against their stronghold in Panjwayi District. Despite this setback, the insurgents showed their flexibility and determination by simply abandoning their attempt to oppose the

Coalition forces through conventional tactics and reverting to IEDs as their main weapon. In the following years, they increased their use of IEDs, making them more sophisticated as time went on. Some of the simplest devices employed in Afghanistan at the beginning were crude pressure-activated bombs constructed by using two hacksaw blades separated by a space; when the blades were pressed together by a person or vehicle passing over the device, a circuit was completed to detonate the explosive. The explosive mixture usually consisted of a common material like ammonium nitrate fertilizer, which was contained in an empty plastic cooking oil jug or a cast-iron pressure cooker. Military munitions such as mortar bombs, artillery shells, and anti-tank mines were also rigged to increase the devastating effect of the explosion. Components not available locally were smuggled in from Pakistan along supply routes that passed through sympathetic villages and across the wastelands of the Registan Desert.

The process was well organized as the Taliban improved their tactics assisted by the arrival of foreign Islamist fighters.[5] The Taliban leaders created a military-style organization located in the lawless Pakistan border region to direct the IED campaign. Under its command, a network of bomb-making cells was set up in Kandahar Province, each one responsible for a specific area. Cell members were assigned duties such as being a builder, supplier, emplacer, or triggerman. Facilities for training bomb makers and gathering supplies were also set up in the safety of the border regions of Pakistan. Materials were then smuggled into Afghanistan over secret routes to reach local bomb-making factories hidden in nondescript rural compounds, along with orders regarding their targets. Not all cells were so well organized, however, since poorly trained local dissidents or unemployed youths were also utilized, the latter lured by rewards for hitting specific targets, such as up to 20,000 Pakistani rupees for blowing up a Coalition vehicle.[6]

When the Canadians and their armoured vehicles first arrived, the Taliban's IEDs were at times not strong enough to destroy these vehicles, especially those that had been designed to survive mine strikes, like the RG-31 Nyala. Insurgents, however, began to design devices with increasing explosive strength until they could judge how strong a charge was needed to affect the vehicle. Unfortunately, they found the answer in July 2007 when an IED made up of artillery shells and anti-tank mines stacked together was command-detonated by a remote Taliban observation team as a Canadian convoy passed along the roadway. The explosion propelled the supposedly blast-resistant, 6,600-kilogram Nyala into the air, killing all six Canadian soldiers inside.[7]

From the beginning of the mission, Canadian soldiers realized they had to be on guard against possible IEDs as soon as they left the gates of KAF or their FOB. When travelling by vehicle, they learned to avoid roads and drive cross-country whenever possible. Similarly, when on foot patrols, soldiers scanned the ground constantly for signs of any suspicious disturbance and took precautions such as walking in the footsteps of the man in front. In firefights Canadian troops found they could beat any insurgent opposition because of their superior training, tactics, and weapons, but they began to be frustrated that they could not easily fight the IEDs. It was like battling an unseen enemy against which they could not hit back. IEDs continued to claim lives, with the majority of combat deaths — 72 percent — resulting from this deadly weapon.[*]

In this new type of warfare, in which merely stepping on the ground became dangerous, the front-line soldier was more often the combat engineer who had been trained in explosives ordnance disposal (EOD). Before Afghanistan these specially trained soldiers had been employed in Canadian peacekeeping operations in zones of conflict where their main duty was the removal of unexploded ordnance. In Afghanistan combat engineers now took on the key responsibility for dealing with the more deadly IEDs. When the first battle group arrived in Kandahar in 2006, it contained a field engineer squadron with an EOD component, and a counter-IED cell was located at KAF. As the threat of IEDs continued and became more pressing, the EOD assets were consolidated in 2007 into a Counter-IED Squadron that reported directly to Task Force Headquarters. The EOD teams of the squadron were thereafter deployed to separate AOs throughout Kandahar Province where they worked with respective battle group elements. These teams were given the responsibility of dealing with

---

* By the end of the combat mission, of the 137 Canadian soldiers killed as a result of combat, 92 were caused by IEDs, according to figures posted on www.icasualties.org.

all IEDs, such as taking over sites where IEDs had already been detonated and the disposal of caches of weapons and IED components.

The work of the EOD operators was no longer limited to simply disposing of the IEDs as they were discovered. As the new threats from asymmetric warfare became increasingly apparent in Iraq and Afghanistan, the U.S. military introduced more sophisticated tactics to take the offensive against the bomb makers. The scientific method of police forensics was introduced, whereby evidence was gathered at blast sites for later use in identifying the bomb maker and ultimately ensuring the destruction of the network. Small clues could be matched with other intelligence that could lead to operations to cut the flow of supplies, block the financing, or destroy manufacturing sites. With this approach, the task of the EOD operator in the field became not only rendering an IED safe, but also removing all of its components and sending them to the forensic laboratory for analysis. In those incidents where the IED had already been detonated, all available evidence was still collected by photographing the scene, measuring the crater, taking samples of the soil for explosives residue, and gathering any pieces of wires, circuit boards, or triggers. All this material was assembled, logged by the EOD team, and then sent to an American forensics lab operating at KAF where it was analyzed and entered into a database for future reference.[8]

This new approach to counter-insurgency warfare was laborious and time-consuming, but it had a payoff. As the numbers of IED attacks increased, however, the American lab became overloaded with evidence. Reports on samples submitted often took too long to get back to the Canadian headquarters, and in some cases, remained indefinitely on the shelves awaiting priority. To resolve this problem and to develop a capability within Task Force Kandahar, a Canadian facility was opened at KAF in the spring of 2009. This was given the label of Multi-Disciplinary Exploitation Capability (MDEC) and was staffed by Canadian Armed Forces personnel who had been trained by the Royal Canadian Mounted Police (RCMP), and were supported by both the RCMP and the Canadian Security Intelligence Service (CSIS). Response times soon became significantly shorter, with critical cases coming back within hours instead of days or months.[9]

With each rotation, Task Force Kandahar's effectiveness in dealing with the IED threat improved; but with each rotation, the Taliban's IED offensive intensified. By 2009 ISAF was finding 50 to 60 percent of IEDs before they were detonated, but the number of IEDs placed had gone up 350 percent, according to Colonel Omer Lavoie, who commanded the Canadian Counter-IED Task Force in Ottawa.[10] Coalition deaths from IEDs in Kandahar had escalated from 40 in 2006 to 76 in 2009, with 27 of the latter being Canadian.[11] In this deadly game where there was no clear front line, the point man facing the IED threat head-on was now the EOD operator. Whenever an IED was found, he was the one who had to leave the safe zone to approach the device by himself, trusting only his training and the tools he carried to find out what awaited him in the rubble. For good reason, the EOD operator's approach to a detected IED became known as "The Long Walk."

✦

As the column of vehicles of the Quick Reaction Force (QRF) geared down to a stop along Route Summit, one soldier looked out on the scene with more interest than the others. Sam* was just starting his tour in Afghanistan as the leader of an EOD team, and this would be the first suspected IED site he investigated. All the training he had had as a combat engineer over the past 20-or-so years would now be put to the test, and it had better be good; he would be dealing with devices designed with the deadly intent to kill or maim, not the more routine unexploded munitions he had dealt with before during his tours in Bosnia or his previous tour in Afghanistan in Kabul.

As Sam climbed out of the team's Cougar, a vehicle specially designed to carry EOD teams while searching for and removing IEDs, he assessed the situation in preparation for his work. The scene seemed a bit strange, not what he had been expecting, but then he reminded himself that this was Afghanistan. The site appeared to be guarded by a motley crew, some in the uniform of the ANP, while others, who he hoped were also police, wore

---

* EOD operators who have been deployed to a conflict zone do not publicly reveal their names to avoid repercussions in Canada.

the usual loose cotton men's clothing called *shalwar kameez*. If the normal protocol had been followed, a cordon should have been set up to secure the site. But these ANP men were scattered in a relaxed manner around it, making them seem more like a bunch of local residents merely hanging out.

The QRF personnel quickly dismounted from their vehicles, with the infantry starting to work around the area to establish the cordon while Sam's team set up a safe zone from which they could begin their work. They had to move quickly to deal with this device because they had received intelligence that insurgents were moving toward them, likely planning to launch an ambush. So Sam decided not to use any of their more sophisticated equipment and to instead approach the device carrying his basic tools of a brush and trowel. He could clearly see where the ANP had already prodded the loose gravel on the shoulder of the asphalt road, so he began his cautious approach to the IED. Reaching the spot, he knelt and started to work on it carefully.

Suddenly, he lost his concentration as a shadow passed over the hole. Glancing up, he saw one of the Afghans leaning over him to watch what he was doing. Sam quickly got over his initial surprise, as he guessed, by the Afghan's posture and expression, that the man was merely curious. But that was not supposed to happen — Sam was not supposed to have an audience while dismantling something that could explode with the first wrong movement. Sam could not help but feel a rise of irritation. Dealing with any IED was dangerous, and one never knew when it might go off. The EOD operator accepted that risk, but it was plain stupid for someone else to come close just to satisfy his curiosity. Trying to be as diplomatic as possible, Sam suppressed his annoyance and waved his arms around to communicate to the intruder to get back. The Afghan finally got the message, and Sam returned to his task, which was to destroy the device with a block of C-4 explosive because of the need to clear the site as rapidly as possible.

That was Sam's first exposure to IED disposal in Afghanistan. The task was successfully completed, and the QRF had returned to Ma'sum Ghar safely. But the job was not carried out as well as Sam would have liked. He had taken mental notes of all the things that had not been done appropriately and set out to change them, because it was going to be a long tour and he could not afford to accept sloppy procedures if he and his team were to come through it safely.

Sam's tour began in August. When his flight from Canada touched down at KAF, Afghanistan was no novelty to him, because he had already been there in late 2005 to help get KAF ready for the arrival of the first Canadian contingent that would be based there for Operation Athena. The task of the combat engineers at that time had been to tear down Camp Julien in Kabul, pack up, and move everything south by convoy over Highway One to Kandahar City. The city and road had been peaceful then. Now he was returning to a province that was the centre of the southern insurgency, this time in charge of one of the EOD teams in Task Force Kandahar's Counter-IED Squadron.

The team spent the best part of the first week going through the usual acclimatization routine, and by the end of that time was simply anxious to get on with the job. They received their orders to move out to an FOB and were packed into the troop compartment of a LAV. It was an uncomfortable introduction to being outside the wire, with the passengers crammed into a claustrophobic space and their only view of the passing countryside via the monitor screen fed by the camera attached to the cannon. The trip was slow as the convoy started and stopped intermittently to check for IEDs. While some of the younger engineers remained tense, Sam realized this might be the last time he had for a while without the burden of responsibility, so he closed his eyes and enjoyed the ride as much as he could. But lingering in the back of his mind was his own sense of priority for this mission; and that was to bring his team back whole without losing anyone.

Sam's team was based at FOB Ma'sum Ghar, and their area of responsibility (AOR) covered the Taliban heartland of Panjwayi and Zharey Districts. Their accommodation was near the back of the base, which they later learned was where the insurgents usually aimed their mortar bombs and rockets. Despite this threat, Sam chose a tent for his sleeping quarters because he found that the close beds in the better-protected sea containers made him feel like everyone was packed in like sardines. The team quickly settled into the base's routines, but soon discovered they were seldom in the base during the day.

EOD teams were basically on call all the time for the entire tour — 24 hours a day, seven days a week — waiting to be notified that an IED had been found somewhere. When such a notice came in, Sam immediately

Sam's EOD team travelled in a Cougar, an MRAP (mine-resistant ambush-protected) vehicle that carried all their specialized equipment for dealing with IEDs when going out to a bomb site with the Quick Response Force.

The Telerob Explosive Ordnance Disposal and Observation Robot, tEODor, goes to work for Task Force Kandahar.

went to the command post to receive the details while everyone else got their gear ready. Upon Sam's return, they piled into the Cougar and headed to the rendezvous point where the QRF was assembling. The Cougar was designated as a mine-resistant ambush-protected (MRAP) armoured vehicle, with its V-shaped hull meant to deflect much of the force of an IED detonating below it and specially designed for carrying EOD teams and their equipment.

The Cougar had enough interior space to transport eight soldiers, but much of it was instead taken up by two bulky EOD pieces of equipment that were the major items in the team's arsenal: a bomb-disposal robot and a mine-protected suit. They called the robot "Teodore," based on its trade name, tEODor, the Telerob Explosive Ordnance Disposal and Observation Robot. Measuring 1.2 metres tall and weighing 375 kilograms, the machine was remotely operated from a safe distance while carrying out tasks required for dealing with an IED. For example, the EOD operator could use the robot's sophisticated vision system, which had several cameras that panned, tilted, or zoomed. These could be employed when approaching an IED

A tEODor demonstrates its capabilities at Camp Nathan Smith, the Provincial Reconstruction Team base in Kandahar City.

An EOD operator wears a bomb suit, which they all used as a required procedure when dealing with an IED.

for the first time to assess its composition and determine what they were dealing with. Then, if the conditions were right, its arm, with a reach of 2.7 metres and a claw at the end, was used to dig, lift, or defuse the device. It was thus of great value in dealing with IEDs because a robot could be replaced if something went wrong, while an EOD operator could not.

Under normal circumstances the robot was utilized as much as possible when dealing with an IED. But to complete the job the EOD operator had to approach the IED himself, taking the Long Walk while wearing a bomb suit, a heavy, all-encompassing system of protective clothing made of ballistic lining and Kevlar. The suit was hot and heavy and could feel claustrophobic. During training, many engineers swore they would never get used to it. There was no doubt that it was awkward, the closest comparison being to what it might feel like wearing a snowmobiler's outfit — heavy jacket and pants, big, warm boots, large gloves, and full helmet with a visor — all under the Afghan sun. Sam did not mind it. To him the suit helped him feel that he had a better chance of survival while dealing with an unknown device, giving him a comforting sensation as if he were in a cocoon.

The EOD team was out practically every day working as part of the QRF. If an IED was located anywhere in the AO, the team had to deal with it and move out with the QRF. But the QRF could be called out for any number of other reasons, from a vehicle breakdown to an ambush. Since the threat of IEDs was constant, the EOD team always went along with the QRF. The size of the QRF depended on the particular task it was summoned to do, but most of the time it was, in effect, a self-contained combat force containing tanks, infantry, combat engineers, recovery assets, medics, and ambulances — everything that might be needed in any situation that arose. It could be a convoy as big as 30 vehicles at times, depending on the mission. When the string of vehicles making up the QRF left the gates of the FOB, no one really knew how long they would be gone outside the wire, because new tasks could come in over the radio even while they were en route to the first mission. For that reason everyone took along extra food and water, a change of clothing, and something to sleep in if they were unable to return that night.

When the QRF headed out of the FOB, the team's Cougar was usually placed somewhere in the middle of the convoy, since it was considered a high-value target. In that position it was better protected if they encountered an ambush along the way. Once all elements of the convoy were marshalled into the order of march, they rolled out of Ma'sum Ghar with the object of getting to the target site as quickly as possible. At the same time the convoy had to proceed with some caution, because there was always the danger of hitting an IED along the route. To try to minimize this occurrence, they avoided known danger areas and travelled off-road as much as they could, even if there was a paved road leading to the target site. But time was always of the essence, because the longer they took to get to the target site, the more time they gave the Taliban to set up an ambush. As a result, they could not check every choke point and culvert along the way as they sped toward the IED site, relying on any useful intelligence reports helped along by any air asset that could provide observation on the route. The trip was always tense, with everyone paying constant attention to the surroundings, searching for bad guys or indicators warning that something might go *bang!* It was no trip along the Trans-Canada Highway!

Upon arriving at the IED site, the pressure continued. While the QRF's infantry worked around the site to set up the cordon, the EOD team established a safe area where they could begin their work. From there Sam started his work by first checking the site from a distance, using either binoculars or the visual systems on the armoured vehicle, or by sending in the robot. At some point in the process he went in alone, usually with the bomb suit on, but not always if an ambush was threatened or if the IED was difficult to access. Even if time was pressing, he approached the IED carefully, always looking to see if anything was out of place or if any Afghan civilian could be seen nearby, watching too intently. When he reached the IED, he pulled whatever tools he needed out of his kit and began to defuse the weapon. The object was to remove absolutely every piece of material from the site and send it back to KAF for analysis. It was easier to remove the threat by blowing up the device in place, but because that destroyed any useful evidence, Sam never did this unless they had to get out fast.

While Sam worked on the IED, the infantry kept watch on the surroundings but stayed well back in case something went wrong. They were

A tEODor approaches an IED site, probably near Ghundey Ghar in Zharey District. Following standard procedures, the EOD team normally sends out the robot for an initial inspection when it reaches a suspected IED site.

quite happy to let the EOD operator take over, although it was not unusual for them to remain anxious. One soldier, for example, went through a number of firefights without any trouble, but readily admitted that if he knew an IED was nearby, even if it had orange tape around it and was two blocks away, he was terrified. As far as infantry soldiers were concerned, the work the EOD operators did was simply too dangerous. They often told Sam, "You're crazy for what you're doing. We find this stuff and we want to get away from it, but you guys go toward it!" Sam merely laughed at their concerns. In his opinion, it all depended on one's definition of "dangerous." He felt his specialty was no different than the risk a policeman or fireman took in their routine line of duty. Yes, it was risky, but he was well trained and confident in his ability to do his job.

The Taliban were shrewd opponents, however, and threats constantly changed, so Sam had to stay ahead of them, forever looking for easier and safer ways to deal with IEDs. He had the habit of doing a self-analysis

An EOD operator in a bomb suit approaches an IED site, probably near Ghundey Ghar in Zharey District.

process after every call, first asking himself, *Well, that didn't work so well this time. I'll do it like this next time.* He also talked to his team or peers, asking, "Here's what I found, and this is how I took care of it. Have you done it differently? Or have you encountered anything like this? If you did, how did you do it?"

While all the combat arms specialties in the military required special skills to carry out their trade most effectively, it was probably most important that EOD operators had personal characteristics that suited the work they did. A good EOD operator had to have the personality type that thought well under stress. When an operator faced a sudden challenge, he had to quickly come up with an inventory of possible solutions to overcome that challenge. He had to know those solutions well, almost instinctively, and be confident in his ability to apply them. At the same time he had to know how to improvise when faced with something that did not fit the usual pattern. Under real-life situations in Afghanistan there was no rule that covered all possibilities. The EOD operator was actually trying to beat the imagination of his opponent, the unseen bomb maker. There were times when the EOD operator had to break the rules he had been taught, but then he had to clearly understand why he was doing so. And the EOD operator had to remain calm both mentally and physically while under stress, which could be caused by the danger posed by the device he was working on, by knowing that an ambush could occur at any time, or by the sights or sounds of casualties caused by an IED that had been set off. Sam had managed to develop this mental sense of calmness under such circumstances, pushing any negative thoughts out of his mind. If he was going to worry about anything, it would be about getting the job in front of him done correctly and safely. Everything else was put on the back burner and was dealt with later.

The personality of EOD specialists came under special scrutiny in an important study done for the U.S. Army in 1980 by Professor Stanley Rachman. The object of the study was to examine the nature of fear and courageous behaviour in soldiers while carrying out highly skilled work in dangerous situations. For this the researchers conducted an analysis of more than 200 British improvised explosive device disposal (IEDD) operators who had seen service in Northern Ireland. In the 10-year period prior to the study, the IED threat in that region of the United Kingdom had risen to an extreme number of IED incidents, averaging more than 3,000 a year. The tests Rachman conducted demonstrated that these operators were notable for having stable personalities and a high level of competence, with psychological health norms that were above average compared to the civilian population. The study concluded that the self-confidence shown by these men in carrying out their hazardous duties came as a result of excellence in training in IEDD practices along with high group morale and cohesion, all of which became the main determinants of courageous behaviour. As a side note of the study, Rachman also observed that experienced operators seemed to have the mental ability to easily "switch off" their emotions when in stressful situations while carrying out their duties, but later allow themselves to "switch on" when off-duty.[12]

These characteristics seemed to be reflected in the ability of Canadian EOD teams in Afghanistan despite the continuous stress they worked under. Once Sam's team began operating out of Ma'sum Ghar, they went full out and were on call seven days a week from September to January with long days outside the wire. On most days they left in the morning and did not come back until late afternoon or after supper. On some days they might be partway through their first call, or just finished one call-out and heading home, when another call came over the radio, sending them to another site.

The team got its first taste of multiple calls early on their tour when they were dispatched to Maiwand District, west of Kandahar City. They arrived at the site around 0900 hours and set up the cordon, while Sam identified the problem as a pair of directionally focused fragmentation charges set back to back and designed to act like claymore mines to target a patrol approaching a culvert from any direction. It was a command-wire IED that could be set off by a triggerman (now long gone) hidden off the road. Tracing the wires, Sam then found another IED attached to the same circuit buried in the mouth of the culvert, this one using a pressure cooker packed full of explosives. While he was still dealing with this problem, he got a call about another IED in a wadi just down the road. He finished clearing the first set of IEDs and started moving to the second site when a call about a third device came in. By the time he dealt with the second IED, he was already dead tired. When he returned to the FOB late that night and tried to write his daily report, he had trouble remembering the details of everything he had done through the fog of his fatigue.

That day set the pace for the whole tour. The long days were tiring, and when the last call came at the end of the day, Sam had to resist going through the steps almost robotically. But his team was not the only one under such pressure. On one day alone 19 calls came in to squadron headquarters, and deciding which team should be assigned to each site became almost like a game of chess. The team even came to consider those days when they were called upon to support a cordon-and-search operation as a nice break. They also noticed during the Muslim religious festival of Ramadan that IED calls decreased noticeably. That should have given them a break, as well, but the team could not relax because they remained on call, edgy all day, thinking, *I know we're going to get a call. Just wait and see!*

Sam was very rigorous in following proper procedures when dealing with all the calls his team received. But the call for which he had to improvise the most was for an IED in a culvert near Ma'sum Ghar. An ANP patrol had spotted a command wire along the roadside, which brought the QRF out to deal with it. For some time the Taliban had found that culverts over which Coalition supply lines passed were great places to emplace explosives. To counter this threat, contracts had been let out for the construction of steel grates that could be attached to the openings to block their use by insurgents. It was a nice solution in theory, but there were too many culverts and not all the grates fitted properly. The culvert for which Sam's team was called out on this particular day seemed to be a favourite of the Taliban. Sam immediately recognized that he had dealt with an IED there only a few weeks earlier. He remembered that at that time the grate had been loose and the IED had been booby-trapped. As he approached it again, he saw that the grate had now disappeared — probably taken by locals for scrap metal — and he knew he had to be extra cautious when dealing with whatever was now inside.

He started off by following the usual routine and could see the trace of a command wire, like an ant trail in the dusty ground as it went along the shoulder and into the culvert opening. To get a first look at what they were facing, the team unloaded the robot with its camera and sent it into the ditch. Unfortunately, they were only able to see that the wire entered a hole in the culvert wall. Under normal circumstances when dealing with an IED site, Sam would put on the bomb suit to approach the device on foot, but that wouldn't work here because the suit was too bulky to allow him to get into the opening. So he had to go inside wearing only his tactical vest to deal with whatever was there.

Sam found that the Taliban had chipped out the concrete on the side of the culvert, cutting and bending the reinforcing steel bar to make an opening big enough to insert a very large cooking pot loaded with explosives. The rebar had then been bent back and the hole covered with chunks of concrete. It was an awkward and tense situation as Sam knew he had to deal with this IED while lying in cramped quarters, unable to turn his head to see all around. With the memory of his previous visit fresh in his mind, he first checked as well as he could to see if the explosive had any anti-tampering device on it. Not finding anything, he then bent the rebar out again and got to work. Although he thought he had defused the device properly, he continued to be cautious with every move, knowing that it could go off if his educated guesses were incorrect. He had thought it was likely a command wire, but now he had doubts. Could that piece be a remote-control antenna? Until he had the whole thing pulled apart, there was no way to know for sure.

Because the IED was jammed into the concrete and was still partly covered by rebar, it required some force to get all of it out. Remaining cautious, he decided to wrap a rope around it, crawl outside, and try to pull the IED out from a safe distance. He tried that approach, but it failed to work; the charge would not move with the rope pulling at an angle. So he walked back to the end of the cordon and tied the rope to a LAV to see if a bit more force could dislodge the thing. The driver in the armoured vehicle started its engine, the slack on the rope was taken up, and the LAV started to pull. But the IED still did not budge — then the rope broke!

What now? He would have to go back in again and work the IED out some other way. As he crawled in, he was still tense, but was also getting annoyed. The bomb emplacer had done his job too well and had made Sam's task very challenging. He resigned himself to the final solution: pulling the device out by hand. He squirmed up to the IED hole in the culvert wall and then wedged himself facing it. The rebar was bent but now poking into his crotch while his head banged on top of the culvert passage. He could only curse the Taliban and everyone else who irked him loudly and think, *Let's get this over with!* His blood pressure had risen, his hearing was alert to every sound, and the perverse thought went through his head that if something went off, he hoped it went quickly, because then he would not feel anything. He put his feet up against the wall, grasped the pot by the handles on either side, and hauled on it, forcing it up over the rebar and out — finally ending another day in the fight to outsmart the bomb emplacers.

After about a month of constant call-outs and daily briefings, Sam developed a sense of which areas were more dangerous than others. To the west the villages of Zangabad, Talukan, and Mushan continued to be dangerous because of the limited Canadian presence there. The battle group was so thinly stretched that it could not properly cover the whole AO, so the Taliban had been given a freer hand to operate in that territory. Two other areas the Taliban seemed to always target were the road between FOB Ma'sum Ghar and Kandahar City, and along Highway One east of Kandahar City. When the team was out travelling with the QRF, Sam found he could relax slightly along stretches where he knew the road was usually clear, but his senses always started tingling upon coming into the next section where he knew a Taliban bomb cell was likely more active. It all depended on which village or which little side track they were passing by.

There were other times when some sixth sense made Sam more alert, like the day when he worked a call near Howz-e-Madad, just off Highway One. He was at a site on a gravel track that led through farm fields, where he was confined by a mud wall on each side as he tried to deal with an IED that was buried in the side of one of the walls. It was an uncomfortable position that could not be cordoned off in the usual way. His concentration was suddenly broken when he got word from one of the turret crews of a LAV on watch that heads of Afghans were starting to pop up over the wall farther down the lane. He was already tense about the location and now the hairs on the back of his neck straightened. The news about these suspicious observers was enough for him to take some kind of precaution, so he began to throw smoke grenades down the lane in the direction he felt there might be a threat. The smoke gave him some cover so that no one could observe what he was doing, but unfortunately it caused a new problem. The smoke was caught between the walls, and as it swirled around in the channel, it moved back toward him, slightly obscuring his vision. He was very relieved when he finally got the IED out and could leave the area.

The area Sam disliked the most was around the village of Sanjaray, about 10 kilometres east of FOB Wilson on Highway One. The team had quite a few calls out to that area during their tour, and every time they went, Sam's senses were always on alert. There were small things out of the ordinary that gave him the feeling something was not right there. About a month after arriving in the theatre most soldiers developed a good sense of what was normal and what was not. So, when they started noticing things strangely becoming abnormal, senses went on high alert. Often it was hard to define what caused the discomfort, but it was usually some subtle pattern. When the QRF arrived in such a location, local Afghans might be around watching while the cordon was set up. Sam and his team knew the Afghans were naturally curious, but when they looked up and all of them had disappeared, then it was time to get the job finished quickly and get out of there.

Sanjaray had not always been hostile territory. Up to the time when Sam's team arrived, it was controlled by a local leader of the Alizai tribe, Habibullah Jan, who remained neutral but allowed the Canadian battle group to carry out operations in his territory. Under his strong leadership the Taliban could not gain any ground in the village, and the tribesmen even fought off passing Taliban. But in July just before Sam's arrival, Jan was assassinated outside his home as the Taliban began a deadly campaign to eliminate tribal leaders who opposed them. With his death the Zharey District leader should have stepped in to exert some personal leadership and not leave a vacuum, but he did not command the same respect among local residents. Consequently, the Taliban soon infiltrated the area to such an extent that prominent Taliban figures began openly attending public prayers in the mosque. Sanjaray was a strategic town for the Taliban, since it was located on the border of Zharey and Arghandab Districts, which meant it was important for the transit of supplies into Kandahar City. The Taliban continued their terror campaign in the area and other pro-government tribal elders were killed in the ensuing months. A Taliban bomb-making cell was soon established in the vicinity of Sanjaray, and it had freedom of movement after dark to become a permanent threat to the critical Highway One. By the end of 2008, Taliban courts were operating out of Sanjaray.[13] Sam had good reason for his sense of discomfort when travelling to this village.

For the first months of Sam's tour, security patrols were successful in uncovering all the IEDs along the critical routes in the AO before any fatalities were sustained. While that resulted in a heavy pace of work for the team, it also gave them a sense of accomplishment that they were successful in combatting the Taliban's IED campaign in their area. That ended on December 5. At around 0800 the first sign of trouble came from a report that a foot patrol near Pashmul had triggered an IED made from a mortar bomb, blowing off the legs of one soldier.[14] Then, an hour later, another call came in that an IED strike had occurred against a Canadian patrol 16 kilometres to the north, just outside Sanjaray, and at least two men had been killed — casualties who had been categorized as VSA (vital signs absent).

The QRF hurriedly formed up and headed north along the connecting highway — Route Summit — to get onto Highway One. They only got partway, however, when they hit a cordon that had been set up by the ANP after they found an IED on the road. So the team had first to deal with that device, unfortunately delaying them a couple of hours. As they finally approached the site, the sky grew oddly gloomy. While they had been driving up, the weather had been sunny, but now black clouds appeared out of nowhere and everything became much darker, giving Sam an eerie feeling that matched what he found there. It was an agitated scene where everyone was under extreme stress, with a lot of people moving around and trying to deal with the casualties while maintaining security at the same time. Fumes of the explosive were still in the air, and pieces of the vehicle littered the site.

Warrant Officer Robert John Wilson, Corporal Mark Robert McLaren, and Private Demetrios Diplaros from 1 RCR had been mentors to an ANA patrol that was searching for IEDs along the highway that morning. Their RG-31 Nyala triggered off a massive blast that threw their vehicle into the air, killing all three and leaving a crater nine metres deep and almost as wide as the road. On the drive up, Sam had been very apprehensive about what he would see because this was his first incident with fatalities. Questions kept swirling in his mind — who had been killed, what would the site look like, how bad was it really going to be, how chaotic was it?

Before being deployed they had all been briefed on such incidents, but he had not been faced with the reality of it until now. He knew that seeing death with his own eyes would be quite different than viewing it through a projector in Canada.

To Sam it was a bit of a shock, but he quickly assessed the site, determined that everything seemed under control, and got on with his job. Because Sam's team had taken so long to get there, another engineer detachment had already arrived from the OMLT's combat outpost and had secured the site. The IED had already been detonated, so the task for Sam and his team now was to scour the area, going through adjacent grape fields to find any components that could help them figure out the cause of the blast as well as recovering weapons the Canadian mentors had been carrying. After the bodies of the three Canadians were medevaced to KAF, the site was cleared and Sam's team headed back to Ma'sum Ghar. On the return ride everyone in the Cougar was very quiet; the sight of the fatalities had driven home the realities of their mission.

But Sam's team was not finished with Sanjaray. Only about a week later, on December 13, they had a call to go to another IED attack there with VSAs again, just a few hundred metres farther west of the strike on December 5. This time the casualties came from the QRF of the PRT at Camp Nathan Smith. That QRF had been called out to deal with reports of suspicious activity near the previous strike site, and one of their LAVs had actually hit the IED they were searching for. Sam's QRF responded again, this time travelling cross-country as much as possible to avoid any interference on the road. When they arrived at the site, it was a similar scene to the last one — a massive hole in the road bigger than anything they had seen up to that point in the tour. They estimated that the IED must have consisted of 18 20-litre jugs full of explosives, tunnelled in from the shoulder into the centre of the road. When they arrived at the site, they found that Corporal Thomas James Hamilton, Private John Michael Roy Curwin, and Private Justin Peter Jones of 2 RCR had been killed, and that other members of the crew as well as passengers had been injured.

Sam's team continued to deal with IEDs throughout Panjwayi and Zharey for the rest of December. The work was intensive, with multiple call-outs every day. Two more IED strikes with fatalities occurred during that time, although Sam's team was not involved because they were away on an operation at FOB Wilson. On Boxing Day Private Michael Freeman was killed and three other soldiers were wounded when their LAV hit an IED while on a security patrol in Zharey District. The next day was even worse: two Canadians were killed and four others were injured when their LAV struck an IED in Panjwayi District. This bad news touched Sam personally because one of the men killed was Sergeant Gregory John Kruse, an experienced combat engineer Sam knew from the 2 Combat Engineer Regiment. Kruse had come out with the QRF to investigate an IED found by Warrant Officer Gaetan Roberge, and both had been killed in the blast. Sam's team just happened to be at FOB Wilson that day. If they had not been there, his team would have gone out with the QRF instead of Kruse's. That was a thought he could not dwell on.

At the end of December reorganization took place in the Counter-IED Squadron. The chain of command decided Sam should have a break from the pace he had been working at — he had done more IED calls than the rest of the teams put together. So on New Year's Day he moved back to Task Force Headquarters in KAF. There he was given the job of coordinating the assignment of EOD teams to incoming calls of IED threats, as well as making sure the teams were fully supplied with what they needed to get their jobs done.

In May his tour was over and he found himself on a flight to Cyprus where he would spend a short time decompressing from the tensions of a combat theatre. Sam had mixed feelings about leaving. It had been no picnic, but he had expected that. As the outbound flight lifted off, he relaxed for the first time since arriving and thought, *Thank God I'm getting out of here!* But he could not help feeling some misgivings. He was leaving friends behind and hoped they would be all right. He was also concerned about his post-deployment reaction to what he had been through — how easily would he be able to come down from the emotional high of being under pressure every day?

In pre-deployment training they had been warned by everyone about the difficulties some would face transitioning back to life in Canada. Sam would have to wait and see how that went. Cyprus would give him a chance to begin that easing off, but landing there was still a bit of culture shock.

He found it took a day or two to fully get over the sense that he needed to carry a weapon, or whether something bad was about to happen. But it did not take him long to adjust to the fact that he was now on a vacation in a Mediterranean country. Being older than most of the other soldiers, he was quite content to relax around the hotel pool drinking beer and do a little sightseeing, and by Day 4 he was ready to go home.

Looking back sometime later, Sam came to believe that his tour in Afghanistan was the high point in his career as a combat engineer. It had allowed him to really understand the importance of all the training in the basic building blocks of ordnance disposal he had received over many years. Before he had gone to Afghanistan he had been told he would face complex situations that would require a lot of improvisation. But on the ground he ended up falling back on those basic skills to deal with the majority of IEDs he encountered. From his point of view, things tended to go wrong when he got fancy with IEDs. At the same time he had learned a lot about his specialty, and after his return to Canada, he ended up working on the training standards for the next generation of combat engineers, helping to make sure they learned the lessons from Afghanistan. The world was not getting any more stable, and the Canadian Armed Forces would have to be ready to deal with asymmetric warfare in future conflicts. Sam could now use his experience to help Canadians fight the next battle.

7

MENTORING THE AFGHAN NATIONAL ARMY:
CAPTAIN ROBERT PEEL

When Canadian troops arrived in Kandahar to begin Phase 2 of Operation Athena, their mission was to assist in the reconstruction of a country that had been devastated politically, economically, and socially by almost three decades of war. The breakdown of a normal society had been assured by the last eight years of rule by the Taliban, who sought to remove all traces of rational government from the country. With the Taliban driven from power and the creation of a new constitutional government, the United Nations recognized there was a great need to rebuild all aspects of the country. The new Islamic Republic of Afghanistan, however, remained fragile as it struggled through the stages of creating a constitution and electing its leaders.

The threat of a return by the Taliban was seemingly remote when the new government was installed in 2004, but threats remained — from strong warlords with their own sizable armies, from other terrorist groups such as Hezb-i-Islam Gulbuddin, and from ongoing intertribal conflict. Therefore, one of the most important steps in creating the new state was to provide sufficient security for the reconstruction to take place, and this required that steps be initiated to help the central government create its own police and military force. Hamid Karzai had already given this task priority in 2002 while he was still interim president by issuing a decree to set up a new Afghan National Army (ANA).

Unfortunately, the Afghan government had neither the tools nor finances to begin forming this new security force, so it had to turn to the United States for assistance. In 2002 an American study team agreed with the need to create an Afghan military force as quickly as possible in order to provide the new government credibility in what was still an unstable country. It recommended that the U.S. military commit a training task force for 18 months, after which the Afghans would carry on with their own resources to build a national army initially targeted at around 50,000 men. As the Taliban started to make a comeback, however, the planned strength of the ANA rose to 171,600 men.[1] As might be expected, the establishment of a new security force was an enormous task: there were great cultural differences to deal with, most recruits were illiterate, desertion rates were initially high, and there were problems of ensuring that an ethnically balanced force was achieved in a country rife with tribal conflicts. Questions also remained as to how Afghanistan would be able to afford such a large military in the coming years.

To create such a large force from raw recruits needed more than basic training. Once in the field, ANA units still needed assistance to carry out all the complexities of larger unit manoeuvres along with establishing the systems to maintain an effective fighting force. To deal with this issue, Embedded Tactical Teams (ETT) were developed based on the American experience in Iraq. In 2006, when operational responsibility for regions of Afghanistan was transferred from U.S. forces to NATO, similar teams were organized by the Coalition and became known as Operational Mentor Liaison Teams (OMLTs). The first Canadian OMLT with a strength of 65 personnel began working with an ANA *kandak* in Kandahar Province in August 2006 as part of Roto 2's 1 RCR Battle Group, taking over the task of mentoring the 2nd Kandak of the 1st Brigade of the ANA 205 Corps from an American ETT.[2]

Expansion of the ANA was not as vigorous as was hoped for. The U.S. government was criticized for not having a comprehensive plan to rebuild the Afghan security forces, and the bulk of the ANA remained unable to operate without Coalition help.[3] Thus, when the Canadian battle group took over responsibility for Kandahar Province in 2006, it found that the numbers of ANA forces assigned to 205 Corps were insufficient to provide support to the battle group in operations against the Taliban. It seemed that the Afghan government was giving priority to the deployment of newly formed *kandaks* in the Kabul area and northern Afghanistan rather than in the south. At the same time 205 Corps, whose AOR covered the three southern provinces, deployed most of its strength to eastern Zabul Province instead of to Kandahar. This left only one infantry *kandak*, a combat support *kandak*, and a combat service support *kandak* remaining for operations in Kandahar Province where the ANA 1st Brigade operated, and these were neither at full strength nor sufficiently trained for sustained operations.[4]

Despite their initial lack of readiness, the Afghan soldiers from the 2nd Kandak, mentored by the Canadians, proved to be brave and easy to get along with, although allowances had to be made for cultural differences. For example, they were all very religious and relied at times more on prayer to influence the outcome of a battle rather than tactics. Their concept of time might make them careless about adhering to schedules. Most had not had any formal education, so they had limited attention spans for lectures, could not read, and were unable to visualize how to use a map. But they were polite and respectful to authority figures and took care to treat the local Afghan population in Kandahar Province with respect. Despite all these issues, the commander of the first Canadian battle group to arrive in Kandahar, Lieutenant-Colonel Ian Hope, would have liked more of them to be available and complimented them: "On operations they proved to be very brave during combat, loyal to those willing to suffer alongside them, quick on their feet, but simple in tactics.... I loved working with the ANA troops."[5]

Kandahar Province was the heartland of the Pashtuns, who easily resented the presence of anyone they considered a "foreigner," a term that could include other Afghan racial groups. Although an effort was made to mix as many Pashtuns into the ANA as possible, a number of men in the 1st Brigade were northern Tajiks and Uzbeks. Despite this, their professionalism soon gained the respect of local people: they did not steal or damage property like the police, and they took care to respect Pashtun customs such as being very careful about approaching local women. Some argued that the ethnic differences might even be an advantage, since the local villagers felt the ANA could be trusted as neutral brokers in conflicts based on tribal differences.

By early 2007, the 2nd Kandak of the 1st Brigade, 205 Corps, had absorbed its training well. Under its own experienced leaders, assisted by the OMLT, it was believed by many to be one of the most effective units in the ANA.[6] When 2 RCR BG arrived for Roto 3, the *kandak* had already been judged as capable of carrying out joint patrols with Canadian units. The first of these occurred on February 23, 2007, when one of its companies moved west from FOB Wilson along Highway One, partnered with a Canadian infantry company and a tank squadron, to clear the hamlet of Howz-e-Madad close to the Taliban heartland.

That summer the OMLT's responsibilities expanded as it began preparations to take over mentoring the entire ANA 1st Brigade. This formation consisted of five *kandaks* — three infantry *kandaks*, a combat support *kandak*, and a combat service *kandak* — so the OMLT for Roto 3 faced a huge task without having sufficient personnel to take on a full brigade completely. However, plans were put into place that allowed Roto 4 to fully mentor the 1st Brigade. An expanded OMLT complement of almost 200 men under Colonel Jean-François Riffou began training in Canada during the summer and fall of 2007.[7] When the OMLT for Roto 5, TF 1-08, arrived in Afghanistan in February 2008, it was fullly prepared to commence its work with teams for each *kandak* as well as for the brigade headquarters. The Canadian mentor staff for each *kandak* now consisted of an OMLT headquarters group of 10 soldiers, which directed four mentoring teams, each of four soldiers led by a captain (one team for each ANA company).[8]

✦

The sky was lighting up nicely as the sun rose above the horizon on a warm June morning. Daylight provided the line of ANA soldiers and their Canadian mentors a clear view of the surrounding fields of grapes and poppies as well as the usual grape-drying buildings. There had been no signs of danger up to now. The column's feeling of security vanished, however, when the sound of gunfire suddenly broke out to the west and an RPG rocket soared into the sky. The moment was fogged with uncertainty. But then, as a bullet smacked into the mud wall nearby, Captain Robert Peel's senses went on full alert. They had been spotted by Taliban. All the training Peel had absorbed since joining the infantry 15 years earlier came into play. This was not a situation he had expected to be in when he received his orders to deploy to Afghanistan in Roto 5, but he had trained for such a moment for years and now easily switched into responding as he had been taught.

Rob grew up in Edmonton. Because his father was an Anglican minister, joining the military had never entered his mind as a future career. After high school, he enrolled in university with the intention of eventually beginning a secure but unexciting occupation as an elementary schoolteacher. But while he was at university the newspapers started to carry stories of international crises in which peacekeepers played a significant role in the protection of helpless civilians. Rob had always had a broader interest in the world at large, and reading about these dramatic events unsettled him. He began to feel his studies were boring and irrelevant.

At the end of his first year of university he set about finding summer work and decided to take up tree planting in the mud of northern Alberta. But, while leaving an interview for this job, he passed a recruiting desk where some soldiers from the Loyal Edmonton Regiment, outfitted in parachute jump smocks and maroon berets, offered an alternative summer job for students by joining the reserves. The sight drew his attention. The recruiters were enthusiastic about what the reserves offered — do your training for the summer, get a good pay, and continue to earn income throughout the winter by attending evening parades. To Rob this sounded better than tree planting! So he signed up and within weeks was off to Camp Wainwright for his basic infantry course.

The military life suited him well. Perhaps his early upbringing had instilled in him a sense of principle to do some good in the world rather than pursue personal gain. This led him to see the military in a different light than many of his fellow students who were busy participating in protest marches. Rob remained impressed by the stories in the press of the military delivering humanitarian aid in the world, so he stayed on in the reserves, volunteering to go to Croatia in 1994, then joining the regular Canadian Armed Forces and going to Kosovo. He returned to the reserves in 2001, volunteering again for a tour in Bosnia in 2002. By 2007 he was ready to go on another overseas deployment, this time having worked his way up to the rank of captain.

The decision to expand the Canadian OMLT to train a full ANA brigade was announced in the summer of 2007, so the military needed more volunteers to fill the expanded organization. Rob liked the sound of the work they would be doing, knew some of the officers and NCOs from the PPCLI who were already in the OMLT, and managed to secure a position on the team. At that time the ANA 1st Brigade was operating with the 1st and 2nd Kandaks in the field — one in Panjwayi and the other in Zharey — while the 3rd was back in KAF still undergoing training and resupply. The OMLT mirrored the brigade deployment, with a field mentor team for each field *kandak* and a training mentor *kandak* back at KAF. Rob had spent so many years training as an infantryman that he wanted a position in one of the field teams, but these were already filled when he put in his request. As a result, when he landed in Afghanistan in February 2008, he was resigned to doing his assignment at KAF with the training team for the duration of Roto 5.

ANA soldiers in prone positions on a range are trained to fire the Canadian C7 rifle.

One of Rob's first tasks was to put together and implement a training program for the *kandak* in KAF to use the C7 rifle. Canada had donated 2,500 C7s to the ANA, a weapon the Afghans had never encountered before. Up to this time, the ANA's weapon of choice was the AK-47, used by many militaries and insurgents throughout the world. Since the time they were born, most Afghans had grown up with this assault rifle and knew it well. But a decision had been made to try to standardize the ANA on NATO weapons, giving them American M16 and Canadian C7 rifles. Introducing the ANA to the Canadian weapon became one of Rob's first tasks during the winter of 2008. It was not an exciting job, but that was fine. He had always taken the attitude that you made the best of whatever job was given to you. Rob was still a junior officer, and he considered training Afghan soldiers as an opportunity to gain more experience.

Training kept Rob busy throughout February and March. In April, however, the time came for the *kandaks* to rotate: the 3rd Kandak moved out of KAF into Zharey District to take over from the 2nd which, according to standard procedure, was given leave for a month. Rob was temporarily at loose ends when an opportunity came up to go outside the wire of KAF. A replacement was needed at FOB Wilson for a mentor who was going away on leave. While this was only a temporary posting, Rob jumped at the chance. The assignment took him out to FOB Wilson where he worked under Major Bob Ritchie. His formal task for this assignment was to look after the administrative and logistical needs for all OMLT responsibilities in Zharey — making sure that rations and food were organized, ammunition was coming in, fuel was in sufficient supply, and all administrative requests from the five outposts that had been established at that time were processed quickly. This was still a rather routine job, but at least he was now out of KAF. It wasn't long, however, before he was offered what he really wanted — the chance to go out on operations.

The task force was made up of four teams, each consisting of four mentors on paper. In practice, though, the teams often had less than that number on hand. When Rob arrived at FOB Wilson, the team under Captain Jon Snyder was quite shorthanded — his second-in-command was on leave and the other two men had been sent out to support another task. As a result, Captain Snyder required temporary replacements to ensure he had a full team when heading outside the wire. So the OMLT commander, Major Bob Ritchie, knowing Rob was keen to go out of the FOB, approached Rob and made him an offer he could not refuse — going out on all the patrols that he wanted to join as long as all the administrative and logistics work got done. That was more than enough motivation for Rob.

It was a fortunate coincidence that Rob now found he could join the OMLT team under Captain Snyder. The two had met some time ago back in Canada, both knew a lot of the same people in the PPCLI, and they got along well. Both of them had a common interest in extreme physical endurance competitions and had trained together with the intention of entering the Canadian military's Mountain Man Exercise in 2007, a contest that required participants to run 32 kilometres carrying a 15-kilogram pack, then portage and canoe 13 kilometres down the North Saskatchewan River, and finally run the last five kilometres to the finish line. They were greatly disappointed when the race was cancelled, but they decided to carry on and enter what was probably an even tougher ultra-marathon, the Great Canadian Death Race in Grand Cache, Alberta. Participants in this foot race followed a 125-kilometre route that passed over several mountain peaks during the course of which they experienced an elevation rise of 5,200 metres. It was an extremely demanding race. In that particular competition, Rob managed to cover 90 kilometres before safety staff pulled him out because of health concerns. Reflecting his naturally competitive nature, Jon, on the other hand, stubbornly pushed on to complete the course, but ended up suffering acute renal failure as a result.

Rob was lucky that he had landed in the same OMLT team as Jon, an officer for whom he had great respect. Jon stood out as an example of a professional soldier who, from an early age, had decided he would follow a career in the military. He had already been on one tour to Afghanistan and had established a reputation in the fighting in Panjwayi during the summer of 2006, and on this tour continued to impress everyone around him. As one example of his dedication to the mission, he had taken the time to learn Pashto to such an extent that he could carry on a conversation with other Afghans without the need of his interpreter. Because of the thoughtfulness with which he treated them, all the Afghans he came into contact with, including his interpreters, had great respect for him.

The OMLT team carried out a number of routine patrols throughout May. Then, two weeks, after Rob's arrival, an order came down for a larger deliberate operation to be initiated on June 4. Jon's team was still short of men, however, and needed to get help from other sources. Where would he find these extra bodies? The usual source was to scrounge them from the Security Force (SECFOR) unit — Task Force Zharey's transportation element, the men who ran the gauntlet of Highway One almost daily to pick up whatever was needed to keep the OMLT going, always alert to the possibility of coming across IEDs or snipers along the route. SECFOR was temporarily based in FOB Wilson, but its job resulted in it shuttling back and forth to KAF and to the outlying combat outposts and police substations in Zharey. In addition to this main responsibility, it had been made available by Task Force Kandahar to augment the operation on Major Ritchie's request. Carrying out these duties, along with basic maintenance on their RG-31 Nyalas, was a heavy workload that left the soldiers of SECFOR with little time for rest. All the same, they were always keen to go beyond the wire unless they were totally exhausted from their other chores.

During a joint ANA-OMLT patrol, curious local children swarm the Afghan company commander when he stops to have some quick food from his ration pack.

The plan for June 4 involved the entire *kandak*. Two companies would lead the advance south into Zharey District from the ANA strongpoint at Howz-e-Madad on Highway One toward the areas of Sangasar and Nalgham, where the villagers' sympathies were strongly aligned with the Taliban. The purpose of the mission was to disrupt insurgent bases by searching for IED and weapons caches, using such a large-scale operation to assess the capability of the newly arrived 3rd Kandak. Sangasar had previously been cleared by the Van Doos in 2007, after which the Canadians had established a combat outpost there to continue to hold the area. Daily patrols out of the outpost had kept the area relatively well controlled, although signs that the Taliban were still present continued to show up in the form of continually discovered weapons caches. In the spring of 2008, insurgent activity had intensified and the Taliban had blown up all the culverts leading to Sangasar. As a result, resupply was difficult and the strongpoint had been abandoned. Sufficient time had now passed since the Canadians had left the area, and the Zharey OMLT felt it was time to show its presence again by mounting a major operation that would see the rifle companies of the 3rd Kandak converge on Sangasar and pass through several intermediate objectives along the way, with the fourth rifle company establishing a blockade to the west.

On the evening of June 3, Jon gathered his ad hoc team for an orders group to lay out the plan for the next day when they would mentor the 3rd Company of the *kandak*, which would be on the left front of the advance. Besides himself, Jon had six other men who he divided into two-man fire teams. In his role as mentor, Jon would move with the Afghan company commander, taking along with him a joint terminal attack controller (JTAC) team consisting of Captain Trevor Pellerine and Corporal Trevor Knight. The JTAC team would provide additional support assets such as artillery and attack aircraft as laid out by the manoeuvre plan. Rob would mentor the lead ANA platoon commander whose unit would act as a fire base in support of the move onto the final objective. One of the SECFOR soldiers, Corporal Cary Baker, would go along with Rob as his fire-team partner, providing security while Rob concentrated on working with the ANA platoon commander. The other two SECFOR soldiers, Corporals Donovan Ball and Steven Bancarz, would provide additional support.

The operation began well, with the column setting out in single file from Highway One on time at around 0230 hours in the morning of June 4, 2008. Moving through the dark night on a network of trails, they made good progress and soon crossed the three large wadis running parallel to Highway One that were often used by Canadian troops to judge their progress on patrols into insurgent territory. But Ball and Bancarz, at the rear, had immediate concerns about the discipline of this ANA unit as they had observed the Afghan troops were not keeping the proper spacing as they moved out along the dark trail into close country where the Taliban had a strong presence.

At around 0500 hours, just as the sky was lightening, the column crossed another wadi and arrived at a location close to their intermediate objective, a cluster of compounds where a weapons cache had previously been uncovered. Here they paused before launching their clearing operation. The Afghan soldiers spread out in a defensive posture along a long north-south wall that followed a typical irrigation ditch reeking of dirty water and manure, with open agriculture fields on all sides. Jon and the company commander met and agreed on a plan for the next advance onto the intermediate objective, which was just past the south end of the wall.

The ANA platoons were beginning to move into position when automatic gunfire and the noise of RPGs burst out to the northwest of their position, with rockets passing overhead. It was unclear at first who the firing was directed at, but it certainly meant that the element of surprise in the early dawn had been lost. Jon quickly met again with the company commander and advised him to move his soldiers back into a defensive posture. However, the commander was not reacting with any urgency, so Jon insisted that he also send some men to the south end of the wall to cover any insurgent advance from the objective, and also north to the wadi they had just crossed to prevent any attempt to cut them off.

The column now started to come under sporadic fire, making it clear they had been spotted by insurgents. They soon identified that machine-gun fire was coming at them across the field from two compounds to the northeast. In the original plan, Jon had given Rob's Afghan platoon the responsibility of setting up a fire base when the company was eventually ready to move onto the objective. With this sudden change in the situation,

Rob now automatically moved with Corporal Cary Baker to get his ANA soldiers around the corner at the south end of the wall from where they could provide covering fire if Jon decided to assault the buildings where the firing was coming from.

Turning the corner of the wall, Rob found himself on a road heading eastward. It was bounded on both sides by mud walls a little more than a metre high, giving him the feeling of being in a First World War trench. He recognized the cover provided as being advantageous, since he could easily move up and down it by ducking a little for protection. Rob needed this protection because he could already hear rounds cracking over his head and hitting the wall behind him. All this time he was on automatic pilot, doing the drills he had practised so many times during his many years in the infantry. It was the first time he was under fire, but he felt no stress and had perfect mental clarity. He knew exactly what to do — listen to the crack of the bullet as it passed by, locate where it hit the wall by the thump it made, then estimate the shooter's position from these sounds and engage the likely location of the threat. He and Cary Baker began moving up and down the walled road, popping up, locating targets, shooting, then dropping down and shifting a metre or so to one side. At one point Rob experienced a sudden jolt of anxiety when Baker dropped like a sack of potatoes. But with a quick check he discovered that Baker had ducked quickly because a round had hit the wall too close for comfort.

While doing all this, Rob looked around for the ANA platoon commander he was assigned to work with but was unable to locate him. Furthermore, none of the NCOs were visible, either. Only he and Baker were returning insurgent fire: the ANA soldiers were hugging the wall, silently staring at Rob, not yelling or taking action as the Canadians were doing. Rob had been told many times in training that, as mentors, they were there only to enable the ANA leaders to command their units, not to give orders. But that went out the window now. The ANA leaders were not present, the soldiers in this platoon were frightened, and they seemed desperate for someone to tell them what to do. So Rob started to give orders, and the Afghan soldiers reacted well. Noticing that some of the enemy were moving around farther down the road to the east and firing at their position, Rob suspected the insurgents were trying to get behind them. He therefore grabbed one of the ANA soldiers and positioned him with a machine gun to cover that approach. Then he placed another soldier at a side road that headed down to the village to the south so no one could surprise them from that direction. At this point he noticed they were now receiving insurgent fire even from their rear.

Back along the north-south wall, Jon also realized they were taking fire from three directions and were in danger of being surrounded. Now that the ANA company had been repositioned in a defensive arrangement, Jon felt the situation was under control and that they had time for the company commander to decide his next move. In the meantime, his JTAC team got on the air and brought down a Predator drone, guiding it to shoot a Hellfire missile at a target they could clearly identify. With this demonstration of firepower, the insurgent fire slackened, but that lasted only briefly, after which it continued to build up. Up to now Jon had remained cool and collected, acting courageously and decisively under intense fire, but now he became impatient when he noticed that, just like Rob's platoon, the ANA soldiers along the wall were not returning fire.

Jon rose over the wall and began to fire back. His action set an example, and the ANA soldiers around him finally returned fire, as well. Things took a turn for the worse, however, when one of the Afghan soldiers was hit in the head and collapsed into the ditch. Jon quickly moved over to him and attempted to apply first aid. The wound, though, was very serious, and with the situation now getting more complicated, Jon decided they should proceed to extract the casualty. He then went over to the ANA commander to find out what the man planned to do next. Unfortunately, the response was quite unsatisfactory — the commander stated he had no intention of moving. The situation was too dangerous and he might get shot, so he was staying where he was!

At this point Jon realized he had to make the necessary decisions himself to get them out of a situation that appeared to be getting worse. He contacted Major Bob Ritchie on the radio to see if they could coordinate a link-up and an air evacuation to give the casualty any hope of surviving. To the north, Major Ritchie had been made aware of the situation at the beginning of the ambush and had attempted to move the reserve ANA company up to support Jon. However, because of that company's location and posture on the ground, he quickly realized they could not reach the beleaguered company in time. Acknowledging the critical nature of the situation, Major Ritchie started the procedure to bring in an air evacuation and launched a five-man Canadian team to head south on foot to establish the link-up.

Glancing at the north end of the wall, Jon saw that their exit route was still being held open by an ANA detachment firing a PKM machine gun toward the compounds where the heaviest insurgent fire originated from. But he also noticed that more insurgents were massing up the wadi leading to the compounds. To cover the withdrawal, the JTAC team arranged for the artillery to fire a smoke mission. But then things fell apart again. Up at the north end of the wall, another Afghan soldier was hit by enemy fire. One of the ANA soldiers began to carry this wounded man back toward the centre of the wall, but as this went on the others in the detachment covering the exit abandoned their position, giving the insurgents an opportunity to advance.

Jon returned to the company commander and explained to him once more that there were now two casualties who needed to be evacuated, but to do so they would have to reoccupy the abandoned cut-off position. He proposed that Corporals Ball and Bancarz take the lead, bringing along with them an ANA detachment carrying the casualties. The rest of the company would then follow while another detachment under Rob and Corporal Baker covered the rear. The ANA company commander seemed to agree with this plan but remained immobile and failed to pass on any orders.

The smoke mission came down as requested and the smoke spread, blocking the insurgents' line of sight as hoped. However, Jon could not get the company commander to act and the ANA soldiers mostly remained stationary. Some of them fired back, but the majority still hugged the wall. A few helped carry the casualties back along the wall but were still intimidated by the insurgent fire passing close over their heads, so they moved only a few feet before dropping the wounded men and running back to the wall. After about 15 minutes of this frustrating effort, the smoke had dissipated and no progress had been made.

Exasperated, Jon decided that the only way they were going to get out of there was for Ball and Bancarz to move off immediately to retake the north exit, motivating the ANA soldiers to assist as much as they could.

He felt they had to move now, because if the insurgents occupied the exit corner the whole column would be trapped. Ball and Bancarz advanced quickly on that order, although they had no idea if the insurgents had already occupied the position. Despite their exhortations, they could not get any of the ANA troops to help so they set out on their own. Upon reaching the corner, they were initially forced down by heavy machine-gun fire, but Ball was able to cross over the road while Bancarz provided covering fire. The ANA soldiers now began moving, and Bancarz managed to grab some of them to set up a fire base positioned to cover the road to the east. They would hold this position to prevent the Taliban from closing in on the column as it withdrew.

Now, with the corner secured, the rest of the company knew it was time to get going. Unfortunately, they failed to bring their casualties along as ordered. Some even complained that trying to evacuate the wounded was pointless, that doing so would only slow them down. The ANA soldiers staggered forward as if stunned, some firing blindly. By now Jon had lost his temper. He later recalled that one ANA man fired and shuffled along in a trance, howling *"Allahu Akbar"* as if he were about to die. Every time the company advanced, the soldiers became exposed and the insurgents brought heavy fire down on them, impeding forward progress until a few ANA troops fired back, causing insurgent fire to slacken temporarily. Each time the enemy fire intensified, however, the soldiers carrying the second casualty let their burden fall, leaving him for others to pick up. It was stop and go — a horrible process.

The chaos finally ended when Rob and Cary Baker, coming up at the rear of the company, stumbled on the wounded soldier on the ground. The Canadians, with bullets still flying close overhead, attempted to get him out by dragging him for a short distance along the wall, but were unable to make much progress. An eerie feeling engulfed Rob as he noticed that while they were struggling with the injured man a gap was widening between them and the rest of the patrol. It gave him the sense that they were being left behind, not a comfortable feeling. He therefore got in contact with Jon over his personal radio (PR) and asked him to send some men to help. Eight Afghans came back, six of them picking up the body while the other two helped Rob and Cary cover the withdrawal. Moving along the irrigation ditch for protection, the small rearguard kept firing at any avenues where they thought insurgents might move in on them, though the enemy was still invisible. Then they got a report fed down from the drone overhead that the insurgents were not following on their heels but were trying to get around them and cut them off.

Despite the breakdown in discipline, the Afghans and Canadians made it out of the firefight without further losses, but it was a struggle, particularly for the Canadians. Corporal Ball, out in front, linked up with a relief force led by Major Ritchie. Two Kiowa Warrior helicopters arrived after being requisitioned by the JTAC, providing additional firepower that held back the insurgents and enabled a UH-60 Blackhawk helicopter to land and get the casualties away safely. The ANA company continued to lack discipline as it streamed back toward Howz-e-Madad, about four kilometres away, and had trouble navigating the return route. Consequently, Jon and Corporal Baker had to move up to the front to guide the column, leaving the other Canadians behind under Major Ritchie to provide rear security. Fortunately, by 0900, all elements of the patrol were safely back at Howz-e-Madad, drained of energy and high on adrenaline.

What had gone wrong on that patrol? Everyone searched their thoughts for the next few days to try to figure it out. The early contact had been unexpected: the last patrols through the area had not found any armed resistance, only discovering weapons caches. They had expected this operation to be similar and it had been meant to give the new *kandak* a good operational trial without complications. It seemed, however, that they had stirred up a hornets' nest. Did this strong resistance indicate they had bumped into a command group? Or, after the close of the combat outpost at Sangasar, had the insurgents in the area been given breathing time to be reinforced and recover their morale? It might have simply been that they had been seen in the early dawn light by spotters and the return of Canadians and ANA was unwelcome. Rob felt that the muezzin call to prayer sounded unusually early and might have signalled a warning that had brought the insurgents swarming out.

Back at the base the cause of the initial firing became clear. The other company leading the advance to the west of Jon's had spotted armed Afghans on their left flank — in other words, between the two companies advancing on the intermediate objective — and began firing at them, bringing Jon's column under their fire from stray rounds. This gunfire would have certainly alerted all the Taliban in the area about the operation, and Jon's company had become the unlucky recipient of their violent response.

How could the collapse of morale in the company be explained? The *kandak* had been in action for some time and had recently been in action in Uruzgan Province, so one might have expected them to react better. But Uruzgan was relatively quiet compared to Kandahar and Helmand Provinces where the insurgents were making their main effort to seize control. As a result, the violent contact on that early morning of June 4 had unnerved the men of the 3rd Company, and the officers and senior NCOs did not display the confident leadership needed to help their men respond as they should have. It was not unusual for soldiers coming under sudden fire to freeze when they lacked confidence in their own ability and in the ability of their leaders. Their performance on June 4 demonstrated that the *kandak* needed more time and more experience before it could be considered ready for independent operations.

While there was more work to be done to improve the performance of the *kandak*'s 3rd Company, the pace of operations continued as usual. A few days later Jon's team was given the task of going out on a patrol. Although he was invited to join it, Rob was unable to go because of other duties he had to complete, but he promised Jon that he would join the next one. Jon replied, "Okay, see you in the morning." Those were the last words Rob ever heard from him.

Captain Jon Snyder led his patrol out just after sunset on June 7. That night there was only a thin crescent moon in the sky, making it so dark that they could hardly see their hands in front of their faces. That meant the patrol had trouble seeing obstacles on the ground they walked over. In particular they had to watch for *kariz*. The farmers in Afghanistan used a unique and ancient means of irrigation called *kariz*, which involved a network of underground tunnels that carried water from a higher elevation to the fields and villages where it was needed. Along the route of tunnels a series of vertical shafts were drilled down from the surface both to collect water and to allow access during the dry season for maintenance. As the patrol crossed one of these fields in the dark, Jon suddenly disappeared. He had stepped into a *kariz* shaft and had fallen 20 metres into the reservoir below. Frantic efforts were made to rescue him, but his heavy kit dragged him down and he drowned before they could get him out. It was a shock to everyone, a terrible loss of someone who was an outstanding leader.

Despite this loss, they all knew the mission had to continue without undue interruption. Several days later Major Ritchie instructed Rob to temporarily take over the OMLT team until he decided who would fill the position. At the end of that week, after consulting with the team's second-in-command, Major Ritchie made his decision and told Rob he would be appointed the permanent leader. The sudden changes over those few days were unsettling. While Rob was excited about being selected for the job, Jon had been his friend. The contradiction remained on his mind, but he dealt with it and got on with his new position.

Rob was a natural fit for the job. He had been training for years and had the skills to meet the challenge. He also had the character for dealing with ANA soldiers, which required flexibility and patience. He was naturally enthusiastic about any job he was given and readily accepted the task of mentoring. Even when he had first been notified that he would be deployed to Afghanistan, he had wanted to understand the culture he was heading into and had taken the time to read all he could about Afghan history. The ANA and its outlook on life could be strange and frustrating to Western eyes. Rob, however, had a lot of respect for the ANA officers he would now deal with. He was especially impressed with the experience many of the officers had — some had fought with the famed Tajik warlord Ahmed Shah Massoud in the Panjshir Valley against both the Soviets and the Taliban, while others had served in the original Afghan army during the Communist regime. So he saw his mentoring task not so much as teaching new skills to them but more to enable these experienced officers to get on with successful operations that would build on their experience.

The tempo of the operations over the next few weeks was intense. It began on the first day of his new job when Rob stepped out on a 10-kilometre patrol. It was a good start, pretty routine into an area over which they had some control and where they talked to local villagers about rumours that some Taliban had passed through during the night. For the Taliban the fighting season had now begun in earnest, but the ANA forces available to the

Major Bob Ritchie (right) commanded Task Force Zharey OMLT, which was responsible for training *kandaks* of the ANA 1st Brigade, 205 Corps. Colonel Sheren Shah (second from left) was one of the most experienced and talented of the ANA officers, and his 2nd Kandak was considered the most effective of these units. Here, Major Ritchie and Colonel Shah cross the Arghandab River on May 1, 2008, during an operation in Panjwayi District.

Canadian battle group were limited — there was only one ANA infantry *kandak* for all of Zharey. Foot patrols now went out every day, covering anywhere from five to 50 kilometres in the AO. The QRF was also frequently called upon because of IED strikes or ambushes. For Rob in his new job it was non-stop and tiring, but he had great help from his second-in-command, Warrant Officer Ryan Cooper, who was now back from leave along with the rest of the OMLT. He had not been prepared for this sudden responsibility but was buoyed by the trust shown in him by Major Ritchie.

The OMLT also had to prepare the *kandak* for the next major operation, making sure the problems revealed on June 4 were corrected. The first operation took place on June 25 and was carried out jointly with C Company of the Canadian battle group. It was very similar to that of June 4, heading south from Highway One across the lines of wadis into an area where insurgents were present. They met resistance as soon as they crossed the first

Major Bob Ritchie of the OMLT (right) and Colonel Sheren Shah of the ANA (left) look at the position of their troops on a map during an operation in Panjwayi District in May 2008.

Canadian soldiers of the OMLT (right) and a soldier of the ANA (left) take a break during the May 2008 operation in Panjwayi District.

One of Task Force Zharey's OMLT units operated out of the ANA strongpoint at Howz-e-Madad. This view from the southwest tower of the strongpoint looks east, showing the living conditions. The ANA troops not stationed in the building lived around the perimeter in makeshift shelters.

Captain John MacDonald (left), an OMLT team leader, with his mentored Afghan company commander and some of his soldiers have stopped to get set in positions during an operation in the vicinity of Sangasar. The locals have brought out food for the ANA troops.

lateral wadi, and the advancing ANA companies had to leapfrog forward from there, one company providing a fire base while another pushed on to the next wadi. The ANA advance continued for five hours under continuous fire, with reports coming in that the Taliban were calling in reinforcements from the flanks. But the *kandak* was better prepared than it had been in the earlier operation and achieved all its objectives, as well as capturing a number of heavy weapons and discovering several underground bunkers. This time Rob worked once more with the 3rd Company, and at the end of the day, gave it full credit for a job well done. In his opinion the problems of June 4 had been corrected and this time the company had performed as well as a Canadian unit might have done. Rob could rightly feel some satisfaction that the OMLT had helped in the ANA company's recovery.

Captain Robert Peel's tour in Afghanistan ended in August 2008. It was an amazing trip for him. When he arrived in the theatre, he had not expected to leave Kandahar Airfield and was prepared to remain confined to that huge base doing a routine job in which he would need few of the

The ANA was generally respected by most Afghan villagers. Here, an ANA company pauses during an operation near Sangasar to take up positions, while young local men gather to talk to the soldiers. The soldier on the left is the company commander.

skills he had accumulated over the years while training for the infantry. But events changed and he managed to get outside the wire — temporarily at first, but then remaining permanently in the field when he lost someone who he considered a friend as well as an officer he looked up to as an exceptional leader. He had gotten on with the job at hand and found his time mentoring Afghan soldiers in the fields of Zharey a satisfying experience he would never forget. Rob believed he had made a difference in that complex land, although it might take a generation to really determine what had been accomplished there. But his experience in Afghanistan changed his life, and he still experiences strong emotions when he recalls what he and his fellow soldiers accomplished there.

Rob returned to the regular force in 2010, with an occupation change from infantry to intelligence officer. He was also accepted into a subsidized university education program which allowed him to attend the University of Victoria to undertake studies in political science. Over the next several years, he managed to balance his military duties, university studies, and personal responsibilities and received his undergraduate degree in 2016. He is looking forward to the challenges of his new trade and possible future deployment opportunities.

8

AMBUSH ON THE ARGHANDAB RIVER: MASTER WARRANT OFFICER RICHARD STACEY

What do you do with a 42-metric-ton tank that is no longer needed? That was the unsettling question the Canadian Armed Forces faced in 2003. It was not only the Canadian Armed Forces asking this question; it was being asked by most militaries in the world as a result of the breakup of the Soviet Union in 1991. If massed armoured warfare on the North German plains was no longer a threat, did Western militaries have any further need for heavy, costly main battle tanks? The threats to security in the world now seemed to be coming from smaller belligerent countries and from radical insurgencies, and these were best handled by more lightly equipped forces.

In 1996, with no clear adversary on the horizon, the Canadian Armed Forces decided that the German-made Leopard 1, its main battle tank, would not be replaced when its period of serviceability ended.[1] The Canadian Armed Forces' experience in peacekeeping operations in Bosnia and Kosovo reinforced the belief that only light armoured vehicles would be needed in future military operations. The debate went on for a decade but seemed finally resolved when, in late 2003, the minister of national defence announced the decision had been made to replace the Leopard tank with a lighter-wheeled combat fighting vehicle called the Mobile Gun System, which he believed would transform the Canadian Armed Forces "into a medium-weight, information age force" better suited to the 21st century.[2]

When Canada took on the responsibility for Kandahar Province in 2006 as part of its mission in Afghanistan, the battle group that arrived for the first rotation was equipped with LAV IIIs. The Canadians began their mission with confidence and optimism that they could achieve their role within Operation Athena to bring security, governance, and economic development to Afghanistan. They quickly discovered, however, that they were challenged by an insurgency more complex and intense than anticipated and were now largely fighting a battle for security. The first months of operations by the Canadians were spent establishing a presence throughout the province, gathering intelligence on the insurgency, and suppressing the buildup of enemy forces in critical areas. This came to a head in the fall of 2006 when Task Force Kandahar confronted and soundly defeated the main Taliban fighting force in Operation Medusa. The Taliban did not withdraw from the area, however, but instead started a campaign of unconventional warfare and remained a threat that had to be countered.

The Canadians learned a number of lessons from Operation Medusa. One was that hard-core Taliban were more dangerous than previously thought. At Pashmul their fighters had constructed well-planned defensive positions with reinforced bunkers and connecting trenches with good zones of fire. The other lesson was the extent to which the terrain favoured the insurgents. While the narrow roads were sure to contain IEDs, cross-country travel was at times impossible for the LAVs because Afghan farm fields were broken up by mud furrows over a metre deep and encircled by strong mud walls. Grape-drying huts with metre-thick walls as well as family compounds often became good fire bases for insurgents. The hard clay used to make these structures had the consistency of concrete, so hard that the LAV III's 27 mm gun could not penetrate them. Facing these obstacles during Operation Medusa, the combat engineers of the battle group, 23 Field Squadron, gathered tracked bulldozers from whatever sources they could find and welded armoured steel plates onto them. These ad hoc armoured vehicles were then able to lead the advance into enemy-held territory, breaking a way through walls and fields for the LAVs of 1 RCR BG to advance. While the engineers were struggling to make these preparations, the commanding general of Regional Command (South) happened to make a visit to the Battle

Group Command Post, and while there, asked them what they needed. Without hesitation they answered, "Tanks!"[3]

By the end of Operation Medusa, Lieutenant-Colonel Omer Lavoie had come to the same conclusion. His battle group had arrived in Afghanistan prepared to fight an insurgency but had been faced with carrying out a conventional battle against an enemy that was prepared to stand and fight. Now, to his own surprise, he had come to the conclusion that he needed both heavy armour with its firepower and armoured engineer vehicles to create access routes to allow his infantry to come to grips with the enemy. The request went swiftly up the chain of command and was accepted without hesitation in Ottawa. On September 15 the Canadian government announced that a squadron of 15 Leopard C2 tanks, four armoured recovery vehicles, and four armoured engineering vehicles would be sent to Afghanistan.

The deployment of tanks was not without its critics. Some argued that the sight of such heavy weapons would alienate the Afghan people and thus be counter-productive to the principles of COIN warfare. Collateral damage to homes or farms caused by the tanks would certainly defeat the work of the Provincial Reconstruction Team, which was seeking to interact with the population and rebuild the country. Others recalled that in the 1980s the Russians had attempted to employ tanks to suppress the insurgency during that period and had failed completely. In the minds of the critics, Canada was about to make the same mistake. In particular, modern anti-tank mines and RPGs with shaped explosive charges could easily damage or destroy tanks that had been designed in the 1960s.

However, critics must have been surprised by the speed of deployment when the first tank of the B Squadron, Lord Strathcona's Horse (Royal Canadians), was unloaded from a heavy-lift U.S. Air Force C-17 Globemaster aircraft at KAF on October 3, only a few weeks after the announcement of the new strategy. In fact, the need for armour had already been considered some time before the official announcement as reports came back to Canada regarding the intensity of the insurgency in Kandahar Province. While the Department of National Defence denied rumours, tanks were being reconditioned for the new environment and B Squadron was doing pre-deployment training at Canadian Armed Forces Base Wainwright.[4]

This advance planning allowed a full tank squadron to deploy in the fall of 2006 over a distance of 14,000 kilometres to an FOB in remote Kandahar Province in only two months, an impressive feat of operational planning.

By early December, the squadron was ready to support the battle group in operations against the Taliban, and they fired their guns for the first time the day after their arrival at the FOB against insurgents sending rockets into the base. Despite this quick first use of the tanks, however, they did not move out of the gates immediately. Task Force Headquarters still had concerns about how such a heavy weapon should be employed, considering the potential collateral damage and the negative effect that could have on their efforts at counter-insurgency warfare.[5] For the simple local farmers of Panjwayi and Zharey, it would be the biggest vehicle they had ever seen — a 42-metric-ton monster that would not easily pass through narrow village lanes, belching enough destruction from its 105 mm gun to pierce the walls of any building suspected of housing unwanted residents. It would be akin to letting a bull loose in a china shop if not handled properly.

Tanks went into action outside the FOB for the first time on December 19, 2006, when they joined up with an infantry company and an armoured engineer troop in an operation to disrupt insurgent fighters in the area of Howz-e-Madad on Highway One. The operation was meant to be less aggressive than Medusa, with a goal this time of driving away the hard-core enemy fighters and influencing less committed insurgents to return to their villages and join a new regional security force opposing the Taliban. The combat team cleared the area without resistance, the presence of tanks seemingly a strong factor in the enemy's decision to quietly withdraw.

In the ensuing weeks, the tanks continued to take part in offensive operations throughout the AO, fully integrated with the infantry. The Leopard's 105 mm gun provided significant fire support, swiftly destroying enemy ambush parties or mortar groups as soon as contact was made and taking on targets as far away as 4,000 metres. The tanks also made a significant contribution to further deliberate operations designed to expand zones of security within Panjwayi and Zharey. Cordon-and-search operations were carried out to find insurgents concealing themselves among the local population, capturing them or at least uncovering their weapons caches. But in areas where insurgents had established a long-term presence and local villagers were sympathetic to them, approach routes were laced with carefully planted IEDs designed to prevent any rapid approach by the Canadians troops and to lure them into ambush sites. Because of the complex Afghan terrain, the combat team had to move toward an objective in single file to minimize the damage from an IED strike. For such movements, the Leopards had special armoured attachments to overcome these Taliban tactics, so now they led the column forward. Depending on the type of terrain, a roller might be attached to the lead tank to detonate any pressure-plate IED encountered on the track, or a bulldozer plough might be attached to breach fields and walls, creating an alternate approach route to an objective.[6]

While the Leopard C2 tanks were proving valuable to the battle group in carrying out its mission, they did have weaknesses. The armour underneath, for example, was the most vulnerable part of the tanks, and as the IED threat in Afghanistan became more intense, extra protection for the Leopards was necessary. Also, the crews were having a difficult time functioning in the extreme heat of the Afghan summer. The outside temperature could typically rise to 50 degrees Celsius on the dusty roads, spiking the temperature inside the steel hulls to more than 60 degrees.[7] Furthermore, with the Leopard C2 tanks now reaching 28 years of age, maintenance became a problem because some spare parts were difficult to obtain.[8] Reaction to these reports was extraordinarily rapid, and as the quickest means to obtaining more suitable tanks, officials in Ottawa looked to other militaries seeking to reduce their armoured forces. Proposals were received from six Western countries and were evaluated using a number of factors, including operational performance, the cost of upgrading, and readiness for delivery.

In April 2007, the Canadian government announced its decision to buy 100 newer Leopard 2A4 tanks from the Netherlands, and while these were being upgraded to Canadian standards, the government also temporarily leased 20 Leopard 2A6M tanks from Germany for quicker deployment. These leased tanks had the advantage of improved mine protection and an electric turret drive that reduced heat in the interiors. The first of the leased German tanks arrived at KAF on August 16, 2007.

The first real test of the new 2A6M tanks occurred on November 2, 2007, when one of them hit an IED. While the Taliban claimed the tank had been destroyed, General Rick Hillier quickly refuted that report, stating the Leopard 2A6M had been repaired and was soon put back into action. He emphasized that in every engagement the new tanks had already taught the Taliban "some very harsh lessons." Indeed, the deployment of tanks to Afghanistan contributed substantially to combatting the insurgency. Intelligence gathered from prisoners and villagers continued to indicate that insurgent fighters were demoralized by the presence of the Leopards. On the other hand, concern that the use of tanks would undermine efforts to gain the trust of the local population proved unwarranted. Throughout all the contacts in which tanks fired on insurgent fighters, no civilian casualties were incurred. The tanks were used carefully only where they benefited an operation with minimal negative effect on the local population, such as in support of planned operations, for reconnaissance, for route clearance tasks, and for clearing the way through broken terrain. Their fire-control systems enabled them to accurately acquire and eliminate enemy targets with minimal collateral damage in situations where artillery or air support had caused far more damage. They saved lives at times by placing themselves between dismounted Canadian soldiers and enemy positions. At the same time the tanks did have some disadvantages, such as high maintenance cost, especially for fuel, and expenses that resulted from reimbursing farmers when damage did happen to their properties.

The tactics developed for Leopard tanks in support of the battle group in this type of asymmetric warfare provided lessons for other countries. The U.S. Marines ignored similar criticisms about the deployment of tanks and introduced them for their operations in Helmand Province after successfully employing them in Iraq. Denmark also deployed a platoon of Leopard tanks in support of its battle group in Helmand Province and found its presence also intimidated insurgents. As a result of the Afghan experience, it seemed the era of the main battle tank was not over yet, but remained to be further evaluated as new forms of warfare evolved in the 21st century. And if that called for the continued use of tanks, the Canadian Armed Forces were better able to respond, since they were now equipped with the Leopard 2A6M modified to Canadian standards.

When one of the lead vehicles of the convoy hit the IED, the sound of the explosion swept down the line of vehicles and an ominous black-and-orange cloud rose into the sky. Master Warrant Officer Richard Stacey's gut dropped and a sinking feeling came over him. He knew that when such a large explosion happened someone had likely been killed. As the convoy had pulled out of Mushan that morning, he had expected they might be ambushed by insurgents equipped with small arms and RPGs, but he had worried more that they might hit an IED somewhere along the route. Now the reason for that worry had actually happened. But Richard had always been able to remain mentally clear and logical under stress, and the shock of the explosion did not shake his focus now. As the squadron sergeant-major (SSM) of the tanks escorting the convoy, he knew the drill that had to be carried out and got on his radio immediately to get his soldiers moving.

When Richard landed in KAF in February 2009, he felt he was ready for whatever he would face during his tour. He had been in Afghanistan already with a reconnaissance squadron in Kabul in 2004, but he was aware that this tour would be different. Since the Korean War, the Canadian Armed Forces had mainly carried out peacemaking or peace-keeping operations, and Richard had participated in a number of these — Haiti in 1995, Bosnia in 1997, and Kosovo in 1999. Now, however, Task Force Kandahar was involved in combat, and for the first time, he was deploying as a sergeant-major of a tank squadron — C Squadron of Lord Strathcona's Horse (Royal Canadians). To him it was a rare opportunity to make use of all the skills he had developed since joining the army 26 years earlier. Not many soldiers got that opportunity. He also believed in the mission and felt he would do something important if he could help create a secure and stable environment for Afghans.

As with all incoming rotations, the squadron spent only a few days in KAF before heading out to FOB Ma'sum Ghar where the tanks were based. They soon took part in operations, providing support for the infantry of 2 R22eR BG in the multitude of tasks required for the type of COIN warfare going on at that time. There had been no further major fighting like that of 2006, but the tanks were required to be part of the Quick Reaction Force, providing protection for the combat engineers clearing IEDs and joining combat teams that were formed for operations throughout Panjwayi,

Zharey, and Maiwand Districts. During these larger operations, designed to stabilize an area where the Taliban still exerted their influence, the tanks were useful in setting up a ring of steel around the objective. There were no significant firefights during these operations since the Taliban continued to avoid major confrontations, but the threat of IEDs was constant.

IEDs remained a source of stress for everyone. The protective armour of the 42-metric-ton Leopard 2A6M tank gave some feeling of safety to their crews against small-arms fire or RPG strikes. And they could adapt to the heat and dust that to some resembled their training experience in Wainwright, Alberta. But it was difficult when it came to IEDs. Each day as they drove out the gate of the FOB they had to wonder, *Am I going to hit one this time?* The driver in a tank always had to deal with the thought of what would happen if 100 litres of homemade explosive went off underneath his seat.

Stress for tank crew members also came from not knowing who the enemy was. They had originally been trained to deal with the armed forces

Local villagers must have been intimidated when they first saw a massive Leopard tank, but they soon got used to it. Here, a Leopard 2A6M main battle tank from the Lord Strathcona's Horse (Royal Canadians), part of the 1 RCR BG, provides over-watch as a family of local Afghans pass by during a battle-group operation.

of a uniformed opponent, but in Afghanistan the opponent could be a 12-year-old boy. So, when they drove their massive tank through the confined roads of a village, crews experienced anxious moments when small children ran up to the roadside. As with children everywhere, it was exciting for them to see such a new and strange vehicle in their remote village, and they wanted to have a better look as it rumbled past. One of Richard's biggest fears was wondering what he would do while out on an operation if he was ever confronted by a young boy with a rifle. He could not imagine how he would react if that situation arose. That was a dark thought he had to put aside, but he was never sure how he would deal with such a threat if it ever occurred.

As the SSM, one of Richard's main duties now was managing the morale and welfare of his soldiers during the rotation — dealing with day-to-day discipline and keeping their thoughts on the mission. Being away from home and family and halfway around the world weighed heavily on some of the younger soldiers on their first overseas deployment. They had concerns about those they had left behind: how were things going back home, was the car getting fixed, had the wife given birth to their baby yet, was the girlfriend getting along in her new job all right? It was natural for soldiers to worry about such things, but Richard had to be sure that when they went out the gate everyone was fully focused on the mission. He had to keep in touch with his soldiers' feelings, asking how they were doing, judging their emotional condition from their replies or expressions, finding out if something else was on their minds.

If one of his men said "I have a problem back home," Richard chatted, discussed what was going on, and determined if something could be done to relieve the soldier's anxiety. Maybe Richard could get the satellite phone for the worried soldier so he could call Canada. Something like a five-minute conversation might fix everything for the man. Like the master warrant officer of any infantry company or artillery battery, Richard felt responsible for everyone under his command. He had to know his soldiers — their personalities, strengths, and weaknesses, as well as something about their families. He had to convey to each soldier his own personal conviction that, as the senior NCO, he would do everything within his power to make sure each man or woman got home no matter what happened in the coming days. To make sure he stayed connected, he made a point of walking around the whole FOB each night, talking to everyone before he went to bed. Then he was up early the next morning to do the same thing again.

Richard, however, had an additional responsibility that others did not have: running an echelon system for the resupply of ammunition, water, foodstuffs, and recovery of vehicles when tanks were operating with a combat team. When the first battle group arrived in Kandahar in 2006, its supply needs were taken care of by the National Support Element, which had been deployed as part of Task Force Kandahar. With the arrival of the tanks, though, the maintenance requirements in the field became more demanding and specialized. The echelon component of the tank squadron soon proved quite capable of sustaining vehicles outside the FOBs, so its responsibilities were broadened to resupply all subunits in the battle group when on extended operations. The echelon was made up of about 12 vehicles, which included trucks carrying fuel, ammunition, water, and rations; the Bison armoured ambulance with its medical team; maintenance vehicles; and armoured recovery vehicles (ARVs). Because they were now fighting an unconventional war in which there were no front lines, the echelon did not follow the forward battle line at a safe distance in the rear as it had done in the Second World War. It now travelled close behind the forward elements with a small protection force and transported all the supplies needed for the combat team for the duration of the operation, which might mean one, two, or even five days in the field with no other resupply.

Near the end of July the squadron received notice to prepare for a three-day operation meant to disrupt the Taliban at Mushan, in the Horn of Panjwayi. Task Force Kandahar had for some time been wrestling with insurgents in this area, as well as in the far western edge of Zharey, across the Arghandab River from Mushan. The population there was predominately from marginalized tribes antagonistic to the Karzai government and its representatives in Kandahar City. Mushan, in particular, near the confluence of the Arghandab and Dowrey Rivers, was a key distribution node in the Taliban ratline that traced its route from Pakistan through Maywand District and north into Shah Wali Kot. For this reason any interference here by Canadians or ISAF forces would not be tolerated.

After the defeat of the Taliban in Operation Medusa in 2006, the Canadians had established a line of police substations and strongpoints

The mine rollers of the tanks were one of the most valuable assets as IEDs proliferated on all routes. A Leopard 2A6M main battle tank with mine rollers from the Lord Strathcona's Horse clears the way during operations in the volatile Panjwayi and Zharey Districts.

Personnel from B Squadron, 1 RCR BG, utilize a Taurus armoured recovery vehicle (ARV) to conduct maintenance tasks on their Leopard C2 tanks. The ARV was part of the armoured squadron's echelon.

between FOB Sperwan Ghar and Mushan to establish their presence and degrade the remaining Taliban influence. However, the Taliban strength was not diminished, and the combat outposts at Talukan, Zangabad, and Mushan were constantly under threat. Resupply of Mushan became impossible even by a convoy led by tanks because of IEDs and ambushes. The Canadian battle group finally realized it was stretched too thinly to cover all areas of the province, so in early 2009 the decision was taken to abandon the strongpoints and concentrate on districts east of FOB Sperwan Ghar. By this time, Task Force Kandahar had been reinforced by additional American forces, and it was hoped that a newly arrived battalion deployed to Maywand District could now take the place of the Mushan combat outpost in interdicting the Taliban ratline.

Three months had now passed, however, since the posts along the Arghandab had been closed, and it was time for Task Force Kandahar to remind the Taliban that they had not been forgotten. A new operation to Mushan to disrupt the Taliban and to seek out arms caches would be carried out by the 1st Battalion of the U.S. 12th Infantry Regiment, which had deployed to the Arghandab Valley in March 2009, supported by tanks of the Strathconas. The infantry would be airlifted into Mushan by helicopter before dawn on August 1 to take the insurgents by surprise, while the infantry's supply echelon would travel overland to link up at the objective.

The operation began early on July 31, staging out of FOB Sperwan Ghar. While the helicopters lifted off in the early morning darkness heading westward, the supply column moved southward out of the FOB's gate at dawn. Getting the column to Mushan was not a simple task, especially for such a large number of vehicles. It consisted of about 10 American five-metric-ton supply trucks, the Ford Ranger trucks of a full ANA infantry company with a Canadian OMLT team, and an escort of six Leopard tanks along with the Strathcona's full echelon, which included an ARV, a Bison armoured ambulance, and a Badger armoured engineering vehicle. The American contingent included an EOD engineer team and a couple of MRAP gun trucks with M60 machine guns or 40 mm chain guns that would be helpful if they encountered an ambush. Once the convoy was on the move, if they took the most obvious route to Mushan, the Taliban would be alerted and would likely set up ambushes or IEDs along the road. For this reason they headed

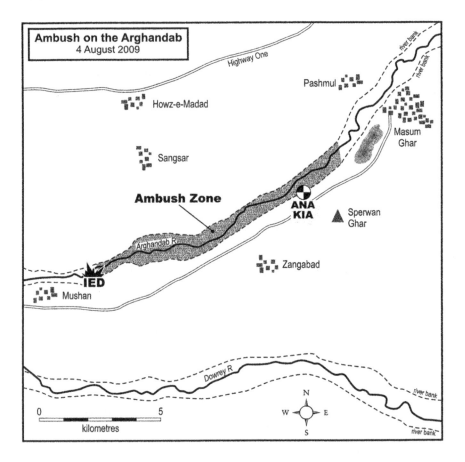

toward the Registan Desert, giving no clues to insurgent spotters concerning their final destination. They turned west only after reaching the dry bed of the Dowrey River, and for the rest of the day bounced along it without any serious incidents — other than some vehicles getting stuck at times — until they reached the vicinity of Mushan. Here they punched up through the riverbank, linked up with the infantry, did the resupply, and were finally able to settle into a defensive leaguer before midnight.

The Strathconas remained based on their leaguer for the rest of the operation, going out very early every morning to support one of the American companies ranging throughout the outlying areas west of Mushan. Operations ceased between about 1000 hours until about 1800 when the midday heat made any movement exhausting, but continued after that

Soldiers from the 1st Battalion, U.S. 12th Regiment, pass behind a tank of C Squadron, Lord Strathcona's Horse, as they advance toward the compound of an Afghan family near Mushan.

Fire by the heavy gun of a Leopard of C Squadron, Lord Strathcona's Horse, is used to destroy an IED workshop discovered near Mushan.

until about 2200. The Taliban reacted to this intrusion sporadically at first, but more intensely as the combat team continued their sweeps. The tanks were involved in only a few firefights during which they quickly eliminated any opposition. But the Taliban, using their usual tactics, remained dangerous. IEDs were always a threat: three Americans on patrol were killed on August 1 outside Mushan when one of them stepped on an IED and the others then came under RPG fire.[9]

The operation was successfully concluded by the night of August 3 with at least one major weapons cache destroyed. Early the next morning Chinook helicopters arrived to pick up the American infantry, leaving the tanks, supply vehicles, some elements of the American infantry battalion, and the ANA troops all on their own. At first light the remaining soldiers of the combat team and supply column woke up and did their accounting for equipment, then the column officer commanding (OC) issued last-minute orders for the move out.

Now with the infantry gone, they faced the problem of how to get back to FOB Ma'sum Ghar. There were few options, none of them ideal. The direct road from Mushan to the FOB was never used because it was

Squadron Sergeant-Major Richard Stacey (centre) prepares the convoy's move back from Mushan, placing ANA vehicles in the proper order.

The convoy of Canadian, American, and ANA troops move along the bed of the Arghandab River after leaving Mushan on August 4, 2009.

The ANA were equipped with Ford Ranger trucks with no armour to protect them from insurgent fire, which made them very vulnerable when ambushed, as happened on August 4, 2009. Here, an ANA Ranger bristles with weapons, including RPGs and a DShK machine gun.

known to have lots of IEDs. Returning by the Dowrey riverbed was foolish because the Taliban had sewn it with IEDs after it was used as the approach route to Mushan. A wider swing south through the Registan Desert was ruled out because the light trucks of the ANA would never make it through the soft sands of the desert. And the route north was not practical — the column would have to pass through the intensely hostile Taliban territory of Sangasar where Coalition forces could not call on help from the QRF at Ma'sum Ghar if needed. As a result, the column's OC, Captain Dave Gottfried, chose the best out of several bad options, returning along the bed of the Arghandab River.

It was already hot when the column headed off at 0530, and everyone was tense because they knew they could expect trouble along the way. Captain Gottfried was not overly worried about being ambushed by insurgents with small arms and RPGs; the convoy could easily take care of these. But he was concerned about hitting an IED, because that could cause them to be trapped in the riverbed. Shortly after they started off, however, it looked as if this was going to be one of those days when things would not go according to plan. Sergeant Steve Connauton's tank normally took the lead in the order of march because it had a roller attached to its front to detonate any IEDs encountered. But now its radio went down. Fortunately, the column had a second tank with rollers, so it replaced Connauton's in the lead. Even so, the gunner in Connauton's tank, Trooper Bill Geernaert, remained on edge because he had not slept well. In fact, he never slept well on operations. As he put it, "You don't sleep deeply at all when you're out. A bug farts and you're awake!" In addition, two trucks had broken down. Captain Gottfried's tank was pulling one of these — an American truck that had a broken tie rod. One of the ANA Rangers also had a broken tie rod, and that vehicle was hoisted onto one of the echelon's portable lift system (PLS) trucks for the return journey. Finally, problems were occurring with one of the American MRAPs that had a mine roller attached. The vehicle kept getting stuck in the riverbed, so they decided to detach the roller and have it towed back by another tank.

They struck the IED at 0800. The insurgent lurking along the riverbank allowed the lead tank to pass over the device without triggering it and then sent a radio signal to detonate the explosive under the second tank in the column, which was now Connauton's vehicle. When the blast happened, Geernaert, seated next to the gun in the turret, suddenly felt himself lift as if he were in a dream. The IED blew up right between him and the driver. He hit the wall and blacked out for few seconds. It appeared he had been thrown up by the blast, somehow somersaulted in the confined space, and ended with his head on the floor and his feet raised near Connauton's seat.

Although confused and stunned, the first thought that came to Geernaert when he regained consciousness was to get out of the vehicle. As he crawled from the hatch and stumbled to the ground, Connauton quickly brought him back to reality by telling him they were under fire and that he should return inside to get his helmet, which had been blown off. Heading back into the tank, Geernaert became concerned that Trooper Jesse Cournoyer, the driver, had failed to emerge. Scrambling onto the hull, he was relieved to find that Cournoyer was conscious and seemed all right. The trooper could not get out of the tank, because the turret was now jammed with the gun blocking his hatch. He was suffering from a severe blow to his leg and was unable to walk. Invigorated by adrenaline, Geernaert and the others dragged Cournoyer out through the gunner's hole. When the engineers arrived and cleared a path free of mines, they carried Cournoyer to an area sheltered from the insurgents' fire.

After the IED had detonated, one of the vehicles at the front had quickly sent out a call over the radio, "IED, IED, IED, stand by!" At that instant the insurgents had launched their ambush. Small-arms and RPG fire erupted from the rear and from both sides of the riverbank all along the length of the convoy, which was spread out in the riverbed over about a kilometre and a half. The insurgents had planned the attack well, disabling a tank at the front, and now expected the soldiers at the rear to become disorganized, which would allow them to inflict heavy casualties on the column. But there was no panic among the Coalition forces. Everyone in the column behaved well, immediately seeking targets on both banks. The radio, however, was full of excited chatter as everyone reported what was happening in their zone. Richard, in his M113 near the end of the column, was encouraged to see the tank in front of him engaging targets on the left bank while an American MRAP covered the right side.

Richard's responsibility now was to take action for the recovery of any damaged vehicles and of any injured soldiers, so he radioed the ARV to stand by to move. Being so far back in the convoy, he would normally await confirmation from the convoy OC that the ARV was needed before moving it up because there might be more IEDs around and they could not afford to lose the ARV. Captain Gottfried's radio had been affected by the heat and was cutting in and out, so Richard decided to get the ARV moving right away. Given all the uncertainties, he had to take the risk of hitting another IED to get the recovery started. As the ARV moved up, Richard pulled out to follow it to the front of the line. But as he did so, things got complicated. He took fire from both banks and had to engage those targets. Then the American MRAP near him was hit by an RPG and became disabled. So he had to stop and deal with that. Fortunately, no one in the MRAP was injured, but the vehicle had to be recovered. With the ARV moving to the front, the tank nearby would have to do the job, so Richard directed it to hook up and tow the disabled vehicle the rest of the way to the FOB.

The situation remained tense as firing continued on all sides. Listening to the radio chatter, Richard could tell that everyone was busy dealing with the threat — the engineers and the medics did their job, while the battle captain and the column OC coordinated the actions of others. Air support was needed and the sooner they got it the better. So Richard got on the radio and put out the message that would bring in attack helicopters. He knew the insurgents feared these weapons so much that they often broke contact as soon as they saw them arrive, and he hoped that would be the case this time. There was no joint terminal attack controller (JTAC) to direct the assets onto targets when they arrived, but Richard had been qualified to do that task over the course of his career and took it on now. He therefore waited in his position in the riverbed with his radio tuned to the right frequency for the helicopters to check in.

While that was going on, Richard's M113 was sitting just behind a tank that was dealing with targets on one side of the riverbed. As Richard scanned the other riverbank on the blind side of the tank, an insurgent with an RPG suddenly walked out from some buildings. The man was completely focused on the back of the tank, obviously intent on firing at it, so he did not see the M113. Richard immediately traversed his C6 machine gun on the insurgent and cut him down before he could fire. As the man fell, two more insurgents appeared from behind the building, and Richard eliminated them, as well.

Within a short time the air assets arrived — two AH-64 Apaches, two OH-58D Kiowas, and an A-10 Warthog ground-attack aircraft. It was surprising, however, that the insurgents did not break off contact with the arrival of the Apaches. The column was still taking fire from the north bank, although Richard was not sure where the insurgents were firing from. Then he saw eight insurgents with weapons run into the back of a two-storey grape hut. Now he had a target! Quickly, he tossed out a red smoke grenade as a reference point and radioed a message that led the helicopters to the target. In the confined space of the riverbed, he now had to send a warning over the radio to the rest of the column, advising them to be prepared for aircraft coming in at a danger-close distance. One of the hovering Apaches turned its attention toward the grape hut, fired a Hellfire missile, and quickly levelled the target with no collateral damage.

The insurgent fire in Richard's area had now been suppressed, but he was aware that the ambush still continued in other areas. His situation was now getting very complicated. Richard knew that controlling air assets was not just a matter of directing them onto a target; he was also responsible for their safety. He had to control the direction from which the aircraft approached, taking into account the danger to the aircraft from ground troops firing at the riverbanks with ammunition ricocheting into the air. Richard was already fully occupied, however, with two radios going, a driver he had to direct, another soldier at the back firing a machine gun, and shooting his own C6 at targets. Throughout all this he remained very aware that his chief responsibilities as SSM were to recover vehicles and take care of injured soldiers at the front. Realizing he was juggling too many tasks, he remembered that someone else could assume control of air support. One of the Americans in a MRAP at the end of the column was qualified as a Fire Support Team (FiST) specialist, so Richard had his driver turn the M113 around and speed back through insurgent fire to the MRAP. There he found the specialist, had him transfer into the M113, and then turned around again to race back through the insurgent fire. Staff

Sergeant Fisher, the FiSTer, stayed with Richard for the remainder of the action, coordinating the Apaches and even manning another machine gun on the M113.

Richard could now focus on his main duties, which were at the head of the column. As his M113 moved forward, he passed tanks and dismounted ANA troops engaging targets, so he had to be careful not to mask their fire. When he finally reached the front, he was momentarily relieved to find everything well in hand. The engineers had come up and cleared the area around the disabled tank to make sure there were no more IEDs. The crew — Connauton, Geernaert, Cournoyer, and Trooper Corey Rogers — seemed to have only minor injuries, although they were in shock. They were functioning but had concussions and were not fit to fight. All the men had gotten out of the tank and were now sheltering beside the Badger armoured engineer vehicle (AEV). The medics reached them, checked them over, and loaded them into the Bison ambulance.

Captain Gottfried contacted the FOB by radio and requested that the QRF get ready to come to their assistance. The captain was quite relieved that there were no critical injuries and was impressed that everyone was performing their responsibilities as if they were on a training exercise.

The question now was how to get the disabled tank back to the FOB. Still under sporadic small-arms fire, they managed to get the ARV hooked up to the tank and the column started moving again by 10:00. Within a few minutes, however, they found that this method was not working. Connauton's tank had lost its right-side track along with the front two road wheels, but the roller was still attached. The Leopard weighed more than 42 metric tons, and they were trying to drag it down a riverbed that was all sand and gravel. The day had become very hot by now, and with the ARV's engine straining at maximum power, it began to overheat. Pulling the Leopard was too much of a load for the ARV on its own. To provide more pulling power, they brought another Leopard to the front, hooked it up, and started off with both vehicles pulling the disabled tank. But that did not work, either. So they stopped and decided to remove the roller from the disabled tank. Because the roller was a precious asset, they made room for it on a PLS truck by taking off the disabled ANA Ranger and blowing it in place. The final solution for saving the disabled Leopard was to create a daisy-chain arrangement — two tanks towing the ARV that was hooked onto the Leopard, with the Badger AEV pushing from behind. In the end, it took four vehicles to recover one tank all the way back to Ma'sum Ghar.

Everyone was relieved that the column was now finally moving, but its speed was agonizingly slow — only going about five or six kilometres per hour as the damaged Leopard dragged its way along the riverbed. The insurgent fire died off for a short time, but that was only a brief pause as the insurgents leapfrogged along the riverbank to keep up with the column's progress. The combined fire of the tanks and the air support had taken its toll on them, but a Taliban radio message was intercepted telling the fighters they had to continue the ambush until everyone in the column was either dead or destroyed. So ambushes commenced again, getting progressively worse for a stretch, easing off, then getting worse again, sometimes from the north bank and other times from the south.

Despite the small-arms and RPG fire, the column made progress, engaging targets whenever possible. Fortunately, they did not encounter any more IEDs, although their anxiety level remained high at every choke point along the route. The column was now spread over a distance of about four kilometres and remained extremely vulnerable. If any of the echelon's ammunition and fuel trucks were hit by an RPG, the resulting explosion would be devastating. As a result, during a lull in enemy fire, the column commander, the battle captain, and Richard discussed getting the soft-skinned vehicles — the lightly armoured and wheeled vehicles, including the ANA trucks — back to the FOB as fast as possible. They decided that these vehicles should be assembled into a group and escorted ahead of the rest by Richard's M113 and an American MRAP. To help protect the tanks, which would then be on their own, the QRF coming out from the FOB would escort them back.

The head of the column had now succeeded getting to within about six kilometres of the FOB, which they could finally see ahead. But as the soft-skinned vehicles gathered together, the column came under insurgent attack once more and this time it included mortar fire. Richard had to get forward quickly to control the situation. As he advanced, he encountered an ANA truck that had stopped, the driver probably frozen with fear because the Ford Rangers had no protection. Richard pulled up to the truck and yelled, "Let's go! You're in a kill zone! Get out of here!" Simultaneously, he spied an American MRAP stuck in the sand nearby, so he drove over to deal with that. Racing up to the MRAP, he shouted, "I'll come back and pull you out of there!" Turning his head to check if the ANA truck had begun to move, he was shocked to see a large explosion blow it up and one of the ANA soldiers flung onto the ground!

Richard's decision was automatic. Everyone in that column was his responsibility. Questions raced through his mind: Were there any other troops in that vehicle? Were they dead or injured? He had to straighten out the mess behind him, so he told his driver to turn and go back through the kill zone. They reached the MRAP first and made hasty efforts to pull it out. These failed, however, since the vehicle was too heavy and was embedded in the mud. But during this frantic recovery attempt, Richard discovered that one of the passengers was an American medic. He ordered the medic into his vehicle and headed back toward the burning ANA truck. Because this vehicle had now come under small-arms fire from the insurgents, he directed his driver to bring the M113 up between the insurgents and the truck to mask the fire and protect any casualties who might still be in it. As the M113 came to a halt, Richard made positive identification (PID) on the insurgents firing at the truck and rapidly shifted his weapon toward them to engage. Then two more mortar bombs fell, so he got Staff Sergeant Fisher to bring in the attack helicopters to eliminate that group of ambushers.

By now he knew his armoured ambulance had no room for additional casualties because it was already carrying Connauton's crew. More medical help was needed, but he did not want to bring another Bison out from the FOB because the convoy was still under such heavy fire. As a first step, he told the American medic and one of his crew to dismount from the M113 and deal with any casualties at the Ranger, giving the medic the information needed to transmit the required nine-line medical message for a helicopter evacuation. At the wreck they found two casualties, one with VSA and one badly injured. Richard got out of his vehicle and helped get the shattered remains of the dead Afghan soldier into a body bag, always a gruesome task. The other injured soldier turned out to be a young Afghan lieutenant with multiple injuries to his hands, feet, and face. While these were serious, Richard had to make an assessment of how to deal with the man and quickly decided the officer could survive if they could get him evacuated within a reasonable time.

Leaving the medic to carry on alone, Richard returned to his vehicle so he could get back on the radio. The M113 was now parked while they tried to deal with the casualties, and the ANA trucks had stopped when their officer was hit. The group of vehicles made an ideal stationary target, and the ANA soldiers were not reacting to the enemy fire now that their platoon leader was a casualty. The ANA company had a Canadian mentor who could have rallied them, but because his vehicle had been damaged he was at the back of the column. The ANA company also had an excellent CO, but he was stuck somewhere in the middle dealing with a multitude of other problems. So the ANA platoon here was on its own — disorganized, confused, and spread all over the area.

The insurgent fire had by now intensified, and Richard realized he had to bring some order to the ANA platoon. So, on top of dealing with casualties, engaging the enemy, and monitoring the recovery, he was now mentoring an ANA platoon, trying to organize it so it could fight back and suppress the enemy ambush party on the north bank. Richard did not know their language but used a lot of English yelling and hand signals and was able to gain control of the situation. The ANA soldiers were actually looking for leadership, which Richard provided. The Afghans listened and reacted. Just as anyone else would do, they had passed through initial shock from seeing their comrades killed and injured, and now their training took over. As the ANA soldiers engaged targets, Richard found an alert ANA section commander among them to provide temporary leadership, then over the radio asked the company commander to come up and take over.

Richard now got back to dealing with the two casualties, wrote the nine-liner needed for an evacuation, and transmitted it. Getting approval for a medevac was not automatic; the air evacuation helicopters did not like coming into a hot site under fire, and who could blame them? They would do it, but they did not want to become another casualty in the process. The controllers therefore had to consider the emergency needs of the casualty as well as the intensity of enemy fire the helicopter crews would face. After some deliberation back at the base, the authority was finally given to release the aircraft.

While he was dealing with all these issues, Richard suddenly spotted a man staggering out of the bushes on the south side of the river behind him, close to the truck that had been destroyed. His pants were burned off and he wore a tattered T-shirt. Was he an insurgent? Richard noticed the man was unarmed, so he held off engaging him with his weapon. He then yelled out a warning to two ANA soldiers nearby, pointing in the direction of the raggedy man, "Who's that?" The Afghans could not understand English, but when they finally comprehended what Richard was shouting about, they ran over to the man and recognized him!

There had been three men in the truck when it had been hit by what was now confirmed as a mortar. While the driver was killed and the officer wounded, the young soldier had been blown out of the truck and thrown about 25 metres into the bushes on the riverbank. The explosion had burned off his clothing, and he had just now recovered his senses and had staggered out to find help. One of the ANA soldiers ran over and administered first aid, putting a bandage on one of the injured man's arms, which was bleeding. As this was being done, Richard pulled out a stretcher from his vehicle and threw it over so they could put the injured man on it. Richard then began to update his casualty list. But while he did this, he saw the injured man collapse. His only visible injury was a cut on one arm, but he had received such severe head injuries that he died that instant.

As this running battle continued along the bed of the Arghandab River, Sergeant Connauton and his crew were relatively safe in the Bison, close to the burning ANA truck. Bill Geernaert, lying on a bench in the vehicle, tried to ignore the noises as mortar bombs fell nearby. But then the medic manning the C6 machine gun in the observation hatch suddenly fell down, clutching his hand. He had been hit by shrapnel and was trying to get a bandage wrapped around the wound to stop the flow of blood. No one else had noticed this, so Geernaert pulled the crew commander standing in the hatch toward the front of the vehicle. "One of your guys has been hit!" he cried.

The crew commander glanced down, saw the medic dealing with his wound, and asked, "Are any of you guys a gunner?"

"Yeah, I'm a gunner," Geernaert replied.

"Okay, you've got the position."

"I'm not doing so hot, but okay. You deal with the wounded medic and I'll carry on with the fighting."

So Geernaert got to his feet and pushed his head through the observer's hatch. As he took a quick survey around to orient himself, he spied the burning ANA truck, and then scanning for any movement along the riverbank, was surprised to see a two-man insurgent mortar team on top of a farmer's compound. Focusing on these insurgents, he saw them fire their last round, run off the roof, and start to cross the alleyway that ran alongside the compound. By this time, Geernaert had swung the C6 onto them and opened fire, hitting both of them. That took care of the mortar crew! He next turned his attention to firing at flashes of enemy fire that he could see in the bushes along both banks of the river.

Despite his injuries, Geernaert experienced no pain. He was still high on adrenaline and in a mental daze that had altered his vision and hearing. Time seemed to slow down. To him everything felt like a scene from a kung fu movie in which bullets passed by in slow motion with exaggerated zipping sounds. Geernaert was, in fact, more seriously injured than either he or the medics realized. He had no obvious wounds or broken bones but actually had hairline fractures in his back, hips, and pelvis, which were discovered only weeks later. Despite any immediate discomfort, he was sufficiently mentally alert to man the weapon, report target grids over the radio, and continue to fire the machine gun until the Bison finally reached the FOB. It was only weeks later that Geernaert's wounds were diagnosed as more severe than fractures — further tests concluded he was suffering from blast-induced traumatic brain injury caused by the concussion of the explosion, for which he eventually required long-term treatment.

At the ambush site the medevac helicopters finally arrived, but by then the ANA officer in the truck hit by the mortar had also died. Richard had checked on him a few times while trying to get the vehicles moving. As the medic had worked on him, the extent of the officer's injuries had become more apparent and Richard had realized the officer was probably not going to make it. As word spread that all three Afghans who had been in the truck were now dead, the ANA soldiers reacted with anger. Richard now had a morale problem to deal with and had to figure out a way to calm the Afghans down.

With the casualties dealt with, Richard began to get his group of soft-skinned vehicles moving again. By now he was becoming uncomfortable that they were somewhat isolated from the rest of the column. They were about 1,200 metres ahead of the tanks, but the QRF advancing down the riverbed from the FOB was still about two kilometres away. So Richard's convoy of wheeled vehicles, escorted only by his M113, the American MRAP, and the small ANA group, was quite vulnerable if the insurgents concentrated on them. All he could do was to keep them moving and hope nothing new happened.

As they approached the FOB, Richard got a message from the MRAP leading the column that he really did not want to hear: "Stand by. I have contact on the north bank of the river!" Richard felt there was something odd about this report. Perhaps it was because they were so close to the FOB, actually passing the heights of Ma'sum Ghar Mountain. He decided to scan the area with his binoculars before making any decision to engage the reported contact. The EOD vehicle then informed again: "Stand by. I have a bunch of squirters." "Squirters" referred to insurgent fighters who fired several bursts of fire and then quickly disappeared into the bushes. The EOD operator was ready to open fire on them, since he expected the column was going to be ambushed again. Richard quickly spotted the target because the group of people were wearing colourful clothing. Training his binoculars on them, he immediately saw that they were actually a bunch of children who had come down to the riverbank to see what all the noise was about. Like everywhere in Afghanistan, children were always curious. The EOD vehicle had not recognized them and was getting ready to engage them with a grenade launcher. Richard's heart almost stopped, and he got on the radio as fast as possible, yelling, "Knock it off! Those are children on the north bank you're looking at!"

The radio was silent for a few seconds and then the EOD operator said softly, "Thanks!"

In the heat of this battle, everyone was tense and ready to fire at anything that looked like a target, but if they had killed a bunch of children, they all would have regretted it forever.

When they finally pulled into the FOB, most of the soldiers were exhausted but relieved. The insurgents had targeted the supply trucks and some were in bad shape. Despite hits from small-arms fire, RPGs, and mortar fire, they had managed to push on with surprisingly few casualties — only the three ANA soldiers in the truck hit by the mortar had been killed. A number of men had been wounded, seven of whom were Canadian.

There were, however, at least two operational stress casualties. One of these came from an American supply truck that had been hit by an RPG. The rocket had been lobbed into the back of the truck but had missed the differential gear so that the vehicle could continue driving. The rocket had blown a hole in the back of the cab, narrowly missing the occupants, and had set their kit bags on fire. The two young American soldiers in the truck knew their vehicle had been hit but had not realized it was on fire. When they drove into the FOB, people yelled and warned them about the fire. The driver and his partner were from the U.S. supply echelon, and as support troops, had not expected to come under insurgent fire during their tour in Afghanistan. Only when the driver got out of the cab in the FOB did he realize his truck was on fire. When Richard came up to him, the driver was in shock with a completely vacant expression and was unable to talk clearly. Richard tried his best to calm the soldier down, telling him that the ambush was over and that he was now safe. None of this registered with the American, however, and Richard had to take him by the shoulder and lead him to the aid post. The soldier was so terrified that he was unable to walk on his own. Eventually, the man was taken to KAF on a medevac flight.

The other stress casualty Richard had to deal with was the American medic who had worked on the ANA casualties from the burning truck. When they all got back to the FOB, the medic had pretty well shut down emotionally. The Afghan officer who had been blown out of the truck had received very severe injuries, with badly mangled hands and feet along with part of his face. The medic had done his best to save him, but the soldier had died and the medic could not help blaming himself for the man's death. Richard tried to convince him that he had done his best to save the Afghan soldier and that it was not his fault the Afghan had died. It turned out that this was the medic's first combat tour and that this was his first casualty since arriving in Afghanistan. Richard had been there when the Afghan soldier had died. Having seen a lot of injuries since arriving in the theatre, he knew that all the U.S. medic could have done was to make the casualty comfortable. He tried to reassure the man, saying, "Look, you did your job. You did everything you were supposed to do. No doctor could have helped him. You're a good medic, you're a good soldier, and these things happen." The medic still had a lot of problems with what had happened, and in the end, was sent for psychological counselling.

After reaching the FOB, Richard did not have any time to think about the day's action himself. He had to deal with his own squadron's casualties and make sure they got treatment for their injuries. Richard then refuelled and rearmed his vehicle, after which he headed back down the riverbed to link up with the tanks that were still coming in. They finally pulled into the gates of the FOB at 1600 hours. He was high on adrenaline for some time. That night he woke up after only four hours of sleep, his mind racing. He still had to do an event field note on the mission, and as soon as he started thinking about that, it was useless to try to sleep again, so he stayed up and wrote his report. By the next day the ambush was no longer on his mind because the squadron had to get ready for the next operation, since the tanks were in high demand. The priority now was to resupply the vehicles, do maintenance, and make sure they were ready to go out of the wire again.

The action on the Arghandab River on August 4, 2009, was the most challenging experience Richard had had during his career in the Canadian Armed Forces. But even after his return to Canada he did not really think about that day until six months later when he was posted to Ottawa. Richard thought about the men who had been killed or seriously injured and regretted that. He found himself questioning the events of that day, wondering if he had done the right things. It had been his decision not to evacuate Sergeant Steve Connauton's crew by helicopter and to take them back in the Bison, but with the best information he had had at the time, their injuries had only been minor. He had regrets about the three Afghan soldiers who had been killed that day, but he had done as much for them as he would have for any Coalition or Canadian soldier.

After some soul-searching and with the passage of time, Richard felt settled in his mind that his squadron had done as good a job on their tour as any unit could have. As for himself, he felt confident he would not have changed anything he had done while leading them as their sergeant major. He believed he had met the challenges he had faced on August 4 because of all the training he had received and from the mentoring he had been given by older soldiers throughout his career. But, most of all, his performance that day was made possible by the skill of the men and women in the squadron who had done the right things at all the critical moments.

On June 10, 2011, His Excellency the Governor General of Canada, on behalf of Her Majesty the Queen of Canada, awarded Master Warrant Officer Richard Stacey the Star of Military Valour for gallantry, perseverance, and valour in the face of an armed enemy for his actions on August 4, 2009. Trooper Bill Geernaert was also awarded the Mention in Dispatches for his heroic actions on August 4, 2009.

9

INFANTRY OPERATIONS IN PANJWAYI: LIEUTENANT SIMON MAILLOUX

E ven as Canadian troops for the first rotation of Operation Athena arrived in Kandahar Province in 2006, officers and soldiers of the R22eR knew they would take part in the combat mission. The Canadian Armed Forces' operational planning process showed that the 3rd Battalion of the Van Doos would form the core of a battle group to be deployed as the fourth rotation in late 2007. The only question was: Who would command the battle group? That question was answered in early 2006 when Lieutenant-Colonel Alain Gauthier was notified that he would be given this responsibility. For Gauthier the opportunity to command a unit being deployed to an overseas theatre was really a privilege, the high point in the career of any professional soldier. But he also knew it was a challenge.

Soon after Gauthier received confirmation of his appointment, the first rotation for Athena (1 PPCLI BG under Lieutenant-Colonel Ian Hope) arrived in Kandahar and information soon came back to Ottawa that the insurgency was stronger than had originally been anticipated. Gauthier read the reports intently as he studied everything he could about this new theatre and the form of warfare that would be encountered. He would not formally take over command of the battle group until June 2006, but he had to develop his pre-deployment training plan right away because he would only have 12 months to get his men ready once the Van Doos' deployment became official.

The Van Doos' rotation, also designated as Task Force (TF) 3-07, would be formed around the headquarters of the 3rd Battalion along with three rifle companies assembled from all battalions of the regiment. As with all rotations, the battle group would include a number of subsidiary units to create an all-arms formation: an engineer squadron from 5e Régiment du génie de combat, an artillery battery from 5e Régiment d'artillerie légère du Canada, a composite Leopard tank squadron from Lord Strathcona's Horse (Royal Canadians) and 12e Régiment blindé du Canada, and a composite armoured reconnaissance troop created from elements of 12e Régiment blindé du Canada and the Royal Canadian Dragoons.

Pre-deployment training began in June 2006 when each subunit started its own three-month period of individual training focused on basic combat skills that would be needed in Afghanistan. The infantry, armour crews, gunners, engineers, and medics then assembled at Camp Valcartier where they were put through collective training in which all subunits lost their individual identities and became familiar in their roles as part of a single formation. Gauthier knew it was a lot like a hockey all-star team in which the best players were put into action but had to synchronize their efforts so they could win the game.

Throughout this period reports continued to come back from Afghanistan confirming the seriousness of the insurgency in Kandahar. From these reports, Lieutenant-Colonel Gauthier came to realize that his soldiers would be arriving at the worst time of the year — the "fighting season" between May and October. This added some urgency to how he structured his training plan to make sure his soldiers were prepared to go into action immediately upon arrival.

The Van Doos' training plan, however, had to include more than individual and collective training. The battle group also had to convert to a mechanized formation. When the Van Doos were tasked for deployment, it was a "light" infantry unit with no armoured vehicles. It would take about three months of the training cycle for the personnel to learn how to use armoured fighting vehicles in Afghanistan. At the same time the battle group had to be introduced to new high-tech equipment that would be employed in the theatre, making it the first Canadian Army unit to be completely digitized. The Athena Tactical System was designed to bring together telephone communications, email, video, and data systems for use throughout the AO. The video capability included video conferencing whereby Lieutenant-Colonel Gauthier could discuss developments in operations as they occurred with senior task force officers at KAF. Video images from UAVs could also be downloaded and displayed so that headquarters staff could follow the progress of battles with the Taliban in real time. Vehicles were equipped with GPS tracking so that headquarters would know exactly where they were at all times, with coloured symbols on their display screens clearly showing the location of reported insurgent forces, IEDs, and other threats. Orders could now be typed at headquarters, a button pushed, and the message would appear on a screen in the vehicle.[1] Younger soldiers could adapt to the new technology quickly, some older ones less easily. This system would allow the battle group to be significantly more tactically effective once it arrived in Afghanistan, but all of these new technologies took more time away from the essential battle tasks in the busy training schedule.

In February 2007, 3 R22eR BG carried out advanced pre-deployment training at Fort Bliss, Texas. Here, medics secure an injured victim on a stretcher during a vehicle explosion simulation that included multiple simulated casualties.

By February 2007, more realism with live-fire exercises was introduced into the battle group's training when it moved to Fort Bliss, Texas, where the terrain was strangely similar to Afghanistan — dry, dusty, and mountainous. Joint and combined exercises, designed to present situations that would be encountered in Kandahar, were carried out from platoon to combat team level. The final phase of training took place in May at the Canadian Army Manoeuvre Training Centre in Wainwright, Alberta, where the battle group underwent its final validation exercises before deployment. Here again the battle group experienced a simulated Afghan village that was given the name "Spin Boldak" and was populated with Afghan Canadians playing the roles of typical villagers such as a mullah or potential insurgents. These actors also spoke Pashto, so the Canadian troops had to communicate through interpreters, just as they soon would in the theatre.

The training seemed to be progressing well as the date for deployment approached. But then, with only a month left, a drastic change was made to Gauthier's battle group. While the main mission of Task Force Afghanistan was to restore security to allow renewed governance and construction to begin, it also had taken on the task of training the ANA so that the mission could eventually be turned over to them. Canadians had first formed a small mentoring team to work with an ANA *kandak* in 2006, but in the summer of 2007 this responsibility expanded and the Canadians began mentoring a full ANA brigade. Additional Canadian troops therefore had to be found to expand the OMLT strength significantly. So the decision was taken to withdraw one of Gauthier's rifle companies and use it to form the OMLT for this rotation. Thus, 3 R22eR BG arrived in Kandahar in the summer of 2007 with a reduced manoeuvre force of only two rifle companies to cover all of Kandahar Province, a huge area of 54,000 square kilometres, about the size of Nova Scotia.

As 3 R22eR BG's deployment date approached, reports coming back from the theatre confirmed that Taliban IED bombings and insurgent-initiated attacks were increasing substantially throughout Afghanistan as a whole.[2] In Kandahar the insurgents had started operating in small groups, targeting the battle group the Van Doos would be relieving, using more powerful explosive devices to disrupt the Canadians' main lines of communication. The 2 RCR BG had actively moved foot patrols out into the districts, making its presence known and disrupting insurgent cells. In doing so it had identified several villages in western Panjwayi and Zharey as the most intransigent centres of Taliban influence, which the Canadians nicknamed "The Belly of the Beast."[3] While the Canadians were able to clear most of these villages with carefully planned operations, they did not have enough troops to remain and hold the cleared areas. The task of keeping the Taliban from infiltrating back was therefore handed over to the ANP, which through a network of checkpoints was supposed to maintain security to allow redevelopment to begin. The handover from the military to the police followed good COIN practice, but unfortunately the ANP detachments proved to be grossly incompetent and were even suspected of being infiltrated by the Taliban. Local villagers resented them because many of the policemen came from other parts of Afghanistan and did not speak Pashto. Underpaid and corrupt, the police resorted to thefts at highway checkpoints. To be fair, however, the police in these outlying checkpoints often did not receive their pay and resorted to extortion to feed themselves. Morale in the ANP collapsed as it became hemmed in among a population that was hostile. As a result, police posts became targets for Taliban attacks. For example, when the most westerly post at Mushan was abandoned in June 2007, 19 of the original garrison of 40 policemen were killed or wounded, and most of the rest had deserted.[4] At the beginning of August when the Van Doos arrived only three police posts remained.

As a result of this deteriorating situation, 3 R22eR BG found itself in a hot situation immediately upon arrival, as Lieutenant-Colonel Gauthier had expected. The Taliban had built up their strength over the winter, and in the spring of 2007 had an estimated 600 fighters in Zharey and Panjwayi.[5] The summer fighting season of 2007 looked as if it might be as dangerous as that of 2006. The plan to use ANP posts to stop Taliban infiltration had collapsed, and the battle group could only be confident of its control around the three major operating bases of Ma'sum Ghar, Sperwan Ghar, and Wilson on Highway One. Even at that, control of these areas was not absolute, since snipers plagued the road to Kandahar and rocket attacks could occur at any time around the FOBs. It did not take long for the Van Doos to suffer casualties.

IEDs remained the main threat. The Van Doos had to deal with these from the start of their tour. Beginning on August 12, they suffered three strikes in eight days. In the first an RG-31 vehicle was blown up on the road to FOB Ma'sum Ghar, injuring five soldiers. Five days later another vehicle hit an explosive device that fortunately only slightly injured two soldiers.[6] Then the first fatality occurred. On August 19, Private Simon Longtin, the driver of the lead LAV escorting a convoy back from Kandahar City, was killed when he struck an IED only five kilometres from Ma'sum Ghar. It was inevitable that casualties would result from the regiment's deployment to Afghanistan, but the first death for the Van Doos was a shock to all personnel in the battle group and created a flood of media reporting back in Canada, particularly in Quebec where a recent poll had shown that the majority of people did not support the mission.[7]

With the IED threat intensifying, Gauthier's challenge now was to quickly re-establish freedom of movement and expand the zones of security. The broad master plan, code-named Garranday Zmaray or "Strong Lion," was to be carried out in stages by the battle group over the entire tour. Combat outposts or police substations were set up along the main transportation routes, this time each having a garrison of 10 policemen, more than had been assigned in the previous posts. The first substations were built to secure the critical length of Highway One, which connected Kandahar City to Helmand Province; the next on Route Fosters to extend ISAF presence into western Panjwayi; and the last on Route Summit, which was the vital supply route connecting FOB Ma'sum Ghar with FOB Wilson on Highway One. The key to success of this strategy was the inclusion of Canadian mentors with the police garrisons to bolster the officers' flagging morale and improve their performance.

The first steps to create a police-mentoring unit similar to that of the OMLT mentoring the ANA were taken during the third rotation as the inability of the ANP to carry out its duties became more obvious. In May 2007, the Canadians assumed responsibility for mentoring the 1st Brigade of the ANA 205 Corps, thus expanding the strength of the OMLT to meet this task. At the most basic level the Canadians began deploying as mentors at each of the newly created ANA outposts and ANP substations. Now, during TF 3-07's tour, some of the Van Doos' OMLT was redeployed for this duty and combined with a platoon of military police from Task Force Kandahar to form small teams that lived and operated with the police units assigned to each substation, ensuring that proper police methods were

Improving the performance of the Afghan National Police was one of the objectives of TF 3-07. Two Afghan men with a motorcycle have been stopped by a patrol in Bazaar-i-Panjwayi. One is being searched by an Afghan policeman while another policeman waits on the road, with a police truck with other police to the right.

One of the major operations carried out by R22eR BG was to establish new ANP substations on critical routes, such as this one at Lakokhel in Zharey.

employed.[8] By reinforcing the police in this manner, the plan called for the garrisons of each post to gradually expand their zones of security until safe buffer zones were established along Route Fosters and Highway One.

For the rest of its rotation, the battle group was very active going after the Taliban, carrying out a major operation about every 10 days. With only two rifle companies available, the battle group was stretched for resources, but for major operations that had priority, Regional Command (South) provided reinforcements from other provinces. At one point Gauthier had a company of the Royal Ghurkha Rifles and a company of the Royal Welsh Fusiliers under his command for about two months.

Similarly, the Canadians were sometimes tasked to assist operations taking place in adjoining provinces, such as helping the British in Helmand to the west, or showing their presence in the Shah Wali Kot to the north when intelligence reported Taliban coming down from the Netherlands Task Force area. Between these operations, each of the company commanders was expected to take the initiative for smaller operations whenever opportunities arose to disrupt insurgent action and interdict their presence, with C Company operating out of FOB Ma'sum Ghar and B Company from FOB Wilson. The Canadians hit targets throughout the province when intelligence sources identified areas of suspicious activity, IED cells, or insurgent command and control centres. Gauthier likened this strategy to a *jeu de marmotte* — the game of whack-a-mole — striking out against Taliban targets with no obvious pattern and keeping them guessing as to where the Canadians would go next.

The first major operation of Garranday Zmaray took place at the end of August in western Zharey, with the objective of clearing a height called Ghundey Ghar. This was a hill of rock and sand reputed to have been built by Alexander the Great in the fourth century B.C. Rising out of the farmlands of Zharey, four kilometres west of the Taliban heartland of Sangasar, it was a critical location because it provided an overview of the region and created a buffer to secure part of Highway One. Elements of 2 RCR BG of TF 1-07 had occupied this strategic height during its tour, using it for surveillance and as a base for operations when attempting to clear the insurgent-ridden village complexes of Nalgham and Sangasar. The Taliban, however, had proven to be too deeply embedded in the area, and now the

A major operation was launched at the end of August 2007 to occupy the height of Ghundey Ghar in Zharey. IEDs were always a threat. Here, Canadian Armed Forces troops on their way to occupy Ghundey Ghar dismount from their LAV III vehicles to investigate the route ahead for possible IEDs.

A sniper lookout position was established on top of Ghundey Ghar after its capture.

Van Doos had to take back Ghundey Ghar. As expected, intruding into this area was like kicking a nest of hornets. The insurgents resisted the move, and it took 13 hours of fighting on August 22 to recapture the objective.

Near the end of the day, after the Canadians had reached the summit, it seemed as if the operation had been successfully completed without suffering any fatalities in the action. That sense of satisfaction was shattered, however, when a disastrous IED strike occurred after the serious fighting had ceased. On news that the summit had been reached, the company sergeant-major had started to move up from the bottom of the hill to resupply the troops and establish better communication. Unfortunately, when his vehicle veered slightly off the cleared route and hit an IED, Master Warrant Officer Mario Mercier and Master Corporal Christian Duchesne, along with their Afghan interpreter, were killed by the resulting blast, while another soldier and two journalists were badly injured. These deaths, especially the company sergeant-major's, shook everyone hard. As professional soldiers, however, they could pause only briefly to mourn their loss and then get on with the mission. That evening and night they were kept busy as the Taliban reacted angrily to their loss of the hill, bringing down mortar and rocket fire on the Canadians.

This reaction showed the importance of the hill, and the Van Doos were determined to hold on to it. At the same time they intended to honour the memory of what the hill had cost them. Soon afterward soldiers from B Company Group and the reconnaissance platoon created a memorial to the men killed at Ghundey Ghar. They carved a wooden cross with chainsaws and erected it with a HESCO container as a base near the top of the hill where the vehicle had been destroyed. A red maple leaf was attached to the cross and wooden plaques were hung from it with the words: *EN MÉMOIRE DE / ADJM MERCIER / CPLC DUCHESNE / NOUS RESTERONS*. Two months later, when Ghundey Ghar was transferred to the responsibility of the ANA, the cross was moved to FOB Wilson where it could better serve as a memorial.[9]

Highway One remained a dangerous route to travel on, and its security was always a priority because it was the main ring road linking Kandahar City to western Afghanistan. About 50 kilometres west of Kandahar City insurgent activity seemed particularly troublesome in the vicinity of the village of Howz-e-Madad. In this area the Taliban constantly infiltrated to the edges of the highway and shot at anything moving along it. The next

This memorial cross on Ghundey Ghar honours Master Warrant Officer Mario Mercier and Master Corporal Christian Duschesne.

operation after Ghundey Ghar created a new strongpoint at Howz-e-Madad manned by ANA troops. In the following weeks of the rotation, further operations took place around Zharey and Panjwayi Districts. By October 30, five police substations had been established to control access on the key roads along with three ANA strongpoints at Ghundey Ghar, Howz-e-Madad, and Mushan in the Horn of Panjwayi. Numerous small temporary checkpoints were also set up between these larger posts to constrain insurgent movement.

ISAF had long recognized that security in Afghanistan could only be achieved by expanding the capability of the country's police and military, so that the task of fighting the insurgency could be eventually turned over to them. One of Task Force 3-07's priorities therefore was to work more effectively in partnership with Afghan forces in the province. FOBs Wilson and Ma'sum Ghar were significantly expanded so that an ANA *kandak* could move into each base, making it easier to carry out joint operations.

A Canadian soldier returns fire when he comes under attack by the Taliban after reaching the
battle group objective during Operation Tashwish Mekawa in Zharey District.

Almost completed, the new Canadian and ANA strongpoint located in Zharey District can
be seen with its razor-wire perimeter fencing, protective HESCO bastion walls, and three
reinforced observation posts, as the sun sets on November 22, 2007. The new compound,
located about 40 kilometres west of Kandahar City, was the next phase of Operation Tashwish
Mekawa. The protective compound was eventually used as a checkpoint by the ANA.

The task of developing Afghan National Security Forces (ANSF) operational capability also extended up the chain of command, with Canadian officers working with Afghan officers at the ANA company, *kandak*, and brigade levels. Lieutenant-Colonel Gauthier knew from lessons learned in previous rotations that any success securing terrain by his battle group alone would not solve the insurgency. It would be simpler if he could carry out his operations on his own initiative. Although it would be more difficult and take longer to include the OMLT and ANA in his plans, he knew that was the only way the mission could really succeed. Fortunately, working with the OMLT was easy because he had known its commander, Lieutenant-Colonel Stéphane Lafaut, back at Camp Valcartier.

As the Van Doos approached the halfway point in their rotation in October, Operation Garranday Zmaray and the installation of new police substations seemed to be going well. The main focus of the battle group remained on Panjwayi and Zharey where experience appeared to confirm the Taliban threat was greatest. This situation changed with stunning rapidity early on October 29 when Gauthier received a phone call from the task force commander, Brigadier-General Guy Laroche, asking him to immediately attend an emergency meeting at the Arghandab District Centre north of Kandahar City. Gauthier happened to be on the road at the time, but he was able to grab his command team and get there within 30 minutes. As he walked into the opulent District Centre building, he realized from the senior level of the other attendees that something serious was going on. Besides the Canadian brigadier-general, the others present included a general of the ANA, the mayor of Kandahar City, the district police chief, and several district leaders. From them Gauthier quickly learned that the Taliban had made a sudden move to take control of the district.

The Arghandab District, situated north of Kandahar City, was one of three agriculturally rich districts in the province. The water from the Arghandab River flowing down from the Dahla Dam provided nutrients that allowed the farms growing fruits and vegetables to flourish. The Taliban had sought to infiltrate the district for some time but had been held back by the Alakozai tribe whose strong leader, Mullah Naqib, had always opposed them. The district was of great strategic importance because it provided an end-run approach for the Taliban to threaten Kandahar City from the north after they had been blocked on the more direct route through Zharey and Panjwayi. Unfortunately, Mullah Naqib had died in the middle of October and the Taliban had wasted no time in taking advantage of the leadership vacuum. As they began to move into the district from the north, they brazenly announced the beginning of an intimidation campaign by phoning the district chief of police in the middle of the night, warning him and his men to get out or they would be slaughtered. The news of the threat spread rapidly by cellphones throughout the farming villages, and panic ensued. As Gauthier assembled his staff to form a battle plan, villagers were already on the main highway fleeing to Kandahar City, with cars ferrying women and children and others on foot herding their animals along with them.[10]

Gauthier would have to scramble to hit back at this Taliban incursion before it could take hold. As an immediate action, the battle group's QRF and a troop of Coyote vehicles from the recce squadron were brought up to secure the District Centre and a key road junction on Highway One by that evening. In preparing his plans, the lieutenant-colonel had to take into account that the terrain was not ideal for any attacker. The sturdy walled compounds resembled fortified strongholds connected by confined roads that were too narrow for LAVs to manoeuvre in. The Van Doos troops would therefore have to dismount and leave their vehicles behind, working their way north using small-unit tactics. Gauthier was short on foot soldiers, but he scraped together everything he could spare, as well as calling up support from other assets that could be made available. Vigorously reacting to the emergency, his battle group was ready to launch a major combat operation to take back the district in less than 12 hours.

Orders went out before midnight, and the strike force began to assemble near the District Centre around 0200 the next morning. Three platoons of the Van Doos' B Company along with some engineers in support would advance in parallel with an ANA infantry company and its Canadian OMLT. This opening phase of the action would take the form of an advance to identify the enemy positions believed to be in several maze-like complexes of compounds. Once the Canadian troops had dismounted, their LAVs would proceed on the east flank along the dry bed of the Arghandab River from where they might be able to provide fire support. Leopard tanks and Coyote reconnaissance vehicles would screen the western flank, while part of an American Special Forces task force was called upon to block any Taliban reinforcements coming from the north. Gauthier provided further support by using his company headquarters group as a small manoeuvre group. A detachment of Canadian 155 mm guns in FOB Wilson was placed on alert, prepared to bring down fire when called upon by the forward observation officers. The Canadian and Afghan troops moved forward by dawn of October 30, and from the first contact, it appeared the Taliban were going to stand on the northern bank of the Arghandab River and fight a conventional battle for the first time since Operation Medusa.[11]

The action lasted three days. The Taliban were well supplied with heavy weapons and showed skill in manoeuvring, attempting to outflank the Canadians and Afghans whenever they could. The advance was difficult because of the close terrain where visibility was limited, and the advancing Canadians needed to clear every objective of booby traps or IEDs. The latter were found on routes leading to the riverbed to block any possible move by the LAVs against the Taliban positions from that flank. Resupply of water, food, and ammunition was also a problem because of the complexity of the terrain.

On the first day, the Taliban stubbornly held on to their ground. Gauthier had to be cautious about the use of his air support and artillery; he knew the area was not normally sympathetic to the Taliban and did not want to antagonize the local population by thoughtlessly destroying their homes or precious pomegranate orchards. During the day, however, one critical strike made a significant difference to the outcome of the battle. The controller of a tactical UAV saw what looked like a cluster of enemy fighters meeting with a commander at a location where no significant collateral damage would result from an air strike. An American tactical fighter on station overhead was therefore given clearance to attack the group. A 227-kilogram laser-guided bomb eliminated the target, likely disrupting an important element in the Taliban command and control.[12]

Radio intercepts the next day indicated that the Taliban force had suffered more casualties than anticipated and that the insurgents were stressed by the rapidity of the Canadian response. The remaining Taliban leaders seemed to have had their confidence shaken and were asking for reinforcements.[13] By the third day, the Canadians and ANA met no further resistance. It soon became apparent that the enemy had given up the fight, splitting into small groups and exfiltrating during the night to escape to other districts. The Canadians were able to occupy all their final objectives and spent one more day making sure all IEDs were cleared. Word that the Taliban were gone spread quickly by cellphone and local villagers began returning almost immediately.[14]

The Battle of Arghandab had been won, but it was not a decisive engagement. The Taliban were in southern Afghanistan to stay, and like all wars of insurgency, this one would be a protracted struggle that would last longer than 3 R22eR BG's tour. The struggle for Afghanistan was an asymmetric war in which the enemy constantly sought to wear down counter-insurgency forces. There was no frontline: the enemy did not dress differently, often did not carry weapons, and were part of the population. At times, as the LAVs trundled out of the front gate of the FOB, the Canadians saw young Afghan males of fighting age sitting alongside the road noting how the Canadian convoy was travelling. The threat of hidden IEDs never ended. By the end of the tour, the battle group had suffered eight deaths from this weapon, along with one from mortar fire and two in an accident that happened during operations.

But Lieutenant-Colonel Gauthier's troops had done their job. They had adapted to COIN warfare and had held back the Taliban from making any further gains. The Van Doos had tried their best to understand the population and protect them as much as they could, whether involved in a firefight one day, providing medical support to a village on another, or assisting in a construction project on yet another day. The ANA was now more integrated with the Canadians for joint operations, and by the end of the Van Doos' tour, a beginning had been made to increase the professional ability of the ANP. The battle group had assisted Task Force Kandahar in carrying out several hundred development projects during the tour. Tangible signs of recovery were appearing: more people frequented the roads, families returned to homes previously abandoned, and the economy seemed to be picking up.

The challenge of the mission was huge, however, and would continue with future rotations. The Van Doos had applied lessons from the previous rotation and had learned new lessons during their time in Afghanistan, which they would pass on to the next battle group as the mission continued. The battle for Kandahar was constantly changing, with the Canadians adapting and analyzing enemy threats as they appeared, and finding better ways of countering the Taliban. The contribution of the 3 R22eR BG to the mission was recognized in 2010 when it was awarded the Commander-in-Chief Unit Commendation for being "instrumental in dismantling improvised explosive device networks, recapturing checkpoints and returning them to Afghan control, enhancing the capacity of Afghan forces, and providing guidance on community building and local governance."

✦

It was just after midnight on a dark cool night in November 2007. All the vehicles of the convoy were lined up with their engines running when Lieutenant Simon Mailloux's senior sergeant gave him the thumbs-up. Orders had been given, everything was loaded, and the checks had been made. "The radios are good to go, sir. We're ready to roll." With that, Mailloux spoke a few last-minute words of motivation to his soldiers lined up in the black of night behind their vehicles, then ordered the lead vehicle of the vanguard to head out the gate of Patrol Base Sperwan Ghar. With this early start they expected to be on Highway One near Howz-e-Madad by first light, when the operation would begin. The vehicles bounced forward along the narrow dirt road, travelling slowly, partly because of the darkness and partly because of the normal routine of scanning through night-vision equipment for suspicious signs on the road and its verges. Simon stood in the sentry hatch of the LAV, keeping particularly alert because his vehicle was one of the last in the column. He remained relaxed, knowing that the road between Sperwan Ghar and Ma'sum Ghar was usually safe and that he had some tanks and engineers leading the column.

They had been travelling along the road for only about 10 minutes when suddenly a massive wave of heat and pressure erupted and hit Simon in the face. That was the last thing he felt before everything went black. When he slowly regained consciousness, everything was confusion and pain. He was on the ground being dragged away from the flames by his driver, Frederic Happell, and was hurting a lot. He tried to make sense of what was happening but couldn't remember where he was and why he was there. His LAV had hit a massive IED, and it would be many weeks before he could really understand what had occurred. He would face many challenges ahead — first to stay alive, and then to learn to walk again. But as he managed to overcome his physical and emotional injuries, the biggest obstacle confronting him was whether he would ever be able to return to Afghanistan. He felt he needed to complete the mission he had started there, but to do that he knew he would have to fight the system; no soldier who had been injured on the combat mission had yet been able to return.

Simon had been attracted to a career in the army since he was a young boy growing up north of Quebec City. When he was only 12 years old, a brochure for the Royal Military College (RMC) caught his eye and he decided that was where he wanted to go. His ambition was realized when he entered RMC in 2001, graduating in 2006 and then being posted as an officer to the 3 R22eR just before the battalion received orders to go to Afghanistan. The battalion was the first Quebec unit to be deployed on the combat mission, which energized everyone. Simon's warrant officer and the older sergeants were particularly keen to go. Over the past few years they had all been deployed on peacekeeping operations, and now, for the first time, they had the chance to demonstrate their capabilities as a combat unit. That was what they had all joined for.

The first elements of the battle group started arriving at KAF at the beginning of August 2007. After the usual period of acclimatization, they moved outside the wire and Simon, with C Company Group, found himself in FOB Ma'sum Ghar. They hardly had time to unpack their rucksacks before their first operation occurred. A frantic call came in from a police station near Howz-e-Madad, appealing for help because it was under attack by the Taliban. As the changeover with the previous rotation was still taking place, a strong QRF made up of units from both battle groups was rapidly assembled. They rushed out of the FOB, taking Route Summit through Pashmul and west along Highway One. When the vanguard of the QRF finally made contact with the police station, the results were somewhat anti-climactic. There were no signs of Taliban attackers. While the situation was being resolved, the convoy sat exposed on a narrow lane, engines running, the soldiers watching their arcs of fire and getting edgy as they felt like sitting ducks. While the threat against the police post had disappeared, the men in the small garrison now declared they were not going to stay at their post any longer because of the death threats from the Taliban they had received. The police packed all their gear into their Ford Rangers and abandoned the cramped three-room compound that served as their post. Ironically, a month later the battle group had to return there to clear the compound after the Taliban had turned it into their own base. For Simon and his platoon, that experience was their introduction to the conflicting realities of the mission.

The handover from the previous rotation was now carried out and C Company Group started getting used to operations out of Ma'sum Ghar. When one company had been withdrawn from the battle group to form the OMLT, the remaining company groups had been somewhat compensated by increasing their strength from three to four platoons. C Company Group could also call on extra help from the armoured and engineer squadrons based at Ma'sum Ghar. Even with these reinforcements, however, Company Group C was still stretched to carry out all its responsibilities. Two platoons would be tied down defending the perimeters of FOBs Ma'sum Ghar and Sperwan Ghar, and another would have to act as the QRF, leaving only one available for tactical activities such as routine COIN patrols or reinforcing B Company Group on an operation. Presence patrols, which included Afghan soldiers or police, were one of their most important activities they would have to carry out, and these went out daily to stay in touch with the population. For Simon's company group, these were most often done around Ma'sum Ghar, but they also headed west along Route Hyena into the Horn of Panjwayi.

Such patrols were the cornerstone of COIN practice to gather intelligence for combatting the insurgency. To make sure the maximum intelligence was brought back by a patrol, soldiers were briefed prior to departure on their mission for the day and what they were to look for. Were children relaxed and out playing? Was the market open and business being transacted as expected? Were the shelves empty or were goods from Kandahar City available? The pace would be leisurely and as unthreatening as possible. They tried to be approachable, stopping where opportunities arose to shake hands and talk. All the while each soldier assessed the environment and everything was noted.

As they passed through a village, there were a lot of different signs the Canadians looked for to assess whether they were winning or losing in that location. The children were very important. If they swarmed around the patrol, Simon and his men could feel there was probably no present threat, but if the kids disappeared, then the patrol knew it was about to be hit. It was harder to assess the mood of the adults, since experience had made them cautious about revealing anything to outsiders, so more effort and patience were required when talking to them. Moods also changed in villages. In a few locations the mood could vary a lot during the tour. In some, people waved at the Canadians at the beginning of the tour but later grew remote and even threw rocks at the LAVs. The change might come after an incident in which a farm was damaged, or simply after a firefight had occurred nearby. But it was in the villages that the war would be won or lost, and the patrols had to continue to show the population that despite any antagonism the Canadians were there to help. It was well understood that both sides were fighting for the support of the population. The main difference was that the Taliban more often used deception, bribery, and death threats as their main tactics.

Participating in *shuras* was not something Simon had learned in basic infantry combat training, but it was very much part of his job in Afghanistan. He had to learn Afghan customs quickly, such as taking off his boots, if he could, or his helmet before entering a village leader's home. Later that became a problem when Captain Trevor Greene, a CIMIC officer, was attacked with an axe during a *shura* in 2006, an incident that left many Canadian soldiers uncomfortable about taking off their protective kit. While the repetition of such an assault was pretty remote, Simon thought it only prudent to bring along one of his biggest sergeants when he conducted a *shura*. The sergeant remained standing in the background, with his fragmentation vest and helmet on and his weapon ready. With that sense of security behind him, Simon could then sit down for the *shura*, take off his helmet, and relax. With this arrangement he participated in a number of *shuras* and was able to develop good relations with some of the Afghan leaders.

One of Simon's personal goals for the mission from the start was to bring all his men back safely. He talked about this with his warrant officer, who he relied on a great deal during the tour. Simon felt if they did their jobs right and worked together they could succeed in this deployment. But once in the theatre, Simon quickly learned that he could not control everything; when things went wrong, his responsibility was to do the best with whatever situation confronted him.

He matured fast. Only a few days after arriving at the FOB, Simon's platoon was given the job of escorting a supply convoy from KAF back to Ma'sum Ghar. The convoy was routine until they were about 15 minutes away from arriving at the safety of the base. Then the leading vehicle struck an IED — the first strike he had experienced. The explosion was shocking and surprising because they were travelling on the section of Route Summit where it was paved. Consequently, he had only expected a possible ambush, since several supply convoys had been hit by small-arms fire but not IEDs. However, the Taliban had found a way to melt the pavement, dig a hole, place the explosive in it, and replace the asphalt to hide what they had done. Simon's vehicle was second in the convoy at the time of the explosion, so it quickly moved in front of the disabled LAV and took up a defensive position. Almost immediately they came under small-arms fire from insurgents hiding south of the road. Simon's vehicle returned fire, which quickly drove off the ambushers. It seemed the insurgents had expected to ambush a supply convoy with lightly armoured vehicles but had been surprised by the unexpected escort of a mechanized infantry platoon.

While Simon was fighting off the ambush, others had initiated their IED drill and were working to extract the casualties from the stricken LAV. The explosion had destroyed the front left wheel of the LAV and distorted its hull. Private Simon Longtin, the driver, had taken the force of the blast and was seriously injured. Everyone worked frantically to get him out of the vehicle, but because the frame of the LAV had been warped, it took some time to extricate him. As soon as the QRF arrived with the Bison armoured ambulance, he was rushed back to Ma'sum Ghar from where the medevac helicopter took him to the Role 3 Multinational Medical Unit in KAF. Unfortunately, the medical staff could not save him.

Simon Longtin's death was the first for the battle group and was emotionally difficult for everyone, particularly for his platoon leader. Mailloux had arrived in Afghanistan thinking they were prepared for anything and that all his men would get through the deployment all right. With his confidence shaken by the tragedy, the ramp ceremony afterward was one of the hardest things he had experienced in his life. It was a very solemn affair, with the coffin carried between two rows of troops that formed a corridor leading to the open ramp of the cargo aircraft that would take the body back to Canada. The platoon leader and warrant officer of the deceased soldier were placed closest to the aircraft and were the last to pay their respects as they watched the coffin go into the cavern-like cargo bay. As the ramp began closing, with bagpipes wailing, Simon's emotions weighed him down. It was only then that he became aware of the full extent of his responsibilities. The men of his platoon were also quiet, and Simon sensed their depression, as well. On forming up their little convoy to return to the FOB, Simon decided he had to do something to help his troops regain their morale. He told his driver that their LAV would take the lead back to the FOB along "IED Alley," and he continued to take this position on patrols over the next few days to give his men some relief as their focus returned to the mission.

Simon's platoon was given a new task at the beginning of October. FOB Sperwan Ghar was a secondary base five kilometres west of Ma'sum Ghar, a mound of a dirt, sand, and dust built by the Russians during their occupation. Rising some 60 metres above a jumbled patchwork of deeply furrowed grape fields, wadis, and villages, the base was strategically import-ant because it protected the western approaches to Ma'sum Ghar. At that time Company Group C could only spare one platoon as Sperwan Ghar's base protection unit, and that became the task of Simon's platoon for the next few weeks. Simon quickly recognized that his small unit did not have a lot of boots on the ground to cover the base adequately, so he decided that whenever he had an opportunity he would put forward the appearance of a stronger force than he actually had.

That opportunity came up very quickly. The leader of the previous base protection platoon had advised Simon that he would have an easy time during his stay, since nothing much had happened there. But on the morn-ing after Simon's arrival Taliban rockets started falling on the base. After a few days of that, Simon decided to head out and hold a *shura* with the local leaders to see if he could get any information about who was firing these rockets. He expected that the local villagers would have contact with the Taliban and that they were probably trying to test the resolve of the new garrison. So Simon decided to make a show of force, gathering all the troops he could spare and arranging for a combat support aircraft to fly past during the meeting. He intended to relay a message that the Canadians were there to help but were not going to put up with harassment by rocket fire.

The *shura* seemed to go well. The local villagers had water problems, which they discussed, and Simon brought along a female medic who was able to sit down separately with the leaders' wives and assist them with any treatment they needed. The diplomacy worked. Simon got some information about where the rocket attacks were coming from and who was carrying them out. Upon returning to the base, he passed this intelligence up the chain of command and requested additional troops so he could go after the source of the rockets. Unfortunately, his company turned him down because it was fully occupied with other operations with higher priorities.

Simon understood that the battle group was short of resources, but the rocket attacks continued to annoy him. His platoon was not the only

Lieutenant Simon Mailloux organized a *shura* with the heads of villages around the Canadian base Sperwan Ghar to discuss security and development concerns. The Canadian contingent in Sperwan Ghar had recently been under sustained rocket and ambush attacks, and winning the support of the population was crucial to eliminate this threat.

combat unit on the base. An ANA company being trained as an artillery unit by American mentors was also stationed at Sperwan Ghar. They did not like the rockets any more than Simon and his men did. The ANA troops were not trained infantrymen, but Simon and the U.S. mentors decided they could probably scrape together enough men to deal with the rocketeers. Simon, in a mood of enthusiasm, agreed. The final composite patrol consisted of a section of Van Doos infantry along with Simon's platoon headquarters, one section of the ANA, the American mentors, and a few Afghan policemen. The result was quite a polyglot miniature battle group, with Van Doos soldiers and Simon speaking French, the Americans talking over the radio in English, and the Afghan interpreter relaying Simon's orders in Dari to the ANA and in Pashto to the ANP.

Initially, the Americans took the lead as they headed into the farmlands, agreeing that if they got into trouble Simon would manoeuvre his troops to outflank any opposition encountered. They travelled west toward a small hill suspected of being the rocket position. It did not take long, however, before events upset their plans. The Americans radioed that they had been ambushed and were now pinned down. The situation did not cause them any great concern at first, since they believed they could eliminate the ambushers if Simon flanked them as planned. Simon started to execute this manoeuvre toward the right with the main body, but the ANP whose morale was often shaky did not react well. After firing a few rounds, they seemed to think they had done enough and stopped moving. Simon still had his own men and so advanced toward the site of the ambush. As he did so, though, the Taliban fire increased in intensity. From the volume of fire and its direction, Simon realized that the enemy force was probably greater in strength than he had anticipated and they were now moving to outflank him!

The patrol was in a bad position: the Americans were trapped, and now some of Simon's own men were pinned down. The unpleasant feeling surfaced in his mind that he, as the hunter, had become the hunted. He now needed help, but he knew from his earlier message that he could not get any from Ma'sum Ghar, so he tried to call in support from the Canadian artillery. They, however, quickly dashed his hopes, as well. He and his men were too close to civilian habitation, so the artillery was prevented by the rules of engagement from providing any significant fire support. The artillery was able to fire some rounds targeted on a smoke grenade Simon was able to throw to mark the insurgent position, as well as some rounds to establish a smokescreen, but these had little effect except only to intensify enemy fire.

Simon was now forced to go on the defensive and begin shifting his men back as much as possible. But the enemy seemed very experienced. As soon as the Canadians fell back, the insurgents followed, extending their flanking moves, as well. To make matters worse, the heat of the day and the tense situation were beginning to affect Simon and his men. They were now moving very slowly, overheated from the extreme heat, soaked with sweat, and weighed down by their heavy kit. Simon made a mental calculation regarding how far they were from Sperwan Ghar and had the chilling realization they might not be able to make it back before the Taliban closed in on them. It was a real possibility that the Taliban might encircle his patrol and pick them off one by one.

At that point Simon heard a faraway sound that raised his spirits. It was familiar — the engine of a LAV III! A vehicle was somewhere out there heading for them, working its way along wadis and scraping through alleyways between compounds. It was his weapons detachment commander leading a small rescue force made up of a LAV III and a tracked T-LAV. Back at Sperwan Ghar, Simon's warrant officer had heard Simon's calls for help on the radio and had ordered the vehicles to push out when he realized the danger they were in. Soon Simon heard the sound of the LAVs' 25 mm guns engaging the enemy. That did it! The insurgents' fire slackened and they backed off. The Americans were able to disengage and rejoin the main party. Relief swept over everyone, and they soon made the link-up with the vehicles. When Simon got back to the FOB, he was on the verge of passing out from heat exhaustion. Adrenaline had gotten him back over the last few hundred metres. The firefight had been a challenge and had given him lessons he would take with him for the rest of his military career.

After staying about a month in Sperwan Ghar, Simon's platoon moved back to Ma'sum Ghar where they continued to participate in the cycle that included patrols, QRF assignments, and combat operations. The next major battle-group-level operation was planned for the middle of November. In Operation Tashwish Mekewa, the Van Doos would strike into the heart of Zharey where Taliban roots remained firmly entrenched. The combat outpost on Ghundey Ghar still held firm, providing a valuable observation post on the whole district, but patrols still could not pass safely through the surrounding villages. Lieutenant-Colonel Gauthier planned to gather all the strength he could muster to strike at Sangasar and establish a police substation from which the security bubble would be expanded to permanently hold the area. Because B Company Group had just carried out the battle to clear the Arghandab District and needed some time to recover, he decided to give the lead for this operation to C Company. The soldiers of C Company were keen to take this on because they had been tied down around Ma'sum Ghar for too long and had suffered too many ambushes without having a chance to strike back.

The combat team for the operation assembled at FOB Sperwan Ghar on November 16. Simon was just back from leave, so the company commander decided to use his platoon for the vanguard. Not long after midnight on November 17, Simon and his LAVs trundled out of the gate as the first packet. But the Taliban were not asleep. Very likely they had spotters hidden in the vineyards around the FOB and from the activity inside had sensed something big was coming. As the vanguard drove north in the dark of the night, an insurgent triggerman lay in wait 50 metres from the narrow road. When the first LAV approached, he waited patiently and let it pass, no doubt looking for a target farther along in the convoy. He found it when the LAV near the end of the packet approached, its aerials marking it as a command vehicle. As it came opposite him, he pressed the trigger.

Simon felt the explosion for a split second and then lost consciousness. The next thing he remembered was lying on the ground and feeling pain. Glancing up, he saw his vehicle in flames and bodies inside. "You need to get them out!" he yelled at the soldier trying to drag him away from the flames.

"I tried and they're just not moving!" was the reply.

Simon attempted to absorb the situation but could not understand what was happening or where he was. He had to struggle merely to speak because his jaw was fractured and swollen. Unable to move his legs at all, he kept slipping in and out of consciousness every few minutes. As the ammunition in his LAV began to explode from the fire, the men in his platoon dragged him behind a concrete wall for protection.

Simon later learned that the rear compartment of his vehicle had taken the main force of the explosion. The blast had come straight up through the floor, destroying the vehicle's differential and creating pressure that violently ejected Simon and Corporal Jimmy Lavallière, his platoon's machine gunner. They had both sustained serious injuries but had at least survived. The other three passengers had died: Corporal Nicholas Beauchamp, the medic; Corporal Michel Lévesque, Simon's signaller; and their Afghan interpreter. Sadly, Simon had never had a chance to learn the interpreter's name, because the man had just been assigned to the platoon that night. The crew commander was also seriously injured but had blocked the force of the blast from hitting the LAV gunner, sitting on the other side. The driver was the most fortunate crew member; his position was usually the most vulnerable, but that night he was only shaken up.

The message about the IED strike went back to the FOB where the main body of the company was still waiting to start off. The company commander immediately pulled the Bison ambulance out of the convoy lineup and headed out to the site. They quickly evacuated the casualties back to Sperwan Ghar where their small aid station could begin dealing with the injuries. Although Simon's leg was in terrible shape, the bleeding had stopped, so the medics concentrated on the machine gunner who was losing a lot of blood. An American Black Hawk helicopter soon arrived, and the casualties were moved out of the aid station on stretchers. Throughout this Simon remained conscious, and as he was carried out, he noticed the soldiers of his platoon standing nearby with their helmets off. He was in a state of shock and high on medication but felt compelled to yell at them over the roar of the helicopter blades in a surge of bravado and anger, "I'll be back in two weeks and we'll get the bastards!"

The medic tried to encourage him by telling him, "You're going to be fine. You just need to be patched up at KAF."

From the medic's words of encouragement, Simon thought he must only have a concussion with a few scratches. He did not understand the seriousness of his injuries yet through the fog of morphine and shock, but his tour on the Afghan mission was over. With the extent of his injuries, his army career might also be finished. He would be lucky if he actually survived. In the hospital in KAF, he continued to drift in and out of consciousness and later had no memory of that time. He could not recall that friends from the Van Doos had visited him there, or remember that he had spoken to Lieutenant-Colonel Gauthier, who had shaken his hand and presented him with his tour medal — the General Campaign Star with ISAF Bar. His flight to Germany and his first days in the big American medical facility at Landstuhl were also a blank. When he finally regained consciousness in Germany, the first thing he felt and would later recall was the pain all over his body.

The pain Simon immediately experienced was caused by the amputation of his left leg, but it also emanated from his fractured jaw and the external fixation device protruding from his broken left femur. Making things worse was his difficulty understanding his surroundings. Simon found everything strange; so many things had been done to his body without his knowledge. He thought he was too much like a character in the novel *Frankenstein*. The medical staff gave him the basics of his situation, but it was only after patient explanations from his girlfriend, who had arrived from Canada, that Simon was able to overcome his confusion. She had been well briefed by the doctors and was able to tell Simon how bad his condition was when he arrived at Landstuhl.

His worst injury was to his lower left leg, which was badly shredded. The doctors had seen many similar traumatic wounds from Afghanistan and Iraq, and felt they could save his leg by transferring some veins from his good leg to get the blood flowing again. But that did not work, so they had to amputate. Once that was done, other, even more serious problems arose. Simon began to suffer acute respiratory distress as his lungs filled with fluid. The doctors immediately briefed his girlfriend and parents, the latter having also arrived, on the situation. The medical staff were very concerned about Simon's ability to survive. He was, as one doctor put it, basically drowning in his own water, but they were not sure of the cause. There were several reasons, but Simon's situation was so bad they didn't think they had time to narrow these down. So they were decided to intervene and employ brute treatment for all possibilities. While this went on, they had to put Simon on a vibrating chest device to provide a regimen of respiratory physiotherapy to prevent him from drowning.

All of this was shocking news for Simon's girlfriend and parents, who could only wait and hope. Fortunately, one of the heavy doses of medication given to Simon worked, and his body recovered from the acute pulmonary edema threatening him. While this was happening, Simon was unaware of the crisis because he was still unconscious. Later, when his girlfriend tried to explain what he had been through, he had trouble believing her. Surely, he would remember such an extreme experience. She convinced him only after drawing his attention to the tiny scars on his chest where the doctors had inserted tubes to vibrate his lungs.

Simon remained in Landstuhl for two weeks until his condition stabilized. Then, when deemed fit enough to travel, he, along with his injured gunner and LAV crew commander, were transferred to Canada in a Canadian Air Force Airbus for further treatment. From there they were whisked away in ambulances as quickly as possible to the major trauma centre of the Hôpital de l'Enfant-Jésus. Here the treatment of his injuries continued under the care of that hospital's wide range of specialists. It was during this period that Simon had to struggle not only against the physical pain he felt but against psychological trauma, as well. He felt extreme frustration that he could not do anything by himself, even for his most basic needs. Now having to rely on others produced a sense of identity loss, since utter dependency was so incompatible with his natural character. And through the confusion of his present circumstances he continued to think about his platoon back in Afghanistan. Simon had left them behind and was not with them as the mission carried on. He went through all possible emotions: discouragement that he might not recover, uncertainty about what his life might be afterward, fear that his health might get worse, and frustration that this was not supposed to happen, that it was not what he had thought the tour was going to be about. There was relief that he had survived, but he also experienced survivor guilt.

He had to learn to deal with all these emotions, succeeding with some better than others. It helped a lot that he had always been a very logical person, someone who tried to think things through calmly, keeping emotions out of the way as much as was practical. Also helpful was the very strong support group he had: not only his girlfriend and family, but friends from RMC who either visited him or if stationed in other provinces sent him letters. Above all, he discovered the strength to deal with his difficulties from the support his girlfriend provided. The new situation was not the relationship either of them had expected before he had left for Afghanistan. But when the doctors told her that he would probably take two years to walk again and would need a lot of care, her reply gave him the strongest support he could have hoped for: "Yes, I'll do it. That's fine."

Simon moved on to begin rehabilitation but had no clear idea what his future life would be like after losing a leg. As they had carried him to the medevac helicopter in Afghanistan, he had called out to his men that he would be back to finish the mission, but he now knew that promise could not be possible. He felt some encouragement when he was visited in the hospital by General Rick Hillier, chief of the defence staff. This gave Simon a chance to explain that he wanted to continue serving in the military and eventually return to Afghanistan. General Hillier appeared sympathetic and promised that Simon could stay in the army at least until the contract to pay back his university studies expired. The general could only add that they would see what was possible about Simon's future after he was released from the hospital. Having had a chance to talk to Hillier helped raise Simon's spirits somewhat, but he still remained anxious that he might have to settle for doing clerical duties in an army administrative unit.

All these concerns came to a head, however, in December on his first trip out in public. As Christmas approached, his girlfriend bundled him up in a wheelchair and they went shopping for Christmas gifts. When his girlfriend wheeled him into the mall, the stump of his leg was quite visible and he became sensitive that many people in the crowd were staring at him. He could image their thoughts: *Oh, that poor person. He needs to be helped!* In an effort to be polite, the crowds moved out of the way of his wheelchair.

The natural sympathy shown by these people did not result in gratitude from Simon but instead created anger. Certain thoughts seared his mind: *Don't do that! I'm not the person you see. This can't be happening! I'm not a useless person who relies on society for help!* That was the moment when he decided he could not accept such an identity. From that point on he worked as hard as he could to regain what he felt was his true character and save his military career.

Intensive rehabilitation with a prosthetic leg began in January 2008. The military gave him all the support he needed. He started with a simple device, learning how to bend the knee, walking on a foot he could not feel, and managing his balance, all the while trying to control the pain such activity generated. Simon had to learn to be confident while walking without looking down, believing that his foot was going to land where it was supposed to land. By February he was doing well enough that he was fitted with a C-Leg, an advanced prosthetic that had a fully microprocessor-controlled knee. This prosthesis was designed to help amputees walk close to normal, but still required an effort by the user to adapt to it. For Simon this was a big challenge. He could never relax even on a casual walk; he had to remain focused on the task of walking on all types of surfaces or risk falling. And he fell often. But he made steady progress and kept his sense of humour through it all. When the rehab centre tried to teach him the proper way of falling, he laughed and told them he had already learned how to do that during the airborne course he had taken before going to Afghanistan. That had been a great preparation for losing a leg!

When Simon finally became comfortable using the new leg, he went back on partial duty with his battalion in Quebec City. But the doctors told him he had to continue focusing on his rehabilitation and not take on too many duties because that would only set back his recovery. Despite these warnings, he became restless without any challenging work. His situation started to unsettle him and he made it known he wanted another posting but had to stay in the infantry. One day, in early 2008, Army Public Affairs contacted him and said that a journalist had requested an interview with someone who had been in Afghanistan. They asked Simon to meet with the journalist. Simon did so, a couple of photos were taken, and he quickly forgot about it. He figured the article would appear on page 50 of some obscure magazine. It turned out that the publication was *L'actualité*, the most widely read French-language magazine in Canada, and he was on the front cover of the February 2008 edition! This interview triggered a surprising sequence of events that, in the end, changed everything for Simon.

The article in *L'actualité* brought Simon to the attention of the Quebec public, and within days he received a request to appear on *Tout le monde en parle*, one of the most popular talk shows in Quebec. From there further requests spiralled upward. Simon was taken aback by all the attention. It seemed that he was the first injured soldier from Quebec to speak about his experience, and the public was impressed by his open attitude. These interviews finally brought him to the attention of Michaëlle Jean, the governor general of Canada. She happened to need an aide-de-camp and asked Simon if he would take on the post. For Simon, finishing his rehabilitation while having a posting outside his battalion would be ideal, so he began these duties at Rideau Hall in Ottawa in July 2008. Gaining this posting was the best thing that could have happened to him. He knew at that time that he still did not fit the physical requirements to redeploy, let alone stay in the army. It would take two good legs to pass a medical examination. He needed to prove without any compromise that he could take on physically demanding duties, and the aide-de-camp job could provide him with that platform.

Despite his enthusiasm, the job was still a huge challenge. When he arrived at Rideau Hall, he could do a full day's work but could not run, and climbing stairs was painful. But facing a full work schedule got him motivated every day. He had to focus on what he had to do and forget about how hard it was. He got lots of practice walking up and down stairs at Rideau Hall and in front of cameras on red carpets where he had to constantly repeat his mantra, "Don't fall! Don't fall!" The physical demands of

In July 2008, Lieutenant Simon Mailloux had the honour of being posted as aide-de-camp to Governor General Michaëlle Jean. The duties were challenging but helped with his rehabilitation. In June 2009, the governor general carried out her first inspection of the 2009 Ceremonial Guard on the grounds of Rideau Hall, Ottawa, attended by Mailloux and Major Hynes from the Guard.

the job were heavy because the governor general travelled extensively. With a very intensive agenda, Simon did not have time to think about his leg and how it was hurting. Rideau Hall remained sensitive to his difficulties and, at times, offered to provide help if he needed it. Simon always turned these down, determined to get through on his own, but was grateful for the faith shown in him. His ability to handle the artificial limb progressed well, and by the end of his 14-month term, he felt ready to go back to the battalion and take on full duties.

The final key to Simon's return to active duty began while he was still acting as aide-de-camp. For some time he had decided he had to go back to Afghanistan. He knew that would be difficult because he still only held the rank of lieutenant and did not fit the medical requirements for deployment. However, as the end of his assignment at Rideau Hall approached, he took every opportunity he could to let people know about his ambition. As aide-de-camp to the governor general, he was in the fortunate position of being able to meet generals and chief warrant officers who attended ceremonies at Rideau Hall. He felt that if he was lucky he would find the ear of someone who could get him back on a deployment. Simon also felt strongly that if he could accomplish this it might set a precedent for other injured soldiers who wanted to stay on active duty.

What finally opened the door for him came about when Simon accompanied Michaëlle Jean to the Citadel in Quebec City where she was to participate in a change-of-command ceremony for colonel-in-chief of R22eR. Just before the ceremony was to start, Brigadier-General Daniel Menard, who was to command the next rotation of the headquarters unit of Task Force Kandahar, took him aside. "There's been a few decisions made," he told Simon, "and I want to make you aware of this. First, you're promoted to captain. Second, if you're okay with that, I'm taking you to Afghanistan." Simon was stunned. He could hardly believe what he had been told, and spent the rest of the ceremony trying to focus on his job, although Afghanistan had taken over his thoughts.

Some time later, a few of the pieces behind the decision became clearer when he saw a chain of email messages. His case had somehow reached General Walter Natynczyk, the new chief of the defence staff, who had taken up Simon's cause. General Natynczyk had sent a message to Lieutenant-General

Andrew Leslie, chief of the land staff, explaining that he considered Simon fit enough and asking Leslie to find Simon a position in Afghanistan. Simon felt honoured that these two senior-ranking officers would give him that much consideration and knew that it was only with their example of leadership that he was going to get his opportunity. If it had not been for their support, it probably would not have been possible. He now felt he had to do his utmost to deserve this honour and prove he was capable.

Simon knew he still had to overcome one big obstacle before achieving his ambition to return to Afghanistan. That was to pass the fitness test that evaluated whether soldiers could meet physical demands they would encounter on operations. Depending on their injury, some soldiers trying to return to Afghanistan might be able to train themselves to pass these tests satisfactorily while for others that would not be possible. For example, Simon could show he had adapted well physically to a prosthesis after losing his leg, but someone who had been injured in the eye would not be able to demonstrate he could fire a C7 rifle accurately. To some extent it was a matter of determination to adapt, and Simon had the drive to do so. He had the weight of responsibility to prove that the decision to send him back was right. He knew that if he succeeded in finishing a tour it would open the door for other injured soldiers to redeploy. It could then be argued that if Simon could do it others could, too. By the time pre-deployment training began in Valcartier, Simon was ready. With his artificial limb he managed to walk 13 kilometres with a 27-kilogram pack on his back, carried another soldier with full kit for 100 metres, and dug a trench. When it came time to carry out these tasks, he did not think about how impossible they seemed; he just set about doing them. He was exhausted after some of them, but he succeeded.

Simon felt a great sense of satisfaction as he landed in KAF for the second time in November 2009. He had left in November 2007 against his will and with a feeling that he had unfinished business there. To mark his return he made sure that the first step he made to exit the aircraft was with his plastic foot. He managed to do that successfully and began his duties as part of the J5 planning staff. He was based in KAF this time and found that it had changed a lot since he had last been there — the base was much bigger and full of American troops now that the surge had started. Life was not physically hard as it had been in the FOB. They had bedrooms in converted sea containers, good food in a cafeteria, showers, and a workday that started at 0700. But it was mentally exhausting. He now worked seven days a week, sometimes up to 15 hours a day, under pressure to constantly evaluate the effectiveness of current plans and to prepare plans for future operations. Every time someone was killed in action, all staff attended the ramp ceremony, and this reminded everyone that the plans they were making, the decisions they were taking, were affecting the men and women on the ground.

For a while it looked as if Simon was going to spend his tour in the confines of the big base. It seemed to be understood that he was not to go out of the wire, since his safety was considered a "sensitive" issue — they wanted to avoid any possibility that he might be injured again while in Afghanistan. However, as the tour continued, there was a need for him to carry out tasks that could only be done outside and he began going out on convoys that travelled the familiar roads to Camp Nathan Smith and even to Panjwayi. That was fine with him. And even KAF was not without the possibility of danger. When the Taliban launched a suicide attack on the base in August, Simon actually felt it was some relief from the usual routine. When he heard the firing and explosions coming from the perimeter, his drill from the first tour returned. He grabbed his weapon, put on his kit, and headed out with several others to connect with other headquarters units that were close by in case they had to deal with any insurgents who had gotten through. He was surprised how instinctive his reaction was and actually enjoyed the sense of being back in action.

Simon completed his tour successfully and returned to Canada in May 2010. Having shown his resilience and determination to minimize any limitations caused by his disability, he remained in the infantry as he had hoped. By 2014 he was promoted to second-in-command of C Company of 1 R22eR. With continuing technical improvements in his prosthesis, he was able to participate in unit field exercises, although some conditions still challenged him. During winter exercises on snowshoes, for example, he did not look good. He would trip and fall more than the other soldiers, but would still do everything by the end of the exercise. He also remained unsure of himself on rough ground, but when he fell his men took the opportunity to joke, asking, "Captain, are you seeing a lot of enemies down there?"

Captain Simon Mailloux carries the baton as he leads the Soldier on Afghanistan Relay Team into a ceremony at the Royal Military College Memorial Arch in Kingston, Ontario, on May 5, 2014. Nineteen previously injured personnel ran the six-day relay through communities from Trenton to Ottawa, where the specially built baton was presented to Prime Minister Stephen Harper.

Despite his handicap, his relations with his men remain good. They are hard-bitten infantrymen, but they give full credit to anyone in the regiment who has been on the combat mission and who has had the courage to go back again, even after having been critically injured in action. They know that Simon has opened the door for others to follow.

After his return from Afghanistan, Simon was determined to continue his career in the infantry as long as he could, but he knows that his file will always have a red flag on it. The system will not lower any standards for him or for anyone else with a disability because the military has to be fully capable of meeting any challenges it faces. But Simon will be forever grateful for upper ranks who took a leadership role in cutting through the normal bureaucracy to help him prove that soldiers with a disability can still contribute. Simon has been able to justify their confidence in him and doesn't see any reason to think that will change.

POSTSCRIPT

A well-known American historian once remarked that a country's wars are often forgotten within two generations. Life changes and too many other things arise in people's consciousness. The news media almost instantly move on to other things. And so the same thing is happening with Afghanistan.

But the combat mission in Afghanistan was significant in Canada, and some traces of its record should be preserved. It was the first real war experienced by the Canadian military in half a century, and in that time the public was lulled into complacency with praises of our leadership in peacekeeping missions. Many argued that peacekeeping should be the main role of our military. But warfare has been a constant part of human history, and this fact was brought back to the attention of the public when Canadian troops arrived in Kandahar in 2006. As our troops began to suffer casualties while carrying out a mission meant to help bring a better life to a faraway people, the Canadian public became conscious of the high standards of performance shown by their servicemen and women. A large number of Canadians remained opposed to the mission, but their respect for their soldiers grew. As the body of each soldier killed in Afghanistan returned home and was carried along Highway 401, crowds assembled spontaneously to pay tribute to those they now considered their fallen heroes. Ordinary civilians began to thank off-duty soldiers on the streets of cities across the country. The military received a seldom-seen recognition for its dedication to duty, courage, and sacrifice.

The media gave good coverage to the combat mission, and the dangers for our troops in Afghanistan were well known. But as the mission progressed, the risks did not stop large numbers of civilians from applying to join the Armed Forces. Canadians have been called an "unmilitary people" by some writers, but Canadians willingly participated in every major war in the 20th century, and they did so again for the combat mission. By the end of the mission, almost 40,000 soldiers had been deployed to Afghanistan, a few even volunteering for up to five tours of duty. Only perhaps a quarter of the troops who went over on any tour would have found themselves in the combat arms or other specialties that confronted the Taliban in actual battle. These were the men and women who felt the full extent of the violence encountered in Afghanistan.

This book has pulled out seven men from the roster of all those who served in the hope that their stories might give other Canadians an understanding of what their soldiers did throughout the combat mission. Master Corporal Sean Chard, Sargeant Sam, Master Warrant Officer Richard Stacey, Lieutenant Simon Mailloux, and Captains Jonathan Mineault and Robert Peel were all career professionals whose skill in their particular specialties helped establish the reputation of our military in Afghanistan, while Corporal François Dupéré was one of those citizens from the general population or part-time reserve army who were ready and eager to volunteer.

At some future date others will fully analyze and write the history of the Canadian Army's involvement in Afghanistan. Only then will the successes and failures of this conflict undertaken in a most complex environment be comprehensively understood. But until that time, my hope is that this book might help to preserve the efforts and sacrifices of the individual men and women who deployed.

NOTES

CHAPTER 1: A CHRONOLOGICAL OVERVIEW OF THE COMBAT MISSION

1. Captain H. Christian Breede, "A Socio-Economic Profile of Afghanistan," *The Canadian Army Journal* 11, no. 3 (Fall 2008): 56.
2. Ibid., 59.
3. Carl Forsberg, *Afghanistan Report 3: The Taliban's Campaign for Kandahar* (Washington, DC: Institute for the Study of War, December 2009), 12. Accessed at www.understandingwar.org/sites/default/files/The_Talibans_Campaign_For_Kandahar.pdf.
4. Winston Churchill, *My Early Life* (London: Fontana Books, 1972), 141.
5. Roland Paris, "The Truth About Canada's Mission in Afghanistan," Centre for International Policy Studies, Policy Brief No. 22, March 2014, University of Ottawa. Accessed at http://cips.uottawa.ca/publications/how-canada-failed-in-afghanistan.
6. "Regional Command South," Institute for the Study of War. Accessed at www.understandingwar.org/region/regional-command-south-0.
7. "Operation ATHENA," Canadian Expeditionary Force Command, Department of National Defence. Accessed at www.cefcom-comfec.forces.gc.ca/pa-ap/ops/athena/index-eng.asp.
8. Major Jason T. Adair, "Learning on the Run," *The Canadian Army Journal* 10, no. 4 (2008): 29.
9. Sean M. Maloney, *Fighting for Afghanistan* (Annapolis, MD: Naval Institute Press, 2011), 147–48; Murray Brewster, *The Savage War* (Mississauga, ON:

John Wiley & Sons, 2011), 137–38.

10. Lieutenant-Colonel Ian Hope, *Dancing with the Dushman* (Kingston, ON: Canadian Defence Academy Press, 2008), 17.

11. Colonel Bernd Horn, *No Lack of Courage: Operation Medusa, Afghanistan* (Toronto: Dundurn, 2010), 31; Forsberg, 13.

12. Report by U.S. Ambassador Ronald Neumann regarding the Policy Action Group meeting of August 16, 2006, WikiLeaks, August 21, 2006. Accessed at www.cablegatesearch.net/cable.php?id=06KABUL3719.

13. Horn, *No Lack of Courage*, 374.

14. Ibid., 39.

15. Ibid., 62.

16. Colonel Bernd Horn, ed., *Fortune Favours the Brave: Tales of Courage and Tenacity in Canadian Military History* (Toronto: Dundurn, 2009), 401.

17. Ibid., 399.

18. Dave Markland, "Operation MEDUSA: Fog of War." Accessed at www.sevenoaksmag.com/features/afghanistanafterMEDUSA.html.

19. Forsberg, 32.

20. Lee Windsor, David Charters, and Brent Mission, *Kandahar Tour* (Mississauga, ON: John Wiley & Sons, 2008), 125.

21. Ibid., 209.

22. Sean M. Maloney, "Panjwayi Alamo," *Canadian Military History* 18, no. 3 (2009): 51.

23. Windsor et al., 92.

24. Adair, 33.

25. Susan Sachs, "Five Years in Afghanistan: Fighting a War Within a Larger War," *Globe and Mail*, July 4, 2011.

26. Seth G. Jones, *Graveyard of Empires* (New York: W.W. Norton, 2010), 248.

27. Forsberg, 6.

28. Ibid., 39.

29. Ibid., 40; Ray Gould, *Worth Dying For* (Toronto: Random House, 2014), 44–46.

30. Forsberg, 49.

31. Brian Hutchinson, "Assignment Kandahar: Interview with Jonathan Vance, Canada's Top Commander in Kandahar," *National Post*, August 13, 2010. Accessed at http://news.nationalpost.com/2010/08/13/assignment-kandahar-interview-with-jonathan-vance-canadas-top-commander-in-kandahar.

32. John Manley et al., *Independent Panel on Canada's Future Role in Afghanistan*

(Ottawa, 2008), 32–35. Accessed at www.collectionscanada.gc.ca/eppp-archive/100/201/301/news_release_lac/2007/08-09/afghanistan/index-e.html.

33. Forsberg, 52.

34. Brian Hutchinson, "The Long Road," *National Post*, June 25, 2011. Accessed at www.familyforce.ca/sites/MainlandBC/EN/Documents/TheLongRoad_1.pdf.

35. Captain Jennifer Kellerman, "Operation KALAY: Moving on to Build in the South," Canadian Expeditionary Force Command, Department of National Defence. Accessed at www.comfec-cefcom.forces.gc.ca/pa-ap/fs-ev/2009/09/18-eng.asp.

36. "5 Canadians Killed in Afghanistan," CBC News, December 30, 2009. Accessed at www.cbc.ca/news/world/5-canadians-killed-in-afghanistan-1.782043.

37. Forsberg, 52.

38. Forsberg, 31–32.

39. Olivia Ward, "Canadians Played Key Role in Marja Attack." Accessed at www.thestar.com/news/world/article/772420--canadians-played-key-role-in-marja-attack; Matthew Fisher, "Canadians Take to Skies for Afghan Offensive." Accessed at http://forums.army.ca/forums/index.php?topic=92118.0.

40. Hutchinson, "The Long Road."

41. Susan Sachs, "Canadians Complete Final Afghanistan Operation," *Globe and Mail*, June 6, 2011.

42. Captain Melina Archambault, "The 1st Battalion Royal 22e Régiment Battle Group in Pakistan: The End of an Era," July 13, 2011. Accessed at www.comfec-cefcom.forces.gc.ca/pa-ap/fs-ev/2011/07/13-eng.asp.

43. Major André Salloum, "Task Force Kandahar Restores Salavat Village School," *The Maple Leaf* 14, no. 4 (January 26, 2011): 1. Accessed at www.forces.gc.ca/site/commun/ml-fe/article-eng.asp?id=6719.

44. Murray Brewster, "Canada Transfers Command of Kandahar to U.S., Ends Five Years of Responsibility," *Brandon Sun*, July 7, 2011. Accessed at www.brandonsun.com/national/breaking-news/canada-transfers-command-of-kandahar-to-us-ending-five-years-of-responsibility.html?thx=y.

CHAPTER 2: COUNTER-INSURGENCY (COIN) WARFARE

1. Ryan Flavelle, *The Patrol* (Toronto: HarperCollins, 2011), 131.

2. Martin van Creveld, *The Changing Face of War: Combat from the Marne to Iraq* (New York: Ballantine, 2008), 229.

3. *Counter-Insurgency Operations*, B-GL-323-004/FP-003 (Ottawa: Department of National Defence, 2008). Accessed at www.scribd.com/doc/31351763/ Canada-Coin.

4. U.S. Joint Chiefs of Staff, *Counterinsurgency: Joint Publication 3–24*, November 22, 2013, ix. Accessed at www.dtic.mil/doctrine/new_pubs/jp3_24.pdf.

5. Quoted in Walter C. Ladwig III, "Managing Counterinsurgency: Lessons from Malaya," *Military Review* 87, no. 3 (May-June 2007): 63. Accessed at http://users.ox.ac.uk/~mert1769/MalayaCOIN.pdf.

6. Major Grégoire Poitron de Boisfleury, "The Origins of Marshal Lyautey's Pacification Doctrine in Morocco from 1912 to 1925," Master's Thesis, U.S. Army Command and General Staff College (2010), 10, 93, 121.

7. Sean M. Maloney, "Taliban Governance: Can Canada Compete?" *Policy Options* (June 2009): 63–68; William Lind, "How the Taliban Take a Village." Accessed at www.military.com/opinion/0,15202,207101_1,00.html.

8. Maloney, *Fighting for Afghanistan*, 122.

9. Anand Gopal, *The Battle for Afghanistan: Militancy and Conflict in Kandahar* (Washington, DC: The New America Foundation, November 2010), 22–24. Accessed at newamerica.net/sites/newamerica.net/files/policydocs/kandahar_ 0.pdf.

10. Horn, ed., *Fortune Favours the Brave*, 371–72.

11. Windsor et al., 168; *Honours and Recognition for Men and Women of the Canadian Forces, 2008* (Ottawa: Department of National Defence, 2009), 23, 72.

12. Hope, 35–37.

13. Sebastian Junger, *War* (Toronto: HarperCollins, 2010), 213.

14. Benjamin Tupper, *Greetings from Afghanistan: Send More Ammo* (New York: New American Library, 2010), 128.

15. Horn, ed., *Fortune Favours the Brave*, 68.

16. Lieutenant-Colonel John Conrad, *What the Thunder Said* (Toronto: Dundurn, 2009), 109.

17. "Joint Task Force Afghanistan Air Wing Closeout Ceremony," CEFCOM NR — 11.011, August 18, 2011. Accessed at www.forces.gc.ca/site/news-nouvelles/ news-nouvelles-eng.asp?id=3907.

18. Captain Ray Wiss, *FOB Doc: A Doctor on the Front Lines in Afghanistan* (Vancouver: Douglas & McIntyre, 2009), 97, 170.

19. Wiss, 37–38.

20. Josh Wingrove, "Last Exit from Kandahar," *Globe and Mail*, March 5, 2010.

Accessed at www.theglobeandmail.com/news/world/last-exit-from-kandahar/article1491529/.

21. Windsor et al., 200.

22. Christie Blatchford, *Fifteen Days* (Toronto: Doubleday, 2007), 104.

23. Adam Day, "Assignment Afghanistan: The Struggle for Salavat — Part 2," *Legion Magazine* (May-June 2010): 32.

CHAPTER 3: INFRASTRUCTURE DEVELOPMENT AT BAZAAR-I-PANJWAYI: LIEUTENANT JONATHAN MINEAULT

1. Sean M. Maloney, "Special Report: On Patrol in Kandahar, Where the Insurgency Is Now More Dangerous, and More International," *Maclean's*, April 30, 2009. Accessed at www.macleans.ca/2009/04/30/inside-the-battle-zone.

2. Major Don Saunders, "Ending Operations, but Not the End of an Era," CHIMO Communiqués. Accessed at www.cmea-agmc.ca/Communiques/11.07.Ending_Op_e.pdf.

3. Paul Watson, "Power Shift in Panjwaii Offers New Hope," *Toronto Star*, January 23, 2011. Accessed at www.thestar.com/news/world/article/926855--power-shift--in-panjwaii-offers-new-hope; Tom A. Peter, "Afghanistan War: The Civics in a Kandahar Governor's Slap," *Christian Science Monitor*, July 22, 2010. Accessed at www.csmonitor.com/World/Asia-South-Central/2010/0722/Afghanistan-war-The-civics-in-a-Kandahar-governor-s-slap.

4. Major Mark Gasparotto, ed., *Clearing the Way* (Self-Published, 2010), 75.

5. Ibid., 113.

6. "Insurgency Has Gone AWOL in Afghanistan," *Toronto Star*, June 27, 2011. Accessed at www.thestar.com/news/world/article/1015736-dimanno-insurgency-has-gone-awol-in-afghanistan.html.

7. Captain Anthony Robb, "The TFK Engineer Regiment and Support to Counter-Insurgency Operations in Kandahar, Afghanistan," *The Canadian Army Journal* 14, No. 1 (Spring 2012): 136; Saunders.

CHAPTER 4: THE PSYOPS WAR AGAINST THE INSURGENCY: CORPORAL FRANÇOIS DUPÉRÉ

1. Bing West, *The Wrong War* (New York: Random House, 2011), 71.

2. Maloney, "Taliban Governance: Can Canada Compete?" 67.

3. Sean M. Maloney, *Confronting the Chaos* (Annapolis, MD: Naval Institute Press, 2009), 43; "Canada Delivers Night Letters of Its Own to Counter Taliban Threats," *Toronto Star*, February 24, 2011. Accessed at www.thestar.com/news/canada/2011/02/24/canada_delivers_night_letters_of_its_own_to_counter_taliban_threats.html.

4. Correspondence with Major Benoit Mainville, September 10, 2013.

5. J. Glenn Gray, *The Warriors* (New York: Harper & Row, 1967), 123.

6. Forsberg, 30. Accessed at www.understandingwar.org/report/talibans-campaign-kandahar.

7. Flavelle, 105.

8. Talukan Bazaar, Canadian Forces Combat Camera, S2011-2006-06, February 23, 2011. Accessed at www.flickr.com/photos/canadianarmy/5514958710/meta.

9. Mainville.

10. The poem Lieutenant Rorke leaves for his son in the 2012 movie *Act of Valor*. Accessed at www.movemequotes.com/9255.

CHAPTER 5: HOLDING THE NORTH — SHAH WALI KOT AND ARGHANDAB: MASTER CORPORAL SEAN CHARD

1. Conrad, 142.

2. Forsberg, 36.

3. Tundra SCA was an Afghan-owned, Canadian-run security company, one of several contracted to provide base security. Its operations raised the ire of President Karzai, who accused the company of stealing staff from the Afghan National Security Forces and of engaging in lawless activities contrary to Coalition aims. Having armed private security guards within a base could still not guarantee the safety of the garrison. On March 9, 2011, a Tundra Security guard at FOB Frontenac opened fire with an AK-47, killing three American soldiers and wounding four others. See "Afghan Hired Guns Bill Tops $41M," Canadian Press, February 8, 2011. Accessed at www.cbc.ca/news/politics/afghan-hired-guns-bill-tops-41m-1.990336. Also see Courtney Kube, "Afghan Security Contractor Accused of Killing U.S. Soldiers," NBC News. Accessed at www.nbcnews.com/id/42203513/ns/world_news-south_and_central_asia/t/afghan-security-contractor-accused-killing-us-soldiers/#.Vdzp15erFgs.

CHAPTER 6: WAR AGAINST THE IEDS: EXPLOSIVE ORDNANCE DISPOSAL

1. Gasparotto, 68.
2. "From Bomb to Bomb Maker," International Center for the Study of Terrorism, January 2013. Accessed at www.icst.psu.edu/docs/3.ExecSum/ICST.B2b. ExecSumm.pdf.
3. "IED Fatalities," Operation Enduring Freedom. Accessed at www.icasualties. org/OEF/index.aspx.
4. Hope, 59.
5. Evan W. Medina, "Roads of War: Paved Highways and the Rise of IED Attacks in Afghanistan" (Philadelphia: University of Pennsylvania, 2011), 10. Accessed at http://repository.upenn.edu/curej/13.
6. Greg, "Bigger, Badder IEDs in Afghanistan," *Defensetech* (March 16, 2010). Accessed at http://defensetech.org/2010/03/16/bigger-badder-ieds-in-afghanistan; Mujib Mashal, "Afghanistan's IED Complex: Inside the Taliban Bomb-Making Industry" (January 2, 2013). Accessed at http:// world.time.com/2013/01/02/afghanistans-ied-complex-inside-the-taliba n-bomb-making-industry.
7. The IED strike on July 4, 2007, killed Captain Matthew Dawe, Captain Jefferson Clifford Francis, Corporal Cole Bartsch, Corporal Jordan Anderson, Private Lane Watkins, and Master Corporal Colin Bason.
8. Tu Thanh Ha, "Canadian Forces Bring Forensics to the Battlefield," *Globe and Mail*, August 5, 2011.
9. *Department of National Defence Performance Report 2008–09, Section II: Analysis of Program Activities by Strategic Outcomes.* Accessed at www.tbs-sct. gc.ca/dpr-rmr/2008-2009/inst/dnd/dnd02-eng.asp; Lieutenant-Colonel D.W. Corbett and Lieutenant (N) K.P. McNamara, "Countering Improvised Explosive Devices in Afghanistan," *Gazette* 73, no. 1. Accessed at www.rcmp-grc.gc.ca/ gazette/vol73n1/esubmission-ereportage1-eng.htm.
10. James Careless, "Countering the IED Threat," *Frontline Defence* (May/June 2009), 16.
11. "Coalition Deaths by Nationality," Operation Enduring Freedom. Assessed at www.icasualties.org/OEF/Nationality.aspx?hndQry=Canada.
12. Stanley Rachman, "The Development of Courage in Military Training and Performance in Combat Situations," United States Army Research Institute for the Behavioral and Social Sciences, ARI Research Note 95-21 (January 1995). Accessed at www.dtic.mil/dtic/tr/fulltext/u2/a296369.pdf; Stanley

Rachman, "Fear and Courage: Some Military Aspects," *Journal of the Royal Army Medical Corps* 128 (1982), 100–04. Accessed at www.ramcjournal.com/content/128/2/100.full.pdf.

13. Graeme Smith, "Taliban Take Hold of Vital Road," *Globe and Mail*, December 5, 2008. Accessed at www.afghanistannewscenter.com/news/2008/december/dec152008.html; Forsberg, 42.

14. Ethan Baron, Mike Blanchfield, and David Akin, "Three Canadian Soldiers Killed in Afghanistan," *National Post*, December 5, 2008. Accessed at www.nationalpost.com/related/topics/Three+Canadian+soldiers+killed+Afghanistan/1036387/story.html.

CHAPTER 7: MENTORING THE AFGHAN NATIONAL ARMY: CAPTAIN ROBERT PEEL

1. Peter Tomsen, *The Wars of Afghanistan: Messianic Terrorism, Tribal Conflicts, and the Failures of Great Powers* (New York: Public Affairs, 2013), 629–34.

2. Windsor et al., 51.

3. Tomsen, 634.

4. Maloney, *Fighting for Afghanistan*, 53–54.

5. Hope, 41–42.

6. Windsor et al., 92. According to American military analyst Carl Forsberg, the 1st Kandak is the second oldest unit in the current Afghan National Army and was highly regarded by its U.S. partners when operating with them in Arghandab District in 2010. See Carl Forsberg, *Counterinsurgency in Kandahar* (Washington, DC: Institute for the Study of War, December 10, 2010), 19.

7. Philip Stavrou, "Canada to Focus on Mentoring Afghan Forces in 2008," December 30, 2007, CTV News. Accessed at www.ctvnews.ca/canada-to-focus-on-mentoring-afghan-forces-in-2008-1.269384.

8. Windsor et al., 199; Colonel Riffou, "The Infantry as Trainers — a Growing Task for the Future," May 23, 2009. Accessed at http://www.ducimus.com/documents/Ser25-InfantryasTrainers(En)2_Riffou.ppt; Sean Maloney, "Panjwayi Alamo: The Defence of Strongpoint Mushan," *Canadian Military History* 14, no. 2 (2009): 50.

CHAPTER 8: AMBUSH ON THE ARGHANDAB RIVER:
MASTER WARRANT OFFICER RICHARD STACEY

1. Major R.D. Dove, "Strategic Foresight in the Canadian Armed Forces Force
    Development of Armour Capabilities: Pursuing the Horizon?" Canadian Armed
    Forces College, Master of Defence Studies JCSP 38 (2012), 20. Accessed at
    www.cfc.forces.gc.ca/259/290/298 /286/dove.pdf.
2. Ibid., 33.
3. Gasparotto, 325.
4. "Canada's Equipment in Afghanistan," CBC News, July 9, 2009. Accessed at
    www.cbc.ca/crossroads-afghanistan/story/2009/07/08/f-canada-military-land-
    vehicles/html.
5. Colonel O.H. Lavoie, "Heavy Armour in Afghanistan: An Infantry BG
    Commander's Perspective," *The Armour Bulletin* (2007–08): 22.
6. Major Trevor Cadieu, "Canadian Armour in Afghanistan," *Canadian Army
    Journal* 10, no. 4 (Winter 2008): 5–25.
7. Ibid., 21.
8. Dove, 61.
9. See http://projects.militarytimes.com/valor/army-pfc-patrick-s-fitzgibbon/
    4221822.

CHAPTER 9: INFANTRY OPERATIONS IN PANJWAYI:
LIEUTENANT SIMON MAILLOUX

1. Matthew Fisher, "Canadian Military Brings High-Tech Warfare to Afghanistan,"
    National Post, October 27, 2007.
2. Seth G. Jones, *In the Graveyard of Empires: America's War in Afghanistan* (New
    York: W.W. Norton, 2010), 207.
3. Windsor et al., 110.
4. Forsberg, *The Campaign for Kandahar*, 28–30.
5. Ibid., 28.
6. "Van Doo Killed in Bombing: Private Is First Member of Famed Regiment
    Killed in Afghanistan," *The Record*, August 20, 2007.
7. See http://milnewstbay.pbworks.com/f/Longtin20Aug07Fr.pdf.
8. Windsor et al., 135, 206; Major Alex D. Haynes, "Opportunity Lost," in
    Colonel Bernd Horn and Dr. Emily Spencer, eds., *No Easy Task: Fighting in*

Afghanistan (Toronto: Dundurn, 2012), 216.

9.   Pierre-André Normandin, "Le siège de Ghundy Ghar raconté," *Le Soleil*, September 20, 2007. Accessed at www.cepes.uqam.ca/spip.php?article1222; Fabrice de Pierrebourg, "Pas d'accommodement pour nos militaires tombés au combat," *Journal de Montréal*, November 1, 2007. Accessed at http://fr.canoe. ca/cgi-bin/imprimer.cgi?id=324702.

10. Sarah Chayes, "A Mullah Dies, and War Comes Knocking," *Washington Post*, November 19, 2007.

11. Sean M. Maloney, "Operation Intizaar Zmarey: The Battle of Arghandab, 30 October–1 November 2007," in Colonel Bernd Horn, ed., *Fortune Favours the Brave: Tales of Courage and Tenacity in Canadian Military History* (Toronto: Dundurn, 2009), 417–35.

12. Ibid., 428–29.

13. Ibid., 431.

14. Ibid., 433–34.

GLOSSARY OF MILITARY ABBREVIATIONS AND ACRONYMS

AEV: Armoured engineer vehicle.

ANA: Afghan National Army.

ANP: Afghan National Police.

ANSF: Afghan National Security Forces.

AO: Area of operations.

AOR: Area of responsibility.

ARV: Armoured recovery vehicle.

BG: Battle group.

CAF: Canadian Armed Forces.

CF: Canadian Forces.

CIMIC: Civil-military co-operation.

CO: Commanding officer.

COIN: Counter-insurgency.

COP: Combat outpost.

CSIS: Canadian Security Intelligence Service.

ECT: Engineer Construction Team.

EOD: Explosive ordnance disposal.

ETT: Embedded Tactical Team.

FAO: Forward artillery observer.

FiST: Fire Support Team.

FOB: Forward operating base.

GPS: Global positioning system.

IED: Improvised explosive device.

IEDD: Improvised explosive device disposal.

ISAF: International Security Assistance Force.

JTAC: Joint terminal attack controller.

JTF: Joint Task Force.

KAF: Kandahar Airfield.

LAV: Light armoured vehicle.

MDEC: Multi-Disciplinary Exploitation Capability.

MRAP: Mine-resistant ambush-protected.

MUAV: Mini unmanned aerial vehicle.

MWO: Master warrant officer.

NATO: North Atlantic Treaty Organization.

NCO: Non-commissioned officer.

NGO: Non-governmental organization.

OC: Officer commanding.

OMLT: Operational Mentor Liaison Team.

PID: Positive identification.

PLS: Portable lift system.

PPCLI: Princess Patricia's Canadian Light Infantry.

PR: Personal radio.

PRT: Provincial Reconstruction Team.

PSYOPS: Psychological operations.

QRF: Quick Reaction Force.

R22eR: Royal 22e Régiment.

RALC: Régiment d'artillerie légère du Canada

RBC: Régiment blindé du Canada.

RCD: Royal Canadian Dragoons.

RCMP: Royal Canadian Mounted Police.

RCR: Royal Canadian Regiment.

Recce: Reconnaissance.

Roto: Rotation.

RPG: Rocket-propelled grenade.

SEAL: Sea, Air, Land.

SECFOR: Security Force.

SSM: Squadron sergeant-major.

TUAV: Tactical unmanned aerial vehicle.

UAV: Unmanned aerial vehicle.

VSA: Vital signs absent.

VTECS: Veteran Trainers to Eradicate the Use of Child Soldiers.

IMAGE CREDITS

Chard, Sean (Master Corporal): 125 (bottom), 126, 127, 130, 131.

Combat Camera, Department of National Defence: 26, 30 (bottom), 32, 45 (top; bottom), 52, 54 (top; bottom), 56, 58, 106, 121 (top), 124 (top), 145 (top; bottom), 146, 147, 179, 180 (top; bottom), 191, 194 (top; bottom), 197 (top; bottom), 198, 199 (top), 216, 222 (top), 225 (top; bottom), 245, 249.

Dupéré, François (Corporal): 93, 109, 110 (top; bottom), 112, 113, 114.

Gauthier, A. (Lieutenant-Colonel, 3 R22eR BG): 149, 150, 220, 222 (bottom), 224.

MacDonald, John (Lieutenant-Colonel): 169, 181 (top; bottom), 182.

Mineault, Jonathan (Captain): 27 (top), 71, 74, 75, 80, 81 (top; bottom), 82, 85.

Strachan, David (George Metcalf Archival Collection, Canadian War Museum): 27 (bottom), 30 (top), 33, 59, 97, 99 (top; bottom), 124 (bottom), 125 (top), 166, 199 (bottom), 220 (top).

Tremblay, Dean (Lieutenant-Colonel [Retired]): 121 (bottom).

INDEX

DUNDURN

VISIT US AT

Dundurn.com
@dundurnpress
Facebook.com/dundurnpress
Pinterest.com/dundurnpress